Smart Home Communication Network Needs

IR (Infrared) Control Network for A/V equipment (using IR cable)

Stuff You Need	Quantity You Need
3 conductor IR cabling	One run from each remote location to the media room
Wall-mounted IR sensors or remote keypads	One sensor or keypad per remote location
IR distribution block (with zone capability for use with multizone audio systems)	One installed in media room
IR emitters	One per audio source device being controlled in media room

Telephone Network

Stuff You Need	Quantity You Need
4 pair Category 5 UTP cabling	One run from wiring closet to each outlet
Modular wall outlets with female RJ-11 jacks	One per telephone extension
Telephone patch cords with male RJ-11 plugs	One per telephone extension
Telephone patch panel mounted in wiring closet	One
CAT 5 UTP cable to connect patch panel to incoming lines from telephone company NID	One run per incoming line
Key Service Unit (KSU) (optional)	One

Computer LAN

Stuff You Need	Quantity You Need
4 pair Category 5 UTP cabling	One run from wiring closet to each outlet
Modular wall outlets with female RJ-45 jacks	One jack per computer or network printer
CAT 5 UTP patch cords with male RJ-45 plugs	One patch cord per computer or network printer
CAT 5 rated Patch Panel mounted in wiring closet	One (can be the same one that works with phone network)
Ethernet hub	Minimum of one (additional hubs can be installed at remote outlets to allow connection of several computors to a single outlet)
Home automation system interface (optional)	One
Cable or DSL Modem/Modem-Router combo (optional)	One

For Dummies®: Bestselling Book Series for Beginners

Smart Homes For Dummies®

Cheat Sheet

Smart Home A/V Needs

Video Distribution Network

Stuff You Need	Quantity You Need
RG-6 coaxial cable with F connectors	Two runs from each viewing room to the central distribution point for a two-way network
Wall outlets	One per remote viewing room housing two female connectors
Video distribution panel	One, located in the central wiring closet
Modulators	Variable, each video source device that you want to distribute must be modulated to an unused frequency, but some modulators handle multiple video inputs

Audio Distribution Network (Single amplifier)

Stuff You Need	Quantity You Need
Single-zone or multizone integrated amplifier or receiver	One (multizone systems contain one stereo amplifier per zone)
Impedence matching system	One
Speakers	Two per room (can be in-wall or free-standing speakers)
In-wall speaker cable (16 AWG minimum)	One run between the media room and each remote location
RCA audio patch cords	(Usually) one set per audio component
In-wall speaker wire outlets	Two per remote area (if in-wall speakers aren't being used)
IR control network (with multizone IR zone distribution block for one multizone system)	

Hungry Minds™

For Dummies®: Bestselling Book Series for Beginners

Smart Homes

FOR

DUMMIES®

Smart Homes

FOR
DUMMIES®

by Danny Briere and Pat Hurley

Hungry Minds™

HUNGRY MINDS, INC.

New York, NY ◆ Cleveland, OH ◆ Indianapolis, IN

Smart Homes For Dummies®

Published by
Hungry Minds, Inc.
909 Third Avenue
New York, NY 10022
www.hungryminds.com
www.dummies.com (Dummies Press Web site)

Library of Congress Catalog Card No.: 99-63104

ISBN: 0-7645-0527-0

Printed in the United States of America

10 9 8 7 6 5

1O/SQ/QS/QR/IN

Distributed in the United States by Hungry Minds, Inc.

Distributed by CDG Books Canada Inc. for Canada; by Transworld Publishers Limited in the United Kingdom; by IDG Norge Books for Norway; by IDG Sweden Books for Sweden; by IDG Books Australia Publishing Corporation Pty. Ltd. for Australia and New Zealand; by TransQuest Publishers Pte Ltd. for Singapore, Malaysia, Thailand, Indonesia, and Hong Kong; by Gotop Information Inc. for Taiwan; by ICG Muse, Inc. for Japan; by Intersoft for South Africa; by Eyrolles for France; by International Thomson Publishing for Germany, Austria and Switzerland; by Distribuidora Cuspide for Argentina; by LR International for Brazil; by Galileo Libros for Chile; by Ediciones ZETA S.C.R. Ltda. for Peru; by WS Computer Publishing Corporation, Inc., for the Philippines; by Contemporanea de Ediciones for Venezuela; by Express Computer Distributors for the Caribbean and West Indies; by Micronesia Media Distributor, Inc. for Micronesia; by Chips Computadoras S.A. de C.V. for Mexico; by Editorial Norma de Panama S.A. for Panama; by American Bookshops for Finland.

For general information on Hungry Minds' products and services please contact our Customer Care Department within the U.S. at 800-762-2974, outside the U.S. at 317-572-3993 or fax 317-572-4002.

For sales inquiries and reseller information, including discounts, premium and bulk quantity sales, and foreign-language translations, please contact our Customer Care Department at 800-434-3422, fax 317-572-4002, or write to Hungry Minds, Inc., Attn: Customer Care Department, 10475 Crosspoint Boulevard, Indianapolis, IN 46256.

For information on licensing foreign or domestic rights, please contact our Sub-Rights Customer Care Department at 650-653-7098.

For authorization to photocopy items for corporate, personal, or educational use, please contact Copyright Clearance Center, 222 Rosewood Drive, Danvers, MA 01923, or fax 978-750-4470.

For information on using Hungry Minds' products and services in the classroom or for ordering examination copies, please contact our Educational Sales Department at 800-434-2086 or fax 317-572-4005.

Please contact our Public Relations Department at 212-884-5163 for press review copies or 212-884-5000 for author interviews and other publicity information or fax 212-884-5400.

Hungry Minds˜ is a trademark of Hungry Minds, Inc.

About the Authors

Danny Briere founded the telecommunications consulting company TeleChoice, Inc. in 1985 and now serves as president of the company. Widely known throughout the telecommunications and networking industry, Danny has written over 1000 articles on telecommunications topics and has authored or edited four books, including the IDG Books title *Internet Telephony For Dummies*. He is frequently quoted by leading publications on telecommunications and technology topics, and can often be seen on the major TV networks providing analysis on the latest communications news and breakthroughs. Danny lives in Stafford Springs, Connecticut with his wife and four children.

Pat Hurley is a consultant with TeleChoice, Inc. specializing in emerging telecommunications technologies. Pat currently concentrates on the emerging field of home networking and on related technologies such as high speed Internet access via cable modems. Pat is co-author of *Internet Telephony For Dummies* (now in its second edition) for IDG Books Worldwide. He lives in Coronado, California with his wife.

Authors' Acknowledgments

It takes a lot of effort, by a lot of people, to put a book together. We probably can't give proper acknowledgement to everyone who's given us advice, opinions and guidance as we've worked on this project, but we'd like to thank a few people.

Katie Clark, Danny's assistant (and minder and keeper), helped us with research and information gathering and much more.

Helen Heneveld, of Heneveld Dynamic Consulting, shared her exceptional insight into the growing home networking marketplace.

Literally dozens of vendors gave us information, tips and techniques (and a few home networking toys to try out). Special thanks go to Matt Taylor at Tut Systems, Pete Schwartz at ChannelPlus, Noel Lee and Daniel Graham at Monster Cable, Patrick Donnelly at ModTap, Adam Stein at Epigram, Gary Lee at Home Wireless Networks, Paul Cunningham at Cunningham Security in Portland, Maine, and George Snyder and Rick Tinker at Home Automated Living.

Finally, we want to thank the IDG Books team who bought into the concept of home networking before it became a "hot" topic, and made sure we crossed our *i's* and dotted our *t's* (or something like that). Thanks especially to Kyle Looper and Sherri Morningstar.

Publisher's Acknowledgments

We're proud of this book; please send us your comments through our Online Registration Form located at www.dummies.com.

Some of the people who helped bring this book to market include the following:

Acquisitions, Editorial, and Media Development

Senior Project Editor: Kyle Looper

Acquisitions Editor: Sherri Morningstar

Copy Editors: Tamara Castleman, Christine Beck, William Barton, Patricia Yuu Pan

Technical Editor: Bryan Sybesma

Editorial Manager: Leah P. Cameron

Media Development Manager: Heather Heath Dinsmore

Editorial Assistant: Beth Parlon

Production

Project Coordinator: Regina Snyder

Layout and Graphics: Linda M. Boyer, Thomas R. Emrick, Chris Herner, Angela F. Hunckler, David McKelvey, Brent Savage, Jacque Schneider, Janet Seib, Rashell Smith, Michael A. Sullivan, Brian Torwelle

Proofreaders: Christine Berman, Joanne Keaton, Marianne Santy, Rebecca Senninger, Janet M. Withers

Indexer: Ty Koontz

Special Help
Joan Whitman

General and Administrative

Hungry Minds, Inc.: John Kilcullen, CEO; Bill Barry, President and COO; John Ball, Executive VP, Operations & Administration; John Harris, CFO

Hungry Minds Technology Publishing Group: Richard Swadley, Senior Vice President and Publisher; Mary Bednarek, Vice President and Publisher, Networking and Certification; Walter R. Bruce III, Vice President and Publisher, General User and Design Professional; Joseph Wikert, Vice President and Publisher, Programming; Mary C. Corder, Editorial Director, Branded Technology Editorial; Andy Cummings, Publishing Director, General User and Design Professional; Barry Pruett, Publishing Director, Visual

Hungry Minds Manufacturing: Ivor Parker, Vice President, Manufacturing

Hungry Minds Marketing: John Helmus, Assistant Vice President, Director of Marketing

Hungry Minds Online Management: Brenda McLaughlin, Executive Vice President, Chief Internet Officer

Hungry Minds Production for Branded Press: Debbie Stailey, Production Director

Hungry Minds Sales: Roland Elgey, Senior Vice President, Sales and Marketing; Michael Violano, Vice President, International Sales and Sub Rights

◆

The publisher would like to give special thanks to Patrick J. McGovern, without whom this book would not have been possible.

◆

Contents at a Glance

Cartoons at a Glance

By Rich Tennant

page 7

page 57

page 129

page 171

page 267

page 231

page 303

Fax: 978-546-774/
E-mail: richtennant@the5thwave.com
World Wide Web: www.the5thwave.com

Table of Contents

• •

Introduction

● ●

*W*elcome to *Smart Homes For Dummies.* This book is the first to specifically tell you how to future proof your home to take advantage of the present and upcoming gee-whiz things that can make your home a 21st century castle.

Very few things can prepare you for the massive changes that are taking place worldwide with the innovations offered by a totally interconnected world. The Internet and electronic commerce are going to change the way we live, the way we work, and the way we play. (Hopefully more of the last one!)

We are so used to going to stores and buying things. To calling toll-free numbers to ask questions and order products. To going to schools to learn. To going to the movies to watch the latest *Star Wars* release. To going to the music store to buy the top-of-the-charts CDs.

Now it's all going to come to us. We can buy things through our TV sets. We can ask questions and videoconference through our computers. We can attend classes through computer-based training. We can click our remote controls to get video-on-demand. We can download new CDs, live, over the Internet.

It's all at our doorstep. The question is, "Can you let it all in?" Without a home network, all of this might stay outside, or in the basement, or trapped in that attic office of yours. A home network today truly opens the world to your entire household, and now more than ever is the time to plan for the future.

That's what *Smart Homes For Dummies* provides — a plan for your networked future.

About This Book

Smart Homes For Dummies isn't a novel. You don't have to read page 1 before going to page 2. So that means that you can just flip around through the book and start wherever you like. You won't feel lost.

You can use the Table of Contents at the front of the book to find out where to look for a topic that interests you, whether it's distributing a VCR signal from your home entertainment center to your bedroom, or making your lights go on and off by themselves. Or, you can search the Index for a particular term that interests you. However you find the information, read and then put the book back on the shelf. That's how this book is meant to be used.

Within the pages of this book, you find a number of technologies and issues relating to developing smart home technologies. Among the things you can find out are:

- ✔ **What a home network is, and what it takes to build one**
- ✔ **What key points to think about before starting to conceptualize a home network design**
- ✔ **What all the various devices and services that you might want to take advantage of with a home network do**
- ✔ **What's involved in making a home entertainment center accessible throughout the house**
- ✔ **What do you need to create a home security network**
- ✔ **What are your various options for dressing up your home telephone capabilities**
- ✔ **What is the best way to design a home data local area network (LAN)**
- ✔ **How you can connect your home to the Internet**
- ✔ **What's coming down the road and into your home over the foreseeable future**

Conventions Used in This Book

Some of the networks and issues that we cover in *Smart Homes For Dummies* are within the realm of the do-it-yourselfer, so we present the big-picture stuff for those readers and give high-level instructions. These instructions don't go into stuff like removing your drywall and running cables through your house. Allow us to recommend *Home Improvement For Dummies* by Gene Hamilton, Katie Hamilton, and the editors of HouseNet (IDG Books, Worldwide, Inc.) if you need help with that stuff.

On the other hand, if you don't feel comfortable running cables through your house, don't feel like you have to do everything yourself, either. Hire a professional!

If you are renovating a home, building a new home, or trying to figure out how to connect anything with anything else in your home, you need *Smart Homes For Dummies*.

Foolish Assumptions

In all practicality, this book is for everyone. Few people don't have a TV, radio, or some sort of computing device that is going to need to be networked in the future. While it is easy to say now that computers are only for families in certain financial brackets, within five years, many TV sets are going to start shipping with all sorts of Internet connectivity options onboard. So, you can buy this book now, or buy it later. But someday, everyone is going to have to read this book or one like it.

You'll get the most out of this book if you're in a position to run wires through your walls, such as when you're thinking about remodeling your house or when your buying a new house. Apartment dwellers can do some of the stuff that we outline in this book (using wireless technologies), and they can get cool ideas for when they do buy their homes, but you get the most out of these technologies if you can run cables through your walls.

How This Book Is Organized

You home has many different systems that have interacted somewhat independently of each other up until now. If you have a home entertainment system and a computer, chances are you have not connected them together.

Part I: Future-Perfect Homes

Part I of _Smart Homes For Dummies_ describes where we're trying to get to — our future-proofed home. In this section, we talk about the different major network zones of your home — your entertainment system, your security system, your phone system, and your computer system. We talk about all of the various other things, too, that you might want to link together, and why you'd want to do that. And finally, we talk about how you can start thinking about the various things you could accomplish with a fully networked home — your smart home.

Part II: Making Your Home an Entertainment Center

Parts II through V look in depth at how to design your home and home network to take advantage of all the neat things coming down the road in each of the major zones, and then Part VI tells you how to interconnect them all.

Part II looks at how to make your home an entertainment center. This is not merely about creating a home theater, but a true home-wide entertainment complex. How do you listen to your favorite CD from anywhere in the house? How do you share a satellite dish among multiple TVs. How about watching your napping baby from your living room TV?

In Part II, we tell you how to sensibly build a media backbone in your home, without breaking your bank account. We make sure to tell you about, and help you plan for, things like flat-screen TVs, intercom systems, whole home audio systems, and satellite systems. We talk about your wiring (and wireless) options for communicating with each part of your home entertainment complex.

Part III: Now We're Communicating!

Part III delves into the world of telephones. Life used to be relatively simple in this area. If you wanted to get a new phone, you could go to the local department store or Radio Shack and pick up a new phone. Now, you have all sorts of complications in this area. There are multiline phones, 900 MHz phones, screen phones, combined phone/fax/printers/scanners, answering machines, central-office-based voice mail services, and a whole lot more. Part IV helps you craft your home telephone network so that you can communicate with anyone from anywhere — and hopefully without all that scratchy static we all hate.

Part IV: Livin' Off the Fat of the LAN

Part IV looks at your computer zone. A smart home has a high-bandwidth backbone connection running throughout the house, so you can tap into your data autobahn from wherever you like — the living room, the bathroom — you pick.

Part IV helps you understand how you can play networked games, share files between computers, print or fax from any computer in the home, or even get the whole family on the Net, at the same time! We look at the world of ISDN, xDSL, cable modems, DirecPC dishes, wireless Internet connections, electrical data connections, and more. Wired or wireless, we help you plan and design your own data local area network (LAN) for your home. We guide you through the maze of wiring options to make sure that if you want to surf the Net while mowing the lawn (which we don't really recommend), you can.

Part V: Keeping the Bad Guys at Bay: Security

Part V takes you through our home-security boot camp and looks at everything you'd want to do to secure and protect your home. This is not just fire and burglar alarms, but also things like video doorbells, closed-circuit TV, and driveway sensors. We help you plan your way to a more secure and protected home.

Part VI: Putting It All Together: Home Automation and Control

Part VI brings it all together — the ultimate guide to home networking. We walk you through a whole-home approach to network design. Part VI gives you home design and layout tips, as well as exposes you to the various products on the market for centralized home networking.

Want to fire up that coffee pot while you're still asleep? Or how about set the mood with automated lighting? We look at all the latest trends and gadgets governing home automation, including the details about X-10 home automation.

Part VII: The Part of Tens

Part VII is our infamous Part of Tens, where we give you Ten Neat Things You Can Network Now, Ten Hints for Designing a Future-Proofed Home, Ten Great Web Resources, Ten Print Publications to Get Your Hands On, and Ten Ways Home Networking Will Get Easier.

Smart Homes For Dummies closes out with one helpful appendix — a glossary of all the key terms we use in the book.

Icons Used in This Book

We would be surprised if this were the first . . .*For Dummies* book that you have read (if so, shame, shame, shame). But in case it is, we use some very helpful graphical icons to point out specific items of interest — sort of like Kodak Picture Spots at Disney World. These icons are meant to encourage you to pause and really take in what we are saying at that point. Here are some of the icons we use:

This is the really fun stuff. This icon highlights neat new technical and other advances that are either just arriving or not too far away. It's like a free pass to the World's Fair and a glimpse at the World of the Future.

This is a helpful reminder to do certain things, which again translates into "we've forgotten to do this so often that we put it here just to remind ourselves."

When you see this icon, you may want to wait to make a decision until the industry decides which way it wants to go. Remember the Beta Max VCR?

A few people in every crowd raise their hands and ask what's underneath the hood, so every now and then we stop to point out some of the neat stuff that makes this technology actually work. (We say "neat" because we're nerdy enough to enjoy writing it, so we'd better think it's neat.)

A shortcut or time-saving secret that we wished someone had told us before we learned it the hard way.

This is never a good icon to see. It means you are working in a part of the Internet or your computer that is dangerous. It's like knowing the Wicked Witch of the West is in your neighborhood and you've got the ruby slippers on. Be careful.

This icon tells you about a wireless technology that you can use without having to rip your walls out.

Where to Go from Here

Whew! As Willy Wonka says, "So much time, so little to do . . . reverse that." Let's get going!

Part I
Future-Perfect Homes

The 5th Wave   By Rich Tennant

SMART HOME OF THE FUTURE

"I'm setting preferences—do you want Oriental or Persian carpets in the living room?"

In this part . . .

*I*n the olden days, your home network was comprised of basically your electrical wires and your phone lines, with a smattering of alarm wiring here and there. Now your home network covers all sorts of wiring and wireless options, to connect any of a number of different devices — including your car and your microwave.

You can connect your home entertainment systems, your security systems, your computer networks, your telephone systems, and your appliances together and come up with all sorts of neat applications to help make your home living simpler and more enjoyable.

In this part, we tell you all about the potential of a home network. We discuss all the major elements of a whole-home network, and describe the advantages of connecting them all together. By the end of this part, you'll be more excited than ever about hooking everything together.

Chapter 1

Mi Casa, Cool Casa

· ·

· ·

*I*f you stop the average person on the street and start talking about home networks, he or she would probably make references to ABC, CBS, NBC, and FOX, or mention the Home Shopping Network or some other cable network show. *Network,* until recently, has meant little else to most people.

But times, they are a changin'. The invasion of telecommunications into all aspects of life is creating a different meaning of the word *network.* Most people have had some contact with a network through their work environment — computer local area networks (LANs) in the office, control networks in factories, telephone networks in many mid-sized or larger businesses.

You can think of networks simply as things that help you do your work. As you concentrate on printing a document, calling up a database, or checking out the price of a product online, the network is invisible. (That is, invisible until it's broken, or you don't have one at all.)

The network concept has begun to move from the workplace to the home, and smart homes builders and remodelers (and forward-looking owners of otherwise perfect existing homes) are starting to think in terms of wiring (or "wirelessing") their homes both to make use of a network today and to future-proof against upcoming requirements.

Before you go any farther, do this little exercise (don't worry, we won't grade you): Write down all the things in your house that you think you may want to network together. Be as creative as you can. Think about your lifestyle and the way your house is set up. When you finish, put the list aside and read on in this chapter. Toward the end, we'll share our list with you.

Living in Your Smart Home

Your smart home can seep into all aspects of your life. It helps you do those day-to-day tasks that can take up so much time — little things like opening the draperies, turning up the lights, and flipping on the Weather Channel to see whether the kids have a snow day.

How far you go with your smart home depends on your lifestyle, your budget, and your personal tastes.

The following sections spend a virtual day in a fictitious smart home. Here's the scenario: You, the reader, are part of a family of six, plus the requisite pet (we prefer dogs). You and your spouse both work, and the kids range in age from 8–17.

Starting your day

Anyone with kids knows the importance of keeping on a schedule. Your home network helps you do just that, in style.

At first light, you wake to your home-controlled *alarm* — a stream of pleasant classical music coming over your home audio network into your bedroom. After a preset length of time, the music fades out and the TV kicks on to your favorite local station, where you can get the weather and traffic reports, and information about any school closings or delays. Down the hall, the kids also awaken to the music of their choice.

In the kitchen, the coffeemaker starts brewing your morning caffeine requirements. Select shades and drapes throughout the house open to let the day's light stream in.

It's winter, so the towel warmers and radiant heat in the bathrooms' floors are turned on. The automatic pet door out back opens and lets the dog out for his morning constitutional.

By this time, you're already in the kitchen making school lunches. Being the nice person that you are, you take a cup of coffee to your spouse who is listening to National Public Radio in the shower.

As you finish laying out the breakfast for the kids, a glance at the upstairs monitors shows that two of the four kids are still in bed. Your eldest son is videoconferencing with his girlfriend on his computer. You punch the intercom and tell them all to get a move on.

As the children cycle in and out the bathroom, the home control system times their showers to make sure that no one hogs the bathroom. The shower's water temperature is just to their liking, but that's hardly a surprise — it's the same setting they use each day this time of year.

As you sit down to breakfast, your spouse comes running through, late for the office. A printout of major headlines and personal stock standings sits in the printer waiting, having been created and downloaded from the Internet overnight.

Your spouse works down the street (we did tell you that you work at home, didn't we?), and your smart home knows you both like a warm car when you get into a 15-degree garage, so the home controller starts the car 15 minutes before the scheduled departure time. Before your spouse climbs inside the toasty car, the home control system gives a verbal reminder to put the bottles and cans next to the curb because today is recycling day.

As your spouse leaves the garage, your home control system talks to your phone system and redirects all of your spouse's home business line calls to the car phone. Once at work, a simple push of a speed dial button on the office phone dials in and redirects the calls again to your spouse's office.

Back at home, you confirm that the kids caught the bus by using the video monitor in the kitchen, and then you get ready for work. You ask the home controller to put the house in your personal mode — in terms of temperature, music, lighting, drape settings, and anything else you may have set.

Getting down to work

You get a second cup of coffee and decide to work for a little while in the sunroom. You tell the home controller where you are, and the controller transfers all your business calls to the extension near the table. Your laptop is wirelessly connected to your server and to the Internet. You check your e-mail and voice mail and make a few conference calls on the home multiline telephone system. While you are on one phone call, you access the online ordering page for that ultra-expensive, posh, take-out shop down the street. Twenty minutes later, the delivery person arrives at the front door; you take your wireless two-line phone — conference call and all — to the door where you pay off the delivery person and retreat back to the sunroom for lunch.

For a mid-afternoon break, you head for the exercise room to work off some of that lunch. When you enter, you announce yourself to your voice-activated home automation system, and it automatically sets the music and other environmental settings to your previously-defined preferences. You sit down at your rowing machine, which is front-ended with a large monitor that shows real-life settings of popular rowing locales.

Halfway through your workout session, a delivery person shows up at your door. An announcement that someone is at the door interrupts the music, and the nearest video display shows a picture of who it is. You don't want to stop mid-workout, so you reply that you are busy and ask him to leave the package inside the door. You prompt for the control system to unlock the front door, and watch as the front door unlocks itself and the delivery person places the packages in the foyer. He leaves, and you start rowing again along Boston's Charles River.

It's your turn for a temperature-controlled shower, where you listen to CNN from the TV set, via moisture-resistant speakers that are mounted in the bath.

Squeaky clean, you go back to work. At 3:00, you have your first videoconference of the day from your office downstairs. While in the basement, you call up your home control system and start the roast cooking in the oven.

The kids drift home in the afternoon and spread out across the house. As you access your corporation's data network, your kids take advantage of the computers at the same time. The youngest kids — twins — play multiplayer games on the home high-speed Internet connection. Your eldest daughter logs onto the school's educational extranet to do research for the midterm paper she has due next week. And your son, when home from football practice, logs onto his school's extranet to collaboratively work with three others on a joint presentation for the next day.

The home controller's voice enunciator reminds you that the roast should be done by now, and you head upstairs.

Internet, intranet, extranet . . . it's all the same stuff

By now, you probably know a good deal about the Internet, but you'll probably hear more and more about intranets and extranets in the future. For the most part, all of these systems ride over the same Internet that you hear about all the time. If you work at home, you may be accessing the Internet, an intranet, and an extranet for various activities.

An *intranet* is merely a secured sublayer of the Internet. Many corporations want to use the Internet for sending information to other locations — out to their remote offices, say — but want to make sure that the communications are secure and private. So they buy intranet gear to create what are called *virtual private networks*, giving the corporations their own internet within the Internet . . . an intranet.

An *extranet* is similar, except it involves parties outside of the corporation as well — say its trading partners. For instance, a large automobile manufacturer may have an extranet that links its suppliers with its various plants and other key locations. Because the link is with firms outside the corporation, it's called an extranet.

Dinner time

Meanwhile, at work, your spouse glances at the clock and remembers in a panic that the family needs groceries. A quick dial into the home LAN yields the grocery list that is on the computerized message board in the kitchen. On the way home, a phone call into the home controller redirects calls back to the car phone in case someone tries to call.

The magnetic driveway sensor tells the home control system to announce your spouse's arrival. As your spouse leaves the garage, the home controller again redirects all calls to the home office, completing the day's cycle. As your spouse brings the groceries into the kitchen, you receive a kiss (sorry, not automated).

Ready to eat, you ask the home controller to set dinner mode in the dining room. A microphone in the light switch hears the command and interfaces with the lights in the room, dimming them, and with the fireplace, turning on the gas-driven fireplace. The home control system selects a family-oriented CD from the CD tower and plays it over the in-wall speakers in the dining room.

After dinner, you start cleaning up as your kids race to their rooms to finish their homework. Later, the kids watch a TV special in the living room, while you take in an old Spencer Tracy movie in your bedroom. In the meantime, your spouse has a late videoconference with Japan in the home office downstairs. Occasionally, you access the picture-in-picture (PIP) capability on your TV set to check around the house, making sure that no one is getting into any trouble. After the movie, you give a simple command to the home controller and the lights go down, the temperature in select zones goes down, shades and draperies close, nightlights come on, and the intercom goes into monitor mode for the youngest kids, in case they're sick during the night. (The sound from those monitors only plays in the master bedroom area.)

Peace at last!

With the kids asleep for the night, you decide to take a nice relaxing bath. You instruct your home control system to prepare the bathroom — dim the lights, open the skylight, run the bath at your favorite temperature, turn off the telephone extensions nearby (route them to voice mail instead), and play your favorite album on the bathroom speakers.

While lounging in bed watching the wide screen TV, your spouse tells the home entertainment system to search the shows it has been archiving every day and play the last episode of *Star Trek Voyager*.

Your house is in off-hours mode. The dog is inside, and the doggy door is secure. All phones have muted ringing volumes; some don't ring at all. All drapes are closed. The temperature is lower to save energy when your family is tucked in tight under the covers. All security systems are now alert, looking for movement outside the house.

After your bath, you climb in bed and read for a while. You finish your electronic book and decide you want to read the sequel right away. You surf the Web from your TV set, find the book, buy it, download it to the home LAN, and thus to your electronic book via a wireless connection.

Your dishwasher kicks on at midnight when the rates are low (you loaded it at dinnertime and turned it on, but the home controller actually activates it when rates drop). All night long, your home controller and its various sensors keep an eye on everything for you. You sleep peacefully.

The Home-Network Revolution

What's brought about this progression of intelligent home networks into everyday life? One word — computers. Computers, computers and more computers. (Oh, we left out the most important one — computers.)

And when we say computers, we don't just mean the PC that's sitting on a desk in a spare bedroom in 40 percent of American homes (although that's an important part of it). We also mean those little blobs of silicon that reside in just about everything in the house — think about phones or televisions or refrigerators, even the car in the garage. Many of these items are already loaded with computer chips, and they get smarter by the minute.

Now, at this juncture, most of these systems use their computing power in isolated and unique ways — islands of computing power plugged into the power outlets of your home. Many of them have no way of talking to each other or sharing the information that these computer chips gather and control.

The network revolution — the home-network revolution — is taking place as these things begin to talk to each other. Imagine, for example, a refrigerator that could talk to your electrical utility and go into its power-hungry defrost mode at exactly the same time that electricity rates are at their lowest. Or how about having all your clocks reset themselves automatically when the power comes back on after an outage, because they are set to "network time."

Well, home networks aren't currently as advanced as the Jetsons' home, but they will be soon. And you're missing the boat if you build a new home, or remodel your existing one, and don't take this kind of future into account.

Home wiring history

Traditionally, homes have been wired for two things only — power and telephones. Add in a couple of haphazardly run cable TV outlets and some doorbells, and you have the whole sum of home wiring for most homes. Some people have an alarm system put in, with its own unique set of wires, and maybe an intercom system, again with its own set of wires. Put it all together, and you have an expensive bunch of wires running throughout your house, each group of them doing their own thing, none of them talking to each other or, for the most part, being good for anything else.

Even more important than the quantity of wires in most homes is the quality. Talk to a home-automation expert, or to a telephone-company engineer who's working on bringing high-speed data services to residences, and you'll find that one of their biggest concerns, if not the biggest, is the quality of the wires inside the walls of most homes. And this problem doesn't just apply to homes that were wired 50 years ago — many brand-new homes are being built with wiring systems that are just plain inadequate for the requirements of today's *wired* citizens. The low-voltage wires (telephone and cable TV wires, for example) don't have adequate capacity for high-speed data use, or for multiple lines. They don't go to enough places in the house, and they have no flexibility of configuration.

In other words, you're stuck with what you have, and if your needs change — and they will! — you'll most likely have to go through and rewire to accommodate them.

Even the electrical power cables in most homes may be inadequate (and not just because you don't have enough outlets where you need them). In fact, many of the leading home-automation and control systems use your power cables to do things like turn on lights and start your coffeemaker, but only if your power system is adequately isolated from interference and line noise. Unfortunately, in many homes, they are not.

Luckily, overcoming these difficulties isn't hard — or even that expensive. All you need is a little knowledge and a good plan!

Predicting the future is difficult — okay, it's impossible — but our culture is definitely moving to a place where a smart home is the norm. So although you can't know today exactly what will be connected to what (and how) tomorrow, you can design a wiring system for your home that will enable you to do the most you can today and be ready for tomorrow's needs.

What's in a Smart Home?

A smart home works because of the advance planning you do. A smart home is a harmonious home, a conglomeration of devices and capabilities working according to the Zen of Home Networking.

At the beginning of this chapter, we suggest that you make a list of all the things you think you may want to network. Table 1-1 shows our list. Notice that practically anything in your home can be, and ultimately will be, networked. That's the whole point of whole-house networking.

Table 1-1	Stuff You Can Network!			
Household Items	*Audio/Video*	*Security*	*Phones*	*Computers*
Drapes/shades	Receivers	Baby monitors	Corded phones	PCs
Gates	Amplifiers	Video cameras	Cordless phones	Macs
Garage doors	Speakers	Surveillance monitors	900Mhz phones	Laptops
Door locks	VCRs	Motion detectors	2.4GHz phones	Modems
Doorbells	CD players	Smoke detectors	Fax machines	Scanners
Lights	DVD players	Occupancy sensors	Answering machines	Printers
Dishwashers	Laserdisc players	Pressure sensors	Screen phones	PDAs
Refrigerators	TVs	Infrared sensors	Video phones	
Heaters	WebTV devices	Intercoms		
Alarm clocks	DSS dishes	Voice enunciators		
Washers	Radios			
Dryers	Remote controls			
Microwaves	Cable TV devices			
Coffeemakers	TV videoconferencing devices			
Hot water systems				
Air conditioners				
Central vacuum systems				
Water controls (shower, sink, and so on)				
Pool covers				
Fireplaces				
Toys				
Lawnmowers				

Household Items	Audio/Video	Security	Phones	Computers
Cars/vehicles				
Pianos				
Weather stations				
Furniture				

Note: Include in the list any phone or electrical outlet in the house.

The key is getting information to and from each of these devices. That takes a network. As explained throughout this book, your home network is actually a collection of networks — communications in and among the different devices travel over various network layers, such as your home telephone network, your computing network, your security network, your electrical communications network (yes, you can talk over your electrical lines, believe it or not), and so on. These collectively are what we call your home network, and you will mix, match, and jump among these network layers as you communicate throughout your household.

Why Network Your Home?

A network allows you to do a bevy of things. For instance, you can

- **Access the Internet from anywhere in your house:** A home network lets everyone share in the broadband wealth, so you can stop fighting over the one computer connected to a cable modem or other high-speed connection. What's more, by having a communications backbone in your house, you can let anything — from your TV set to your car — tap in and make use of that connectivity. After you install your home network, an increasing number of devices will use it to make your life easier.

- **Remotely control your home:** After your home network is connected to your other networks, like the Internet, you can suddenly do amazing things from almost any interconnected spot. The ability to control a device after it is hooked up to the network is limited only by the openness of the device itself. (As the number of home networks grows, you can expect more devices to be open to remote control as well.) Want to turn off the lights downstairs from the bedroom? Click your remote control, and out go the lights. Want to check the babysitter while at your neighbor's July 4th bash? Just log onto their machine and check up on things.

✔ **Save time:** Think about how much time you take every day to open the shades, turn on the morning news, let the dog out, and so on. Wouldn't you like to do all that (and more) with one command? By programming these chores into task profiles, you can.

✔ **Save money on electronics:** With a true home network, you have to buy fewer devices to outfit your home. Instead of having a VCR hooked to every TV set, for instance, you can centralize this functionality and distribute the signal around the house via remote control as you need it. The same is true of almost any network-connected device — tape decks, DSS receivers, cable boxes, and so on.

✔ **Save money on communications costs:** By centralizing access to certain telecommunications services, you can cut your monthly service costs. For instance, with a home-network backbone, both you and your spouse can connect to the Internet on separate computers while sharing one line and one account. What's more, you can now get a high bandwidth option — like a cable modem, DSL link, or DirecPC-type satellite service — to share with the whole family.

✔ **Save money on your home expenses:** A wired home can turn back those thermostats when you're cuddled under your blankets at night or away on vacation. It can turn lights off automatically, too. Over time, you may save a surprising amount in heating, cooling, and electricity expenses.

✔ **Save money on the future:** At different times in your life, you may find yourself changing the way you use certain rooms — a guest room becomes a nursery or the garage becomes an office, for example. Changes like these can be expensive if you try to bring your network along for the ride. Rerunning wiring through walls can be expensive and sometimes impossible. Wireless options can be limiting in what they offer in terms of bandwidth and distance. Planning ahead by having an *articulated* home network strategy — one that is future-proofed for all sorts of contingencies — simply saves you money down the road.

✔ **Be more flexible, and comfortable, with your technological assets:** A home network frees you from being tied to one spot for one activity. For instance, when working late at night, we sometimes like to move the laptop to a comfy recliner instead of a damp basement office. However, without a distributed means to access the Internet (and therefore our centralized e-mail, calendars, and contact databases), we would have no choice but to stay *in the office.*

✔ **Lose more fat:** A smart home won't stop you from eating chocolate cake, but it will spice up that exercise room of yours. You can run Internet access, CNN, or exercise videos over your home network to help you keep pace and pass the time on that treadmill or bicycle. And, with your Internet access, you can access many of the neat new software programs that combine with new exercise equipment to provide you with passing scenery or live competitors as you row, row, row, your rowing machine!

Bill Gates' home — totally smart!

If you are going to get wired, you may as well know how extremely wired you can be. No one's as wired as Bill Gates — at least we don't think so.

Bill started to lay the foundation for his home in 1992 on five acres of land, situated on the shores of Lake Washington near Seattle. When it was ultimately completed, its final price tag was around $100 million. Included in the plans for this home, besides the 500-year-old oak timber, are some of the newest technologies. Check out these hot home-networking technologies:

✔ **The electric pin:** Can you say "Gates to Enterprise"? As you come in the front door, you get an electronic pin to wear. This pin drives your Gates home experience, because the house always knows the location of your pin, whether you are in the main house, the guest house, or even touring the grounds. If a phone call comes for you, it can be transferred to the extension nearest your current location. As you move throughout Bill's home, the lights turn on just ahead of you and fade just behind you, and room temperatures adjust to make you comfortable. When you enter a room, the art on the walls changes to match your taste, because wall-mounted display screens exhibit the art. And if you're listening to music, the audio system plays the kinds of music you like. If two or more pins are in the same room, the computer responds with a mix of styles.

✔ **Home controls:** Augmenting the electric pin are conspicuously-placed touch pads that allow you to change the lighting, temperature, and music in various rooms. These controls enable the computer to create a profile of your preferences. The next time you visit, the home control system adjusts everything as you walk in the door. Or, you can use a handheld remote control to communicate with the house and be in control of your overall environment.

✔ **Home theater/business rooms:** You wanna talk about a home entertainment system? Included in Bill's guest wing is a 20-seat art deco theater. The screen is HDTV capable. That area also has a conference room, a couple of offices, and a computer room.

✔ **Wires everywhere:** Miles of communication wires run throughout the home — most of it fiber connections but some copper cabling — connecting the various devices and elements with a group of computer servers running, of course, on Windows NT operating systems.

✔ **Servers everywhere:** You find a smattering of regular PCs throughout the house — home printers and other peripherals connected to high-capacity T1 access connections for online access and for the phone system. These PCs make exhaustive use of Microsoft software for a wide range of home applications. In addition to Microsoft Office, this software includes such titles as Cinemania interactive movie guide, Music Central interactive music, and various reference guides. These specialty programs allow you to access a movie or a song — not only by the title or the artist, but also by indicating that you want to listen to all the songs that have the word "yellow" in the title, or all the Number One hits in 1979.

✔ **Heat everywhere:** All of the floors, as well as the driveway, are heated, so you don't have to worry about cold floors in the morning or shoveling your driveway after a snowfall.

More specific details about Bill's home network — the security system in particular — are kept confidential. We guess, however, that if you have the right pin, you can get access to anything you want to know in Bill's house. Sounds like a job for *Mission Impossible!*

Chapter 2

Zen and the Art of Whole-Home Networking

. . . .

In This Chapter

▶ Turning on to whole-home networking

▶ Hiding ugly cables and components

▶ Designing a space for entertainment equipment

▶ Looking at all-in-one cabling solutions

. . . .

As you think about your home network, you need to think in terms of the big picture. Instead of trying to extend your cable TV signal from one room to another, think about a video-distribution strategy for the whole house. Instead of talking about how to link one computer to another, think about a computer network that extends to every room. Instead of discussing your home entertainment center, map out a media backbone for your entire home.

In this chapter, we want to give you that holistic view — looking at networks in a broader, whole-home sense. Specifically, we want to spend a bit of time talking about how *all* of the networks in your home fit together physically, and how you can make home networking easier by designing a central location (or two) to house all of your networking equipment.

We also discuss some of the *structured cabling* solutions available to home-owners — packages of bundled cabling and distribution panels that can take care of most of your home-networking infrastructure needs in one easy-to-buy-and-install (or have installed) single vendor system.

All Together Now!

Try envisioning your new home network. Your home infrastructure may consist of one or more of the following networks:

- ✔ A phone network

- ✔ A data network (small networks are often called *local area networks,* or LANs)

- ✔ An electrical network

- ✔ A security network

- ✔ An intercom network (may be part of your phone network)

- ✔ An entertainment network

- ✔ A home automation/management capability that allows your house to do common tasks on its own

- ✔ Access to the Internet and other external programming sources (like satellite broadcasts, cable, telephone services, and so on)

You may not want or need all these different networks in your home application, but if you are at a point in the construction or remodeling of your home where running cables is easy, you should seriously consider running all the cables necessary to allow you (or someone who owns your home later) to add these capabilities at a later date. Doing so protects the value of your home against obsolescence. Many people buy homes that have extra bedrooms that they don't need at the time because they may have a use for them in the future or a future buyer may be looking for that number of rooms.

Thinking of networks in different ways

One of the difficulties that confronts you when you think about home networking is the aggravating way that networks tend to overlap. At various times, you need to be able to think about the networks in your home in the way that gives you the best information. Here are some important ways to think about your home networks:

- ✔ **Physical configuration.** When you're thinking about running cables, making connections, and buying specific pieces of equipment, you're thinking about the physical aspects of your network. This is where all the detail work comes in.

✔ **Logical configuration.** Thinking of networks logically means simplifying networks and how they function by using a model. One way of thinking about your home networks logically is to envision each network as a single object (such as a phone network or a video network) rather than getting bogged down in all the cables, connectors, and devices. Doing so allows you to more easily process the big picture of your networks.

Additionally, you can think of each network's layout logically, by using a network model. Most of the networks we discuss in this book use a star model, in which all the cables you run meet at the same junction point, just as the spokes of a wagon wheel meet at the hub. While your network may not actually look much like a star (or a wheel, for that matter), the star model tells you that all those cables have to connect *somewhere*.

✔ **Application.** Sometimes networks become so intermixed that you need to step back and think in terms of the network's purpose or application and what connections you need to make that purpose happen. Your entertainment network, for example, may represent a combination of different physical components and logical entities all aimed at distributing audio and video around your house. A typical system includes audio and video devices such as VCRs and tape players, a broadcast satellite that runs to receivers that require phone line access, and maybe even home-management software to control the network's functionality.

Although we present the various ways of looking at networks as they are most easy to understand, you generally conceive of your networks in the opposite manner. You usually begin by thinking of what you want to accomplish (the applications), move on to considering each individual network and its layout (logical), and then get to the nitty-gritty of cables, connectors, and specific hardware components (physical).

Thinking of networks by application, logically, and physically can reveal ways to save money, time, and headaches. For example, if you think strictly in terms of the phone network and data network being logically different networks, you could overlook the possibility that these networks may be able to transmit over the same cable runs at different frequencies. By mixing and matching these different views, you can really reach home-networking nirvana, getting more capabilities for less money.

Caution: Merging networks

Someday, in the not-so-distant future, homeowners will be able to install an integrated, unified network that carries voice, video, data, audio, and home control signals over a single kind of cable. When that day comes, we'll write a really short version of *Smart Homes For Dummies,* and spend more time on the golf course or basketball court.

Unfortunately (for Pat's jump shot and Danny's swing), that day is still quite a ways off. Today's home network is actually a number of independent networks, each doing their own thing, over their own set of wires and cables. That's not to say that there aren't places where today's individual home networks come together — and work together.

In fact, there are a whole bunch of these network interconnection points in a typical house, making these separate networks behave somewhat like a unified, single network. There are three ways that networks can physically interconnect in a home:

- ✔ **Networks can share the same media (or cables) to carry different kinds of signals at different frequencies.** For example, telephone wiring can potentially be used to carry both telephone service and data networking using a phone-line networking system.

- ✔ **Specific devices can connect to multiple networks.** A DSS satellite receiver, for example, connects to both video and telephone networks.

- ✔ **Incoming service provider feeds can carry multiple services and connect to different networks in the home.** For example, a cable company could potentially provide television, Internet access, and telephone service over three different home networks.

Home Design/Layout Tips

The best time to start thinking about home networks is early on in the home design (or remodeling planning) process. You can, using wireless equipment or really talented installers, add a home-network infrastructure to an existing home or one that's already pretty far along in the building process, but doing so tends to be more expensive and more fraught with compromise. Remember the six P's: Proper planning prevents pretty poor performance. (Actually, it's not *pretty,* but let's just pretend that it is.)

The two keys things to keep in mind when integrating a home network into your home design or remodeling plans are

- ✔ Designating an appropriate location for all of your network's central distribution equipment.

- ✔ Making sure that you have an adequate quality and quantity of network cabling running to each potential network outlet in your home.

Bringing your network out of the closet

If you're building your house or remodeling your home with a whole-home network in mind, talk to your builder or remodeler about designating space as a *central wiring closet* (or, in the case of remodels, it often makes sense to have multiple locations). The wiring closet should be a place that is out of site but is also easily accessible. It needs to have plenty of space and adequate power to run a great deal of equipment.

By designating a central wiring closet, you gain some huge benefits:

- **Hiding wires:** A truly wired home has a lot of cables in the walls. You're talking about wires for a phone network, a video network, an audio network, a computer network, a security network, and a remote-control network. Add in the connections to the outside phone lines, cable TV, and satellite feeds, and it can become a bowl of spaghetti pretty quickly. You don't want to have to tuck these wires behind your furniture if you can avoid it.

- **Hiding hardware:** Much of the hardware that facilitates home networking, such as distribution panels, punchdown blocks, and so on, is designed with function in mind rather than form. (Not to say that a CAT-5 patch panel isn't a pretty thing — in some people's minds at least — but neither is it something you want to have hanging on the living-room wall above that Queen Anne console or even next to that velvet painting of Elvis.) A central wiring closet can put this hardware out of view.

- **Connecting at a single point:** In the section titled "Thinking of networks in different ways," earlier in this chapter, we tell you that most of the networks we describe in this book are based on a star model and that these networks all connect at a single central location. Why not have all these networks connect in the same area to make it easier to do things like connect your Internet line to your computer network?

- **Providing easy access:** When you want to change the capabilities of your networks or troubleshoot a problem, having everything neatly arranged and easily accessible can eliminate a source of frustration.

What goes in your wiring closet?

Most — but not all — of the cabling and infrastructure components of a home's networks can and should be installed in the area of your home designated as your wiring closet. A few items — mainly parts of your home entertainment network — are better located elsewhere (we'll get to the concept of a *media center* in just a moment). There are also a few systems that you may install in your home network that are inherently decentralized, like X-10 components, intercom systems, and wireless phone or data network systems. These devices don't necessarily have central control units, or they have control units that are supposed to be out in the open, readily accessible, and not hidden away in a wiring closet.

The devices that *should* go in a wiring closet include

 ✔ Your coaxial video-distribution panel (see Chapter 6)

 ✔ Patch panels for CAT-5 phone and data wiring (see Chapter 10)

 ✔ Central controllers for KSU telephone systems (see Chapter 10)

 ✔ Cable, DSL, or ISDN modems and routers (see Chapter 13)

 ✔ Ethernet hubs or switches (see Chapter 14)

 ✔ Stand-alone home-automation control units (see Chapter 19)

Some newer cable and DSL modems utilize a USB instead of an Ethernet interface. Although this simplifies connecting one of these modems to a single computer, it makes it just about impossible to directly connect them to a centralized LAN hub. If your service provider leases or sells you one of these modems, it will have to be collocated with a server computer in your home office or other location.

Choosing a location for your wiring closet

In the best-case scenario (like when you've struck it rich and are building a custom-designed home), you can create a dedicated room for your networking equipment — a central wiring closet just like modern offices and other commercial buildings have.

If we were starting a home from scratch this way, we'd try to design the wiring closet

 ✔ On the main floor of the house.

 ✔ Near an outside wall for easy interconnection to incoming service feeds.

 ✔ Above an accessible part of the basement (if you have a basement).

 ✔ With adequate lighting, ventilation, and climate protection (not in the garage, in other words).

 ✔ With adequate AC power line receptacles to power devices like video amplifiers, Ethernet hubs, and key phone systems.

Such a closet needn't be too large. An 8-x-8-foot room would be more than adequate to handle all of the centrally located network equipment for even the largest home, and you could get away with half that floor space if you needed to.

Of course, the vast majority of home builders or remodelers simply don't have the luxury of adding this kind of dedicated space for a network wiring closet. In these cases, you have to try to make some other part of the house do double duty as your wiring closet. Here are some other places to consider locating your wiring closet:

- ✔ **The utility or laundry room:** The biggest disadvantage of this location is the potential for high humidity — so make sure your clothes dryer is well ventilated to the outdoors.

- ✔ **A protected garage:** The potential for dust and extreme temperatures may make this location less than optimal for some homes, but the garage can be a useful location.

- ✔ **The basement:** Many people choose the basement for a central wiring node because it's easy to run wires through a drop ceiling. Basements can be a very good locations, but keep in mind that basements can be both dusty and damp.

- ✔ **A weather-protected outdoor closet:** We recommend this location only as a last resort, but it could be acceptable in a place with a mild climate. We wouldn't recommend putting any active electronics, like Ethernet hubs or phone systems out here, however.

An important thing to keep in mind is that the natural enemies of electrical and electronic equipment are moisture, dust, and temperature extremes — so locations that may work for someone in Florida or California may not make as much sense for your house in Maine.

Feeding audio and video from the media center

Although most of the network systems in your house — specifically the data wiring, phone wiring, and the coaxial video-distribution wiring — are best located in a wiring closet, the parts of your network that provide the audio and video signals you send through your house are more appropriately centralized in the room where you use them the most. We call this area the *media center.*

What components fit into a media center?

Chances are, you want to be able to quickly access your CD player (unless it's one of those CD juke boxes that holds 200 CDs) and your video source equipment (like the VCR and DVD player) to change discs or tapes and for local (in-room) listening and viewing. So it makes sense to centrally locate your audio network and the source equipment for your video network in a separate place from the rest of your wiring closet. We like to call this location the media center, but if that sounds a bit too much like CNN Central in Atlanta, you can just call it the "room with all the fun toys."

What goes into a media center? Basically all of your audio and video equipment:

✔ Video source devices such as VCRs, DVDs, laserdisc players, and *ReplayTV boxes,* which we describe in Chapter 5

✔ Audio source devices such as CD players, radio tuners, cassette decks, and turntables

✔ Video modulators (see Chapter 6)

✔ Audio amplifiers and controllers for your whole-home audio system (see Chapter 8)

✔ Impedance-matching panels for audio amplifiers (see Chapter 8)

✔ Connecting blocks and emitters from your IR control network (see Chapter 19)

Your video-distribution panel doesn't go in this room — just the source equipment and a modulator that can distribute signals back over your two-way coaxial network to the panel located in the wiring closet.

In addition to the audio/video equipment that you're distributing across your network, you want to have all of the stuff needed to do local listening and viewing in your media center. In other words, you want a television or video monitor of some sort, speakers and a surround sound receiver or controller/amplifier system in this room.

Setting up a media center

Getting all of this gear (and related wiring) discreetly located in your media center can be a bit problematic. This room, unlike a wiring closet, is meant to be a public space in your house, not a place where you can hide away unsightly bundles of wire and racks of equipment. So your aesthetic requirements will be a bit higher.

The best solution to this problem is to design the room so that you have an enclosed equipment-and-connection area where you can put your *whole-home equipment* — the equipment that you don't need to access to watch a program or listen to something — such as impedance matching equipment, modulators, and so on. Your equipment and connection area could be a well-ventilated closet, if one is available. We've even seen really sophisticated setups with a false wall behind the TV and equipment racks to allow access to the backs of all of the gear. If you can't find a separate space for your whole-home equipment, you can connect all of your outgoing speaker wires and IR cables to wall outlets behind your equipment rack, and use short cables to connect these outlets to the equipment itself.

If you really can't find an aesthetically pleasing way of getting all of this stuff in your media center, you might consider putting the audio amplification and impedance matching equipment in your wiring closet (along with all of your whole-house speaker wire connections). Use the shortest run possible of high quality, shielded audio interconnects to connect these amps to the audio source equipment back in your media center. We believe in keeping interconnect runs as short as possible, but sometimes you have just have to make do.

You may face one more issue in equipping your media center: how to integrate source components both into your whole-home audio and video networks and into the TVs, receivers, and amps that you use locally in the media center. For example, you may want to connect your DVD player to both your video-distribution panel (through a modulator) and to a multichannel surround sound receiver and widescreen TV for home theater use in the media center. Or you may want to connect your CD player to the same receiver for listening over those fancy speakers in the media center and also connect it a multi-room audio system. Most of this source equipment has only a single set of outputs, so how do you connect it to two separate systems? There are a few ways:

- ✔ For video source devices, try to choose modulators that have a loop-through connection, so you can run a set of A/V cables from the source to the modulator, and another set from the modulator to your surround sound receiver and TV.

- ✔ Many of the newest DVD players include two sets of A/V outputs, so you can send one set to the modulator and another to the surround sound receiver and TV.

- ✔ Audio-only sources — like CD players — are a bit more tricky. There are two ways of getting them into both systems:

  - • If you're using a distribution amplifier to feed the output of the source device to several amplifiers for a multizoned or multi-amped whole-house audio network, you can use one of the distribution amplifier's outputs to feed the surround sound receiver.

  - • You can skip the CD player entirely if you have a DVD player — just about every DVD player made can also play audio CDs.

You can't prewire too much

Here are things we've *never* heard anyone say after building or rewiring a house:

- ✔ Boy, I wish I hadn't run that extra computer network cable to my home office.
- ✔ Gee, I'm really ticked off that I have a video outlet in all of the bedrooms.

On the other hand, we *do* hear the exact opposite — often accompanied by a Homer Simpson sound — *Doh!*

The bottom line is that wiring your house just to be good usually fails. Even with prior planning and forethought, you're likely to run across some spot in your house, some day, where you'll urgently need some wire that you simply forgot to run.

But you can minimize this kind of situation by prewiring your home while you have the opportunity. Even if you don't plan on doing anything with it, get the wire in the walls before the drywall is up, painted, stenciled, and wallpapered, and before the pictures are hanging. Relatively speaking, wire is cheap; labor to cut the walls open and start over is expensive.

Let practicality be your guide. If you know beyond a doubt that you'll never watch TV in the bathroom (maybe you have some philosophical opposition to that concept), then don't run coaxial cable to the bathroom. Keep in mind, however, that you won't own your home forever, and the potential next owner may be looking at two homes just like yours, and that person may love to watch TV while soaking in the Jacuzzi.

If you're newly constructing a house, you can do a couple of things to make running future wires easier. First, have a drop ceiling installed in your basement. Second, have a PVC pipe run from your wiring closet to your attic. These steps make running future wires much easier. For more futureproofing tips, see Chapter 22.

One factor that may mitigate the need to do a lot of prewiring in a home is the rapid development of wireless and existing wire technologies. Advances in these fields may someday, in the not-so-distant future, put wireless systems on an equal footing with wired ones, in terms of price and performance. When, or if, this happens, it won't make your wired networks any less useful, however. And you can do all sorts of things better with wired networks in the here and now, and probably well into the future.

Fiber-optic faux pas?

Perhaps you've been skipping around the book, reading up on the stuff that goes into all the different networks in a home, and you've been scratching your head (or maybe even composing a nasty e-mail) and wondering why you can't find any mention at all about installing fiber-optic cabling in the home.

Well . . . we didn't forget about it. Instead, we made a conscious decision not to recommend installing fiber in the home. The main reason for this is the simple fact that there are somewhere around zero actual applications for fiber among all the thousands of consumer electronics devices sold today. The only place that fiber really ever comes into play is for some very specialized digital audio interconnects, the kind used to connect CD and DVD players to external Digital to Analog Converters. That's really it.

But isn't fiber the future — and isn't this book all about taking a long-term view? The answers to those questions are "Yes and yes, but. . . ." Although someday in the future, fiber-optic cable may be the most common cabling for connecting home audio, video, data, and phone networks, today, no clear standards govern which of the many various kinds of fiber will be commonly used to connect home devices, and no consensus has been reached on how fiber will be connected and laid out in a home.

We do recommend that you give yourself a head start by designing your home in such a way that adding new cable types like fiber will be easier when the time comes (see Chapter 22 for more on that). But for now, we think that running fiber in a home is probably a waste of time and money.

Investigating "All-in-One Solutions"

Although you may only want to install one type of network that we describe in this book (such as a phone network or a home-automation network), we believe that most homeowners will want to install, at a bare minimum, a home network that will be able to handle the three main types of network applications (that is, telephones, data, and video). We're not alone in that belief. Most of the major wiring and network infrastructure vendors seem to believe it too, and they're beginning to offer all-in-one *structured cabling systems*. These systems let you choose a single vendor to supply (and in many cases, install) a complete, integrated home-networking infrastructure.

What are structured cabling systems all about?

Most structured cabling systems for the home are offshoots of similar (and more complicated) packages of hardware and wiring that networking system vendors have been offering their corporate customers for years. The concept is simple — go to the vendor, tell them what your needs are, and they give you an off-the-shelf, soup-to-nuts system, ready for installation.

For the most part, structured cabling systems are made up of exactly the same parts that you'd use if you were building separate home networks by yourself. Specifically, you'll find that most contain the following components:

- ✔ **A service center:** Usually modular, wall-mounted components, service centers combine phone and data *patch panels* (handy devices for quickly connecting many wires in a single place) and a *video distribution center* (a device that enables one or more video signals to be sent to multiple TVs via a video network) into a single unit — making for a neater installation.

- ✔ **All-in-one cables:** Most structured cabling systems include cabling that combines telephone and data cabling and coaxial cable for video in a single cable jacket. Some systems even include fiber-optic cables in the same jacket (for future uses — see the sidebar "Fiber-optic faux pas?" for our opinion on the matter).

- ✔ **Customized wall outlet plates:** Matched up with the all-in-one cable, these faceplates provide modular connectors for your phone, data and video outlets.

As you can see, nothing about these systems is really different from the pieces you'd install if you were designing your own home networks. They're simply put together in one big kit to facilitate buying, designing, and installing your network infrastructure.

What you can (and can't) use all-in-one systems for

If you read the product literature from most of these manufacturers (we tell you where to find it in just a moment), you get the impression that a structured cabling system can do everything but clean the kitchen sink. That's not untrue — we're not accusing anyone of lying — but some of the capabilities and applications that you see listed for these systems are based on forward-looking marketing projections rather than on what you can actually do in the here and now. Many of the applications that these systems support don't really exist in the marketplace yet — things like CEBUS (Consumer Electronics Bus — a proposed standard for home networking) standard audio over UTP cabling, for example.

We mention this not to disparage the structured cabling system, but rather to warn you that installing one may not take care of all of your home networking needs. For example, the following applications usually are not easily supported by most structured systems:

✔ **Alarm systems:** While some security features, like security cameras, can fit into a structured cabling system, a full-featured, monitored, hard-wired security system will require its own wiring — usually installed by a registered professional installer. Your structured wiring systems will, however, allow you to interface the alarm to an outgoing telephone system for monitoring purposes.

✔ **Whole-home hi-fi audio:** Structured wiring systems are designed to allow low-fi, intercom-style audio distribution throughout your home, but they don't include the speaker wiring and distribution systems to get hi-fi audio around your home.

✔ **Remote-control distribution for audio and video systems:** Most systems do not support this functionality. Only a few systems provide for it, either by providing IR signaling over the video coaxial cable or by letting you use unused pairs of wire on your telephone network to carry IR signaling data.

So, you're probably thinking, what *do* these systems support? Quite a lot, actually. At a bare minimum, a structured cabling system should

✔ **Provide a flexible telephone network** using high-quality unshielded twisted-pair (UTP) phone cabling, and a modular, configurable termination system at the service center.

✔ **Provide a similar computer network** of Category 5 (high-speed rated) UTP cabling for data networking.

✔ **Provide a centrally distributed coaxial cable (usually RG6) network** for distributing video signals.

✔ **Provide an all-in-one modular termination panel** to neatly terminate all of this network wiring in your wiring closet.

Additional applications — such as alarms, hi-fi audio, and infrared networking — may be supported by these systems if systems like CEBUS become popular.

Who makes all-in-one systems?

Just about every company that specializes in network cabling has begun to offer a residential structured cabling system. Those that haven't are sure to begin soon. So keeping in mind the fact that this is a growing marketplace, here's a list of some of the major vendors and their Web pages:

✔ Monster Cable Products (Monster WireAmerica): www.monstercable.com

✔ ModTap RCS (Residential Cabling Systems): www.modtap.com

✔ Lucent HomeStar: www.lucent.com/netsys/homestar

- ✔ ChannelPlus: `www.channelplus.com`
- ✔ Siemon Home Cabling Systems: `www.siemon.com`
- ✔ AMP OnQ: `www.ampincorporated.com/product/onq.html`
- ✔ FutureSmart: `www.futuresmart.com`
- ✔ USTec: `www.ustec.inter.net`

Chapter 3

Cool Stuff Home Networks Can Do

● ●

● ●

> *"I am platform neutral — it doesn't matter to me whether people receive telecommunication services by cable, satellite, streaming, wires, wireless cable, or mental telepathy."*
>
> *— Rep. Tom Bliley, Chairman, Senate Commerce Committee regarding 1999 telecommunications network regulation*

We can't help you create a future-proofed plan for mental telepathy, but we certainly can help you with the rest. We'll just have to assume that mental telepathy falls into the wireless category and move on from there.

All the rest of the telecommunication services that Representative Bliley speaks of, however, are going to be coming to your home. Soon, that same home network will enable you to do numerous things that you never thought were possible.

Neat Phone Tricks

When you define a phone in its historical sense — that is, a device with a handset and a base unit — there are lots of options available to the home networker. You can

> ✔ **Go multiline.** Why install a second home phone line that only goes to one phone? With the proper wiring, you could access that second line from any outlet in the house. Two lines not enough? How about three, four, or more lines?

✔ **Get distinctive.** How about giving all the members of the household their own distinctive ringing tones so that they know who the call is for when the phone rings? You can use certain phone-company features along with your home phone network to avoid buying extra phone lines for your household.

✔ **Get conferenced.** Though it may sound really corporate, consumer-grade conferencing systems make sense where the speakerphones of most phones don't do the trick. These systems come in handy when calling Grandma and Grandpa, and they're more fun too!

✔ **Get transferred.** With a home phone system, you can transfer calls around the house. Know that your spouse is in the garage? Send the call out there.

✔ **Intercom someone.** A home phone system is a great way to get a home-wide intercom system. You can access different rooms by entering different extensions. And you can monitor rooms, too. By tying the system to your front door, you can have visitors leave a message on your phone system when you're not home.

✔ **Answer your door.** Use one of the new Doorcom systems to answer the door when you're away. These systems have a doorbell, speakerphone and microphone, and with a smart home, they can call you where you are vacationing to let you speak with the person at the door via the telephone.

✔ **Get video.** With a videophone, you can see who you are talking to. (Depending on the time of day, that may or may not be a good thing.) Some videophones link up with your TV set for even better viewing — but still use regular phone lines.

✔ **Go wireless.** A home phone is only as good as the length of its cord, but cordless phones can really give you freedom when you need to run all over the house. That's not new. But what is new is the convergence of home cordless base stations with cellular or PCS type phones — so-called dual mode phones that allow you to talk all you want for free (at least no airtime charges) when you are near your base station, but switch over to cellular or PCS frequencies when you leave your home. The phone — and your phone number — goes with you wherever you go.

✔ **Get some sleep.** You can program your home telephone system to automatically route inbound calls to an answering machine without ringing any of the phones in the house. Or, you can selectively ring only certain phones in certain places.

Today, however, the definition of *phone* is being stretched. You can make phone calls from your PC through a microphone and headset, or watch the called party on your computer screen. There are screen phones that allow you to do everything from home banking to grocery shopping — from the comfort of your nearest phone outlet.

The convergence of the computer and telephone realms is driving the telephones to look and act more like computers, and computers to work more like phones. Phones are starting to be able to send and receive e-mail or send faxes. And computers allow you, as mentioned, to make phone calls.

A properly designed home network will let you do whatever you want with any of these devices.

Entertainment Everywhere

Your home entertainment system can cost a lot of money, but when you go to your bedroom at night, that stack of electronics equipment in the living room is pretty much useless. A home network allows you to tap into that media complex instead of duplicating it in each room. A great home network will take that showcase of an entertainment center and distribute it around the house. That makes each room a showcase.

A smart home allows you to:

- **Be free to roam the house:** Want to watch a movie on the living room VCR in your bedroom, or CNN while cooking dinner? By running your home network to these rooms, you can distribute the audio and video signals to these locations as easily as you route the signal to your TV set in the living room.

- **Get flexible:** How about starting to watch a movie on demand in the living room, but going to the bedroom to watch the ending? No longer are you a slave to where the device is located.

- **Get creative:** How about using the picture-in-picture capability of your TV set to monitor the kids in the playroom while you're watching HBO? By linking your video monitoring capability with your television systems, you can have the best of both possible worlds.

- **Stay sane:** Want to listen to that holiday music over your intercom system, instead of blasting the stereo loud enough on the first floor so you can hear it in your office on the third floor?

- **Focus your investments:** By making the most use of the devices you have, you can focus future investments on only those pieces that enable you to take maximum advantage of your existing equipment. Already have a VCR, DSS receiver, tape deck, CD player, and receiver? Great, put your money into a great display or widescreen TV, and let those other devices drive the new video capabilities over the home network.

Technologies are quickly arriving that will allow you to hang your high-quality, flat-panel TV set on the wall, perhaps over the fireplace. Moreover, this same TV set will be able to function as your computer screen and video monitor. The components of today's computers tend to be close together (generally sitting right on top of each other or at least taking up a general area of a desk), but tomorrow's computer components will be able to be farther away from each other, communicating via a wireless connection. So you'll be free to sit in a comfortable place with your wireless keyboard.

Because video is such a critical feature of most households worldwide, it makes sense to make sure you can maximize your pleasure through an entertainment network in your home.

Internet Outlets

For years, *getting connected* meant that you were having a phone line installed. Today, it means getting hooked up to the Internet.

What makes the Internet so influential is that it is everywhere. The Internet is very quickly reaching the point of ubiquity worldwide. It took decades for that to happen with regular phone service. The Internet is becoming commonplace all over the globe.

No joke. You can watch people climb Mount Everest; the transmissions are coming live, from the mountain itself, compliments of the Internet. British millionaire Richard Branson was connected to the Internet from his balloon floating 25,000 feet high in the sky — allowing him to write blow-by-blow (so to speak) reports of his efforts to be the first to fly around the world in a balloon. The new BMW prototypes provide web surfing via monitors that are built into the backs of their car seats. The Internet is everywhere.

By the year 2005, look for Internet access to be as common in households as electricity and water. By then, the Internet will be a utility like all other utilities. Many apartments will be rented with Internet access included. You'll get Internet access in your hotel rooms and on your planes.

The question is then, "How do I get access to the Internet from the various parts of my home?" The answer: "With a smart home!"

A truly smart home turns electrical, telephone, cable, and other wired interfaces into Internet outlets — tunnels through your brick and mortar to the wired world beyond. And it's not just wireline access, it's wireless, too.

With a smart home, you can

 ✔ **Network your computing resources:** If you want to have multiple PCs operating on an internal home LAN, that's part and parcel of what we are talking about here. Why have a printer at each home workstation when printers are not used that much? Share one printer, one scanner, and Internet access among multiple devices and save money and make your overall data LAN simpler.

- ✔ **Simultaneously access the Internet:** You could be working in your office downstairs, accessing the corporate internal network (intranet). Your spouse could be in the living room on the couch ordering groceries from the local grocery store's online Web site. Your 12-year old son could be upstairs in his bedroom playing Quake II on a multiplayer Internet network. And your studious 10-year old daughter might be accessing her school's extranet, working on homework with other kids. All of this could happen at the same time, over the same network.

If you think that you are going to have a lot of people in your household accessing the Internet at the same time, you might want to consider getting a high-speed access option, like a cable modem or DSL link. We tell you more about that in Chapter 20.

- ✔ **Make and receive phone calls via the Internet:** With the right endpoint equipment, you can send and receive phone calls over the Internet. You could use your PC, an adapter for your phone, an adapter for your fax machine, a videophone, or a special Internet Telephony appliance (that essentially looks like a phone). Any of these things will allow you to communicate over the Internet, for free (or nearly so), with parties conceivably very far away.

The quality of your Internet telephony will vary substantially based on the type of device used and the distance you are trying to call. The more hops that your data takes as it traverses the Internet, the more delay that can occur, causing poor quality. If you want to send and receive calls via the Internet, we highly recommend that you read *Internet Telephony For Dummies* (IDG Books Worldwide, Inc.). Of course, we're biased . . . we wrote it.

The true benefits of Internet connectivity come later on down the road, where all sorts of devices start expecting Internet connectivity to be there. More in the next chapter on this.

Remote Control of Everything (Just About)

Another great thing about a smart home is the control that you have. Depending on how complex a home automation system you put in place, you could be controlling everything from the drapes to the heating system. A smart home allows you to add more and more control in the future by tapping the endpoints, so you can start off modestly.

With a home network, you can

- ✔ **Control your lights:** Simple X-10 home-automation systems attach to the electrical system and allow you to control your electrical devices from a common computing platform. So, you can turn lights on and off and check out the heating levels in different zones, by using an X-10 compliant system.

- ✔ **Control your remote controls:** We hate to admit it, but one of us (we won't tell who) has *five* remote controls in one room of his house. Extending that functionality to other rooms in the house will take a lot of remote controls. But with a truly smart home, you can extend control over those devices to other rooms, either by radio frequency or infrared extension units, so that you maintain the same level of control that you would have if you were in the same room. We recommend (at least one of us does) that you get a universal remote control for those rooms, however. (Five . . . jeez.)

- ✔ **Control your computers:** One of the benefits of having connectivity to your various computers on the same network is that you can do things in a coordinated way. For instance, suppose you wanted to back up the computers on a regular basis. You can create a schedule on one computer, and have it access the hard disks of the other computers on the LAN and create a copy of key files. A truly wired user will store these files off site, in the case of fire or theft of the machines. You can also coordinate new software upgrades and virus/junk e-mail protection. Being connected makes a lot of functionality possible in the computer realm.

- ✔ **Control your environment:** Too often, people are slaves to their various devices. If you don't know how to set the time on the VCR, you'll get that darn blinking 12:00. (No, neither of us has that, thank you.) Most people cannot tape programs with their VCRs, and many have problems coordinating among various interconnected devices, like getting the cable box to change to Channel 29 so they can tape *Star Trek Voyager* at 9:00! While the solution is not instantaneous — as there is still a lot more work to be done in this area — having a home network makes it easier for you to control all of this stuff. Whether it is your entertainment system, your computer, your security system, your telephone network, your appliances, whatever, we're working toward a more friendly user interface that uses your computer or TV set to control your home around you. For those of us who have used single-line LCDs for years to program complex things, this new interface cannot come soon enough.

- ✔ **Control your life:** Some home-management systems have automated annunciators that can tell you things you ought to know, like today is your mother's birthday, or today is the day to take the trash cans to the street. Linked with the Internet, telephone, or intercom systems, these commands can be sent to very specific locations — like catching you as you walk out the door.

To Infinity and Beyond!

The home network is an enabler. The bullet list in the preceding section are all things you can do today, to one degree or another. After you are interconnected, you will find ways to make your life easier (at least until the power goes out). Getting interconnected is your first step, but as Neil Armstrong said, "That's one giant leap for mankind!"

So conceptualize that you have a home network interspersed and interconnected in your home. Now let's see what we will be able to do with it in the near future.

Connecting your kitchen appliances and more

Being interconnected is going to change things rather dramatically. You will be able to use common consumer devices to do seemingly odd things, but things that really make sense when you think about them:

- ✔ **Check your e-mail via refrigerator:** New thin, touch-screen, flat-screen computer monitors will fit nicely into your refrigerator door — which is mostly insulation anyway — without compromising much. Add the appropriate computer chip and LAN access to the innards, and you have a very heavy computer that also serves ice. Now you will have a place to keep your shopping lists, send and receive e-mails, and maintain all your phone numbers.

- ✔ **Surf the Web on your microwave:** We have no idea why you'd want to use this feature, but trial products are on the market that allow you to surf the Web from your microwave. Waiting three minutes for your coffee to warm up can be a pain, but that's probably not enough time to check a Web site. Still, you could wake up to warming coffee with closing stock quotes, appointment reminders, weather predictions, school closings, and so on. Personally, we'd go with the refrigerator.

- ✔ **Tie your sprinkler system to** www.weather.com: Never get caught watering your lawn in the rain again! By tying your sprinkler to the Internet, you'll be able to check the weather predictions and let your sprinkler system decide whether to water the lawn as scheduled. During extremely high temperature periods, the system may decide to water a little more frequently. And if you're in a drought area, it can forgo a cycle by monitoring any bans on watering lawns.

- ✔ **Keep your car tuned:** Most new cars have computer chips that track the vehicle's health. Imagine driving into your garage each night and having a remote sensor interrogate your automobile about its day — and interact with remote databases and troubleshooting systems at your car's manufacturing facility located 1,300 miles away. This system will be able to track your oil change needs and automatically schedule an appointment with your dealership. You'll also be able to have it download the latest maps for your area to your car's hard disk, along with your updated calendar and revised phone contacts for your car's cell phone to use.

✔ **Talk to your TV:** New technology coming out of the voice recognition industry is going to turn your home into *Star Trek*'s USS Enterprise. If your smart home happens to have a microphone in each room, you can say, "Computer, put the incoming message on the screen," just like Captain Picard. (By the way, in case you haven't figured it out yet, our lives revolve around *Star Trek* and Disney World!) For more information on this brave new technology, check out the sidebar titled "A speech odyssey."

✔ **Stay healthy:** Interconnecting your kitchen and your computer resources in your house and on the Internet will give you great access to all sorts of nutritional information and online recipe sites. Imagine tracking your diet on a device in your kitchen, and asking for a suggested dinner based on what you ate last week and what you have in the pantry right now. You will be able to converse with your *virtual chef* to refine the menu given your tastes for the evening.

Let your TV show you the Web

Because people without computers are very keen on using their familiar television interface to surf the Internet, manufacturers have been scurrying to bring the Web to your TV screen.

A smart home allows you to directly access the Web through your TV set. The current technology works almost like a toggle switch — you can either view the TV or surf the Internet, but not necessarily at the same time (except maybe by using picture-in-picture capability).

A speech odyssey

Dijima, a California company, promises to allow you to communicate with the stuff in your house in the same way that you communicate with people. Dijima's software will allow you to operate TVs, VCRs, CD and tape players, and other household components just by ordering them around. Dijima uses core technology from IBM and Dragon Systems, two leaders in voice recognition, combined with its own speech-to-text software, to send commands to the designated devices. If the system doesn't understand you, it will prompt you to be more specific, with questions like, "Did you mean a tape from the VCR or a tape from your audio tape player? . . . Dave? . . . Dave? . . . ."

The leg bone's connected to the what?

Smart homes are going to be big for a single, critical reason: All the major consumer appliance manufacturers and electronic goods manufacturers want them to be big. They believe that consumers will choose to buy an Internet-capable dishwasher over fixing their old, broken one. The manufacturers are practicing a form of planned obsolescence.

Think about the benefits to the manufacturers. Against the grain of consumer privacy advocates — who won't be happy at all — manufacturers will be able to more readily determine how you use an appliance, when you use it, how frequently you use it, and so on.

But more importantly, manufacturers will be able to support the customers as long as they own the appliance. Manufacturers will be able to tell when you install the device and then automate registration. They will know when the appliance breaks, probably before you know yourself. With the right, internal diagnostic chips, the manufacturer will be able to identify the problem and send a properly trained repairman out to your house, complete with the part she needs in hand. Manufacturers will recognize when the overall unit is failing and make proactive recommendations to upgrade. Imagine getting a special offer from Whirlpool to swap out your dryer because it has reached a 10,000 cycle point!

This feat will be possible because the foot bone's (the dryer) connected to the ankle bone (the home network); the ankle bone's connected to the leg bone (the Internet); the leg bone's connected to the thigh bone (the manufacturer); the thigh bone's connected to the backbone (all the manufacturer's repair and sales offices); and you know how the rest of the song goes.

What's coming down the pike is a wonderful combination of the two together, and the sky is truly the limit here. Here are some things you'll be able to do:

- ✔ **Click on your favorite actor:** Ever watched a movie and said, "I know that actor from somewhere," and then racked your brain for the rest of the movie trying to figure out who the guy is? With this technology, all you'll have to do point to the actor and click on his image to access his resume, complete with prior roles. Want to go to that actor's fan site? Click on an icon allocated for that purpose. Want to send the actor an e-mail? Click on another icon. When your TV and the Web are connected, they can intertwine shows and databases to create awesome opportunities.

- ✔ **Click on your favorite product:** Imagine watching a 30-second commercial and wanting to find out more about the product being shown. With this technology, you'll be able to click on the product and go to a Web site that lists the product's features and characteristics. Click on another place and see reviews from leading publications like *Consumer Reports*. Click on an icon and see the lowest prices for that product. Like the new gadget James Bond is using in his film? Find out where to buy one by clicking on it. The appearance of specific products on TV shows will change drastically, going well beyond the crass commercialism in *The Truman Show*.

✔ **Click on Grandma:** Combining a small video camera and microphone with your TV monitor creates an instant videoconferencing opportunity. Using your smart home's data backbone, you will be able to hop on the Internet and conference with others. Let Grandma share in your Christmas by enabling her to watch her grandchildren open their presents on the screen. Remarkably, this technology is not all that expensive today, and, combined with high-speed digital access links into the home, it can have surprisingly high quality. Click on Brother and Sister, too, and have a family videoconference. What a great way to show everyone the new baby!

Make phone calls on your computer

You may not realize that your phone calls are really data calls. When you speak into your telephone, your local phone company most likely digitizes your call and sends it across its massive telephone network to either another phone locally or another local or long distance carrier for completion. These telephone networks are basically carrying data — bits of your phone conversation.

So when people first started talking about carrying voice calls over data networks, many said, "What's new about that? Businesses have been doing that for a while." In reality, not much is new about that, except that the data networks for consumers are a new thing. Being able to call someone from your computer is a new experience for the average consumer.

Most new computers can come outfitted with a multimedia configuration, which includes high-quality speakers, a video camera, and a microphone. Well, if you think about what makes up your telephone, you have a microphone and a speaker.

When you make a phone call, your words are converted into data bits and sent to your telephone company's network of computers. From there, your phone company may transfer the call from network to network until the signal reaches the person you're calling. New computers with their speakers and microphones work much like telephones; the Internet is a massive network. For the first time, consumers can combine the two technologies to make telephone calls from their home computers.

Making calls from your computer is also extremely functional. Look at what you can do:

✔ **Have a home PBX:** A *private branch exchange,* or PBX, switch — which most companies use to run their phone networks — is like a mini telephone-company switch that allows stuff like transferring calls from one extension to another, voice mail, call parking, and so on. By running your home phones on your data network instead of your phone network, you can provide each handset with very sophisticated features that you may not otherwise be able to afford. Some of the newest services on the market, such as those from Rhythms NetConnections (`www.rhythms.net`), enable firms to extend their PBX functionality to employees' homes via high-speed, local-access connections. You could have one or more extensions at home that look and operate the same as at work, including allowing interextension dialing within the corporation.

✔ **Receive faxes on your TV:** Just like phone calls, fax transmissions are beginning to move to the Internet. You can currently buy equipment or services that translate faxed documents into digital Internet packets and send them over the Net. At the receiving end, you can choose to print the fax on a fax machine or receive the document as an e-mail attachment. When your TV becomes part of your home's Internet connection — and that will happen soon — you'll be able to preview and read your incoming faxes right on your TV screen. (Later, you can print them out over your home computer network.)

✔ **Shop in Hong Kong:** Envision going to a booth at your local mall, having your body's dimensions scanned, and then using this information to shop anywhere in the world. No more too-short shirts! You will be able to surf the Internet on your TV, find the outfits you want, pick out the color patterns, and then order a custom-fitting garment. You will even be able to use your videoconferencing link or Internet telephony capability to talk with the tailors about your suit. But the interesting thing about the textile industry is that many larger firms cut their garments by using computer-driven lasers. Imagine having your scan feed directly into that!

Check up on your house over the Net

Although they've been around for a long time, home-automation systems are still in their infancy. Most of the systems available now are either old technology (the inexpensive X-10 systems) or very expensive, custom-built systems.

However, you'll soon begin to see home control systems that integrate more fully into your data and telephone networks, enabling you to control them remotely. Right now, a few of the custom systems have a telephone interface that enables you to dial in and use the keypad (or even your voice in some instances) to issue commands to the system controller. The next logical step in this process is to provide a Web interface.

Imagine that one of your home's PCs, using an always-on Net connection like a fast *digital subscriber line* connection or a cable modem, also powers your home control systems. This home control software functions as a Web server to allow you to access your home control system from your office desktop, an airport kiosk, or even your Web-enabled handheld PC. You'll simply have to bring up the URL of your home server, log in, and then navigate through the home control Web page to turn on lights, turn up the heat, or even fire up the hot tub. Pretty cool, huh?

Here are just a few of the things this kind of interface will allow:

- ✔ **Control your appliances' usage:** More and more, companies will start giving you incentives to behave in certain ways. For instance, the power company may encourage you to run laundry at certain hours of the day. A smart home-automation system will be able to interact with the power company's pricing systems to determine the best time of the day to do certain things, and can run them according to those schedules, if that is what you want. Already power companies have different rate periods in some parts of the country.

- ✔ **See-through walls:** Your home-network security system will include a video monitor for the front door, allowing you to see who's there before you open the door. By further interconnecting your security system with Internet access, you can monitor your home remotely, from any Web interface. Suppose that you're at work but think that someone sent an important, overnight package to your home office by accident. With this technology, you will be able to call up your smart home's Web page and check out the video picture of your front stoop. If your hunch is correct, you can go home and get the package. You will also be able to monitor your nanny from work, to make sure that she's not reenacting a scene from some horror movie. (Incidentally, you can also check that the kids aren't throwing wild parties while you're away!)

- ✔ **Turn up the heat:** With a good smart-home design, your telephone system will be interconnected with your heating and cooling systems, which will allow you to monitor and control those systems remotely. Going to go up to your smart vacation home for the weekend? With this technology, you will be able to call ahead and turn the heat on.

- ✔ **Check who's home alone:** Or, have your system dial out to your own pager number when someone (maybe a burglar) enters the back door. With an interconnected system, almost anything is possible.

Chapter 4

Getting It Done: Timelines and Budgets

*Y*our home-network adventure starts in two places — in your head and in your wallet. You need to know where you are going and how much you are willing to spend to get there.

Home networking has an additional aspect to it, like many home decisions: You need to figure out how much of this project you are willing to do yourself versus having others help out. If you really want to, you can build your own home-automation gateway, buying up the various resistors, capacitors, and other components that you need to build the device.

Most of you probably don't want to build your own device, but all sorts of consultants, systems integrators, contractors, and others can help you ensure smart-home success. This chapter helps you figure out when to use these folks and when not to as well as helps you determine the budgetary and timeline considerations involved.

New or Existing Home?

Although we discuss many home-networking options throughout this book, building *your* home network is going to be a very customized effort. You need to winnow these options down to fit your particular situation.

The most important issue when wiring your home is your house's condition; the approaches that you take with a new home and an existing one are quite different. Given that a new home's wiring effort is likely to be more extensive — because you can do more when you are starting from scratch — we generally present all the options possible in a home that you're wiring from scratch. Then we discuss choices (such as wireless options) that you can pursue if a whole-home wiring solution isn't possible in all parts of your home.

Even if you own an existing home, wired solutions aren't necessarily out of the question. Every day, contractors around the world enter houses and snake cables through walls to install alarms, intercoms, phone systems, data networks, automation systems, and so on. Don't assume that you can't reach your home-networking nirvana just because you are not building a house from scratch. But your approach is different from the approach for a new home.

For example, in an existing home, you may want to convert some existing space, like part of a closet or utility room, into your wiring closet. You may also want to rely more heavily on wireless systems, or ones that utilize existing wires. Or you may want to bite the bullet, decide to run new wires, and search around for an experienced telephone or alarm installer who can find some creative ways to run and hide new wires without having to rip walls open and refinish them.

What Do You Want from Your Home Network?

The first step in planning your home network is determining what you want it to do. Do you want a fully automated home, with lights that turn themselves on, drapes that open and shut on their own, and a remotely controlled HVAC (heating, ventilation, and air conditioning system)? Do you want a high-speed computer network that lets you plug a PC or laptop into a jack anywhere in the house and get Internet access? Do you want a sophisticated communications system, with multiple telephone lines, video monitors at the doors, and intercoms throughout your home?

If you're anything like us, all of these things probably sound cool, but going for broke (literally) from the beginning is neither necessary nor wise. You are wise, however, to use any wiring or rewiring opportunity (like a newly constructed home, or one that you're ripping apart for remodeling) to get enough wires to enough places to enable your home network to grow with your needs, without the hassle and expense of doing the wiring thing all over again. If you're installing your home network in your existing home, make sure that you understand how much stringing wire through the walls is going to cost, or plan to install new wireless options.

Whatever you decide to do, a home network is the type of project that works best when accomplished all at once in a well-thought-out fashion. Home networking in a haphazard way results in, well, what most ad hoc do-it-yourselfers' wiring projects end up looking like — a mess.

So before you begin designing (or letting an installer or contractor design) a network and wiring plan for your home, think through how you're going to use each and every room in the home. Do so with an eye toward the future — that spare bedroom that only needs a phone jack and a cable TV outlet may someday be your home office. Then you'll need wiring for an extra phone, as well as some computer networking capabilities. Or perhaps the room will be a nursery; then you'll want an intercom — maybe even a video monitor set up. And when the kids get older, they may need a place to hook up a computer or to plug in the home entertainment system.

As you explore your many home-networking options, aim toward flexibility for the future.

Deciding How Much to Spend

Thinking ahead and prewiring your entire home for every foreseeable contingency may not be as expensive as you think. Several well-respected vendors offer all-in-one kits that put high-speed data communications, telephony, video, home entertainment, and (in some cases) security wiring in place with little or no thinking on your part. Check out Chapter 2 for more information on all-in-one cable solutions.

On the other hand, you can apply the everything-everywhere solution and run high-speed data cables, coaxial video cables, speaker cables, and even fiber-optic cable to several jacks in every room of your home; many homeowners actually go this route. When you come right down to it, home wiring is like money or chocolate — you can never have too much.

The key is to balance your needs, both present and future, against your resources. Bill Gates' house is wired from stem to stern. He also has more money than anyone else in the world. Your own goals — and your funding — may be slightly more modest.

Just because you have to make choices about what you can do right now, doesn't mean that you should forget about building a robust, futureproof wiring system into your home. In fact, the cost of running higher-quality, more capable wiring to most of your home isn't all that much more than running those old-fashioned telephone and cable TV wires that you were going to install in the first place. And while you're at it, you can take certain steps to make running cables easier in the future, should you find that you need more (who knows when you'll need fiber-optic cable in the guest bathroom?).

One of the great things about building a smart home is that many of the network's components are already part of the home's structure — things like wiring panels, cable runs, keypads, switches, and so on — which means that you can usually finance this cost as part of your mortgage. This option helps you stretch out the up-front cost of installing these systems. Some aggressive financing companies also allow you to roll in things like your home entertainment system — you have to ask. A good home builder thinks of these things for you, and often builds such capabilities into the core cost of the house, making the financing very easy for you.

Going Over the Costs

Like everything else, the cost of your network varies depending on the costs in your particular area, inflation, how fancy you get, and so on, but we provide you here with some general information about how much you can expect to spend.

We are basing our pricing on a typical home — two floors, three bedrooms, two-and-a-half baths, and a partially finished basement. However, you can cover a much larger home with very little real impact to our hypothetical budget numbers. To cover a larger area, you do need to add in the cost of extra wiring runs and some extra endpoints, but the real expenses — the source equipment like CD players and central control equipment — are largely fixed, unless you start doubling the size of the house.

Most of the cost in an audio and video distribution system comes from the audio and video equipment itself (rather than the networking infrastructure and components). The audio and video equipment is usually housed in the home entertainment/home theater room. (Part II explains this equipment in detail.) Here are some general costs:

✔ **Home theater:** A home theater can cost you as little as $1,500 if you go with a moderate-sized TV set, a fairly integrated stereo system, and a nice set of home-theater speakers. You can really spend some money in this area, though not as much as you may think. A really great home-theater system runs you about $10,000 to $20,000. Installation costs about 10 percent of your component parts. Nine out of ten home-theater installation jobs fall in this price range.

✔ **Audio/video devices:** Your stereo receivers, DVD players, tape players, laserdisc players, VCRs, and other sources that you find in a home-theater area add between $200 and $400 each.

✔ **Coaxial distribution panel:** Expect to spend about $300 to $400 for a coaxial distribution panel for your home network.

✔ **Modulators:** The modulators that create in-home, video TV channels start off at about $150 for simple single channel models and go up to about $800 for models that can create several channels of stereo TV for your in-home TV network.

✔ **Intercom system:** If you want a stand-alone intercom system, expect to add another $1,200 to $1,500.

Other networks in your home involve the following costs:

✔ **Phone system:** A phone system generally costs around $50–$100 per outlet, or from $500 to $1,500 for a centralized whole-home phone system.

✔ **Data network:** Data networks are relatively inexpensive — less than $200 to buy and install the necessary central components and about $50–$100 per cable run, including cable, connectors, face plates, and so on.

✔ **Home security system:** A home security system averages about $1,200 to install. You also pay about $25 a month for monitoring fees.

✔ **Home-automation system:** By its nature, the cost of your home-automation system can vary all over the place. The cost to turn some lights on and off with a computer-controlled timer is much less than the cost to have androids serve breakfast in bed, for example. The average home-automation project costs around $1,000, but you really do get a bang for your buck.

A moderately smart home generally runs in the neighborhood of $2,000–$4,000 (not including the house of course!).

Depending on what you need to do, you may be able to get away with paying less than this amount. But, we'd rather scare you with big numbers first — while showing you all the ways that you can step down in price and still have a great home network — than to throw unrealistically low numbers your way and set the wrong expectations.

Whatever you do, don't start the process by saying, "I don't want to spend a lot of money on this project." With that defeatist attitude, you end up going for a jury-rigged home network that's not up to snuff. Instead, approach this process with an open mind: Think about what features you'd like to have, share that information with some home-networking experts, and see what happens from there.

The Home Team

The people involved in your project vary according to what you are trying to accomplish. If you are going to put a major home theater in your home — complete with theater seats, a popcorn and candy stand, and screen curtains — then you may bring a home-theater consultant into the process. Most people don't want or need to go to that level.

The cast of characters for your home-networking project can include the following:

✔ **Architect:** This person helps you lay out the initial plans for your home and coordinate with other designers — interior, kitchen, audio/video, lighting, security, and so on — to get their respective visions on paper. Architects create these plans that guide all the activity in the house, but they need the contribution of your individual contractors. Many architects don't have the level of specialty necessary to finalize those drawings. But the architect's drawings are key to making sure that all your speakers, for example, are correctly placed in your home entertainment theater.

✔ **Audio/video consultant:** Your audio/video (A/V) consultant helps you select the right mix of components for your sight and sound systems and helps you integrate all these components together. Your A/V consultant makes sure that the appropriate wiring is run to support your installations and installs the gear in when you're ready. If you're installing a home theater, expect your A/V consultant to get involved with the architect early on too, making recommendations for room sizes, building materials, and so on.

✔ **Builder/contractor:** The general contractor/builders' role is to direct the various other specialty contractors, and make sure that they carry out the intent of the designers. Passing correct information from one contractor (like the home-theater consultant) to the people actually doing the work (like the cabinetmaker who builds the home-theater cabinetry) is crucial. The details are what count here, like cutting out the right size cubby-hole for the kitchen media center.

✔ **Cabinetmaker:** This craftsperson creates cabinets and furniture to meet the special needs of your various systems. As you plan on adding more and more components and subsystems into your home, you'll find that not a lot of off-the-shelf cabinetry meets your needs.

✔ **Computer-systems contractor:** If you work at home or simply have complex computer-networking needs, bringing in a computer-systems contractor to network your computer hardware and interface it to the appropriate systems can be a great time-saver. Also, few electrical contractors really know how to install and test the wiring required to maximize your computing resources, so having a computer-systems contractor install your system may actually substantially increase your systems' performance over time.

✔ **Electrical contractor:** The electrical contractor is a staple of any new home project, but in particular your smart home will require a lot of new items, like surge protectors, extra outlets, direct electrical runs for sensitive equipment (to avoid spikes and surges on the lines), and more. Hiring an electrical contractor who is experienced with smart homes is a definite plus.

✔ **Heating/cooling contractor:** Having a smart home is not just about having a home control system that turns fans on and off. There are many nuances to having a smart heating and cooling system — different zones for maximum control or specialized controls for specific areas (like that wine cellar you were thinking about). Your heating/cooling contractor can help plan out the requirements of your system, making sure that it is as energy-efficient as possible, while at the same time meeting your smart-home requirements.

✔ **Home systems integrator:** This person takes charge of integrating all the different electronic systems in your house, but may or may not do the actual install; specialists for each subsystem may also do part of the work. The integrator should be able to provide your architect with recommendations for where to put your centralized wiring closet, or where to run the wires for specific applications. The home systems integrator also plans with the interior designer to address layout and appearance issues.

✔ **Home-theater consultant:** If you're installing a home theater, getting expert advice is almost a necessity to make sure that your money is well spent. Some A/V consultants can handle this task, but for the pricey systems, you may want to look to an even more specialized group of consultants that only do home theaters. These consultants advise you on everything from audio and video components and placement, to construction guidelines, to the seats and popcorn machine you buy.

✔ **Interior designer:** This person is responsible for making sure that your home-network technology doesn't stick out like a proverbial sore thumb (installing a state-of-the-art home entertainment center in the living room is one thing — making it fit with the overall scheme of your home is another). The interior designer works with your consultants to ensure that what is visible is pleasing to the eye.

✔ **Kitchen designer:** This expert helps you figure out not only a sensible layout for your kitchen, but also your options for integrating the latest technologies into your smart-home design. This designer should work closely with the home systems integrator.

✔ **Landscape architect:** This person ensures that your exterior home automation fits with the way in which your house sits on your property. Together, you discuss things like driveway gates, pathway lighting, automated fountains — even outdoor speakers hidden in rocks. Your landscape architect should work with your security consultant to ensure that lighting is maximized for visual coverage. The landscape architect helps your smart home extend out into your yard, accentuating your outdoor features with selective use of technology.

✔ **Lighting consultant:** Lighting design is often one of the overlooked tasks on your to-do checklist, but it can be one of the most important systems that affects the mood of your home. Home-automation systems work interactively with various light subsystems to control the ambiance, so considering specialized lighting in key areas is important when you want to control the atmosphere. A lighting consultant works early on with the home systems integrator and the architect to define the lighting control requirements and to select a system. The actual wiring, however, is typically handled by the electrical contractor or home systems integrator — unless the lighting arrangement is complex, in which case a specialized lighting contractor may be called in.

- ✔ **Plumbing contractor:** Like the electrical contractor, the plumbing contractor is a must-have for any new home construction. However, the plumber should work with your home systems integrator to plan and install things like temperature controls for your faucets.

- ✔ **Security consultant:** Your security consultants/contractors design a system specifically for your home, and install it. They make sure you have the right coverage to meet your security goals and ensure that the system interfaces with whatever other subsystems are necessary, such as with the telephone lines for calling out to the central station when a burglar trips a sensor.

Whew! Did we leave anyone out? Depending on the amount of money you want to spend, you may indeed have this many people making your smart home a reality. Of course, a more modest project has a more modest number of people stomping around your house. Also, many of the previously mentioned professionals — like kitchen designers, for example — include their services when you purchase their equipment.

Each of these professionals adds something different to the process, but you can actually do many of these tasks with no external help. However, a more intense project does require outside advice. And if you want to ensure that your project is done the right way, the first time, we do recommend that you get help.

Make sure that you pick advisors who share your vision of an ideal smart home. The people you choose should have some experience with this sort of thing. Look at their portfolios to see whether their previous work represents your vision. An old commercial has a less-than-bright-looking mechanic eyeing an automatic transmission, scratching his head, and saying, "I always wanted to fix one of these. . . ." Don't make that mistake.

Get out your napkin

Your first step in building your whole-home network is to visualize what you want. Then you need to sit down with your designers and consultants to refine your vision into a cost-effective reality.

The following list is a rough timeline you can use as you're planning and building your wired home. Your personal timeline may take half as long — or twice as long — so feel free to compact or stretch this as you must.

- ✔ **Month 1:** Meet and interview various architects and key consultants; hire your choices; visit demonstration rooms; visit libraries and bookstores for ideas and cappuccino. (By the way, you'll be doing great if you can keep this effort to a month.)

✔ **Month 2:** If you're part of the 1 percent who can afford a truly custom-designed home, then you're ready now to sit down with your architect and start brainstorming design. Plan to spend a month or two, at least, in this process. Finding a floor plan and front elevation that you like isn't too difficult, provided you can make a few modifications. Now the architect just needs to re-create the plan with your specific needs in mind, bringing the time frame and the price tag way down. Although still early in the process, you may also want to choose an interior designer and landscape architect.

✔ **Month 3:** Final (you hope) refinement of plans. Typically, the architect draws up not only the floor plans, but also the electrical wiring plans for key subsystems. Unfortunately, very few architects will read this book before designing your system, so they may provide a standard "been doing it since the '60s" plan. You, most likely, will bring much of the technical knowledge and terminology to the process. So, you either need to find a home-networking specialist or you need to work closely with the architect to describe the needs of each room and the system as a whole.

✔ **Month 4:** Request for bids and selection of builder/contractor; finalization of budget and plans; detailed drawings of wiring schematics and special construction are approved with builder; the builder applies for and receives permits. These things may take more than a month, but we're optimists.

✔ **Month 5:** Lot cleared; foundation dug; security team on hand to do site survey and external installs; pipe and wiring installed under foundation; foundation poured.

✔ **Months 6–8:** Framing is done; windows and roof are installed; key consultants tour the site for revisions and planning; plumbing and heating contractors install their wiring, piping, and conduit. (If your new house is big or the weather is bad, you may be talking longer than two months here. Building a new house truly teaches the virtue of patience.)

✔ **Month 9:** Various contractors install wiring for data, telephone, security, audio, video, and other special wiring such as for an intercom, before and after the electrician does the electrical work. Insulation goes in.

✔ **Months 10–12:** Sheetrock and plaster are installed; interior wood and finishing work begins, including any special cabinetry; interior subsystem installs take place as well, including:

- A/V contractor installs any in-wall speakers and intercom systems

- Telephone/data systems team installs data/telephone systems

- Security contractor installs endpoint devices and control system

- Electrical contractor/lighting designers install lighting and controls

- Plumber installs fixtures

- Home-automation expert coordinates system install

✔ **Month 13:** Final construction work on interior of house; painting, tiles, carpet, wallpaper, and all the stuff you spent hours agonizing over; final subsystem contractor; testing; system checks. You're probably closer to Month 18 by now, and you've probably blown your budget by a bit. But the important part is to make it through alive and with your marriage intact.

Don't forget about the building inspector. The best-laid plans can succumb to a busy building inspector whose approval is often required to go to the next stage of your multistage project.

The final push

After the plumbing and electrical is in (and in some cases, just before), your various contractors busily rough in their wiring and other conduit systems before the insulation goes in.

Your building contractor and/or systems integrator should coordinate the majority of this final stage of the project. Because many of the smart-home systems stand alone at this point — you mostly have a slew of wiring going from various points in the house back to a concentration point in your base-ment or other designated area — you don't need to worry about much coordination among these players.

You do need to coordinate what you run through any special conduits placed to make running wires easier. For instance, running electrical wiring in the same conduit as your telephone, data, and/or A/V wiring is a very bad move. The electrical lines create electromagnetic flux that ruins your data and video throughput, not to mention your phone calls. This is surprisingly common in many new-home construction projects, so look out for it.

After all the rough-in work is complete (and you have wires all over the place), the sheetrock and other wall coverings go up. The house is finished, and although some items, such as in-wall speakers, go in before all the finish work is complete, much of it goes in only after everything else is just about done. You connect all your components to their connection points, and the control panels are installed.

Testing can be exhaustive (not to mention loud in the case of the stereo), but you can never test too much before accepting a house from your collec-tive of contractors. Make sure to hook equipment to all your outlets and test, test, test.

Part II
Making Your Home an Entertainment Center

The 5th Wave
By Rich Tennant

"The kids are getting up right now. When we wired the house, we added vibrating pager technology to their bunkbeds."

In this part . . .

*F*ace it: The television is a major focus of almost any home, worldwide. In our business, we've traveled all over the globe. We've seen tents in the desert with camels parked out back, dinner cooking over a fire, and a TV set inside. People like and want their video. Those enamored with audio feel just as strongly.

The key is building your home entertainment system so that you can enjoy it everywhere you want to . . . not just in the confines of a particular room or a particular space. Your home entertainment system should be in the whole home — omnipresent to the point of total flexibility.

In this part, we tell you all about how to create your home entertainment backbone in your house. We discuss all the major elements of a whole-home audio/video network and the advantages of connecting all the multimedia elements together. We talk about all the different inputs and outputs required, as well as some tips and tricks for ensuring the success of your home entertainment system.

Chapter 5

Breaking the Entertainment Bottleneck (Without Breaking the Bank)

. . . .

In This Chapter

▶ Making your home more fun

▶ Getting centered

▶ Understanding tubes, screens, and thinner media

▶ Shaking your house with sound

▶ Plugging into the outside world

. . . .

*M*ost homes contain a plethora of entertainment equipment — televisions, radios, CD players, stereo receivers, and so on. (If you're like us, you still have vinyl record turntables sitting prominently on a shelf someplace.) Historically speaking, people have had a tendency to think of home entertainment gear as stuff that is used in a particular room — a stereo in the living room, televisions in the family room and bedroom, and maybe a radio in the kitchen.

The best home entertainment system is a network that leverages your investments in expensive audio and video equipment and lets you enjoy it wherever you are in the home. Think of this gear as part of a *whole-home network*. The bulk of the equipment is located in a common media center (like a home-theater room), and a suitable network infrastructure (whether it be wired or wireless or something else entirely) is set up throughout your home to distribute the audio and video that you want to see and hear.

In this chapter, we discuss the necessary components for your home audio and video network — many of which you probably already have sitting around the house now.

TV and Video Systems

This section takes a look at some of the radical changes that television is undergoing — and we're not talking about programming.

Digital is coming

Like most other devices before it, television is currently on the verge of making the leap from the analog to the digital world. In North America, an analog system known as NTSC (National Television Standards Committee) has been in place for decades — in fact, it hasn't been changed or updated since the advent of color television in the 1960s. Although this system is capable of producing a surprisingly good picture under ideal circumstances, its analog nature makes it susceptible to various kinds of interference and signal degradation. Consequently, the picture can be downright awful by the time it actually gets to your television.

Luckily, broadcasters, equipment manufacturers, and the Federal Commun ications Commission (FCC) haven't ignored the benefits of the digital revolu tion. A new digital television standard has been approved and will slowly be rolled out throughout the country in the next few years. The new system is actually several systems rolled into one. Broadcasters and program providers will be able to choose from among several different digital television (DTV) formats, all of which can be viewed by forthcoming digital televisions.

Analog TV isn't dead yet

Even with the advent of digital broadcasts, the old-fashioned analog television system still has quite a few years left to live.

The FCC is assigning an entirely new tele-vision channel frequency to all existing, licensed broadcasters for digital broadcasts. Broadcasters must begin airing these broad-casts according to a schedule that the FCC provides. As long as they use this channel for digital television purposes, the broadcasters have to pay absolutely nothing for the right to use it. (In the past, the FCC has auctioned the rights for new frequencies — many companies have paid hundreds of millions of dollars, for example, to get the rights to install digital PCS communications networks.)

The other part of the bargain is that TV broad-casters get to keep — and must continue broadcasting on — their existing analog TV channels until at least 2006 (though many pun-dits believe that broadcasters will convince the FCC to let them keep using these channels even longer). So, the analog NTSC television that you purchase today will happily receive over-the-air television signals for at least seven more years.

After the switch over to digital TV is complete, you shouldn't have to pitch all of your old TVs. Digital TV converter boxes will allow you to watch DTV programming on older TVs. Of course, the picture quality and resolution won't be as high as it would be with a new digital set, but you can't have everything.

Alphabet soup

Just as the NTSC standard is common in North America (and Japan), a couple of other standards — known as PAL and SECAM — are common in other parts of the world. Most of these regions are undergoing their own upheavals as they begin to migrate to digital television systems, and many are adopting digital television standards of their own that are different from the U.S. system.

Defining High Definition TV

Broadcasters can best use their assigned digital television channel by sending a single *High Definition (HDTV)* signal, which provides CD-quality digital, multichannel audio, and a super high-resolution picture that rivals what you see on a movie screen. The difference in quality is astounding. In very general terms, two key factors determine how clear and crisp a video display — like a television — looks to the eye: the TV's *resolution* and the TV's *scanning refresh rate* and *method*.

You may be familiar with the concept of resolution if you own a PC, because PC displays are usually rated in terms of their resolution, or more specifically, the number of *pixels* (individual points of light and color in the display) that you can see. For example, most home PC displays are set to show 800 pixels across by 600 pixels vertically, with larger displays often set to show 1,024 across by 768 vertically.

Television manufacturers don't usually mention the number of pixels across the screen, but they do list the vertical number — the *lines of resolution.* Today's analog TV systems usually max out at 480 lines of resolution. Tomorrow's High Definition systems will have more — although the total number is still a matter of great controversy between and among broadcasters, set manufacturers, cable TV providers, and others.

For the most part, these groups consider a DTV signal "high resolution" if it has either 720 or 1,080 lines of resolution. Figure 5-1 shows the difference between 480, 720, and 1,080 lines of resolution on the same-sized screen.

When looking at two screens of the same size, the more lines of resolution, the better the picture.

The other factor in determining the quality of a television or video signal is the scanning refresh rate and method. People generally talk about PC monitors and video systems in terms of their screen refresh rates — often a number like 75 hertz. This figure means that the picture on your PC's video screen is updated 75 times every second. When talking about televisions, people discuss the *scan line refresh rate* to illustrate the same principle.

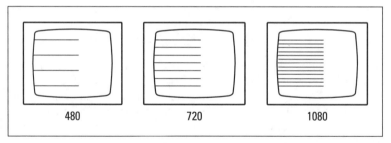

Figure 5-1:
Some lines,
more lines,
lots of lines.

480 720 1080

TV puts an interesting twist on the scan line refresh rate, however. A TV with a *progressive scan display* refreshes all of its lines of resolution during a cycle (TVs average 24 to 30 cycles per second). Other TVs offer *interlaced scan display,* which means that they refresh half the screen — every other line — each cycle.

Why don't interlaced pictures on a TV look all messed up? Mainly because the two halves of the picture are updated so frequently that your eyes can't really register the time delay. That said, however, a progressive scan picture generally looks better than an interlaced one when all other variables (like total lines of resolution and refresh rate) are the same.

Computers use the progressive mode to refresh their displays, while current analog TVs use the interlaced mode. Now the computer companies and the broadcast companies are lining up against each other regarding which version of HDTV should be most common.

Other flavors of Digital TV

The variations of HDTV that we discuss in the preceding section are only a few of the options available to broadcasters as they begin to send out DTV programming. If they wish, broadcasters can forgo HDTV entirely, choosing instead a lower resolution format (which uses less of their assigned bandwidth), and send several different video programs on one channel. Broadcasters can also use part of their digital television channels to broadcast computer data to your television.

The FCC has no hard-and-fast rules designating exactly how television broadcasters must use their digital TV channels. Expect different broadcasters to either choose from among these options or mix and match various formats depending on the kind of programming they are broadcasting (perhaps using HDTV for movies, and multiple lower resolution formats for other programming).

To take advantage of all of digital TV's benefits, you'll eventually have to re-place all of your televisions. Today's televisions don't have the internal circuitry to decode digital TV signals, and they generally don't have screens that can display HDTV pictures in all their glory. In fact, today's TVs aren't even the right shape, because HDTV signals have a wider *aspect ratio* — the ratio of screen width to height — than NTSC signals (NTSC is 4:3; HDTV is 16:9). Figure 5-2 shows the difference in aspect ratios between NTSC and DTV — the DTV screen will be much closer to the width of most movie screens.

Figure 5-2:
A DTV
screen will
be this
much wider
than today's
NTSC
screen.

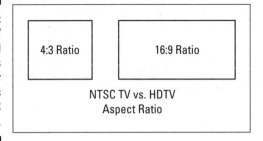

4:3 Ratio   16:9 Ratio

NTSC TV vs. HDTV
Aspect Ratio

These new television sets, which became available at the end of 1998, are quite a bit more expensive than traditional sets. Although prices should eventually come down, the interim solution is a digital set-top box that can convert digital television signals to analog NTSC. You won't get all of the benefits of an actual HDTV-capable digital TV, but at least you can continue to use your existing TVs until you're ready to replace them.

What about cable and satellite television providers? Unlike over-the-air broadcasters, the FCC isn't going to require these companies to provide digital television signals right away. Although DBS television systems (see the section "Direct broadcast satellite TV [DBS]," later in this chapter) are already using a digital system, and cable television systems are beginning to move toward the same type of system, neither is yet offering systems that are capable of taking advantage of the full HDTV-style standard. Doing so will require rather substantial system upgrades — both within their infrastructures and in the systems found in your home. How soon they upgrade to the latest and greatest digital systems depends on several factors, most significantly consumer demand for HDTV. If customers see HDTV, love it, and de-mand it from their service providers, it will probably appear sooner rather than later.

TV types

For a long, long time, televisions have all been pretty much identical in form, with only cosmetic and internal electronic differences — as well as quality of construction — to differentiate them. The advent of new technologies from the computer world, along with the desire of many consumers to build home theaters that use large-screen TVs has dramatically altered this situation.

Tubes for all: Direct-view TVs

The traditional television — or video display of any kind, for that matter — has always been the direct view, picture-tube type. The screen you see is actually the front of a specially treated glass tube with an *electron gun* built into the back end of the tube. This system basically works by shooting electrons from the gun, through some electronically controlled devices that aim them, and onto the back of the picture tube's screen. When these electrons hit the specially treated glass, it lights up in different colors and intensities, depending upon how the electrons are aimed, and creates your picture.

Tubes are a mature technology — having been on the market in large quantities for about 50 years — and they work pretty darn well. They do have a few disadvantages though:

- ✔ They're big (in depth) and heavy (ever try to move a 35-inch television?).
- ✔ The technology itself limits screen size (very few direct-view televisions are larger than about 40 inches measured diagonally).
- ✔ Picture tubes large enough to handle HDTV's high resolutions are difficult to build (though Sony does have such a model on the market).

We're quite confident that picture-tube TVs will remain the standard for quite a few more years, but look for some of the alternatives that we list in the following sections to really take off in the next few years.

Projection TVs

After you move beyond pretty-large big-screen TVs (35 inches or so) into really huge, oh-my-goodness, big-screen TVs, the form of the television changes from direct-view to projection, or *PTV.*

Projection TVs come in two main types, as shown in Figure 5-3:

- ✔ **Front projection models:** These high-end models consist of a projector mounted on the ceiling and a separate screen. These units project the TV video onto the front of the screen (basically just like a movie projector does).
- ✔ **Rear projection models:** The screen and the projection systems are in the same chassis in these all-in-one units. These models beam the TV image onto the back of a screen, like a direct-view TV does.

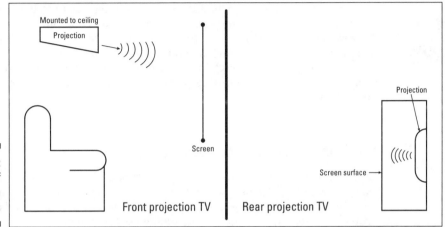

Figure 5-3:
Two types of projection TVs.

The actual pieces and parts of these systems can vary from brand to brand and model to model — some, for example, use liquid crystal displays (LCDs) in the projector, while others use picture tubes. Generally speaking, though, PTV sets start where the top-of-the-line direct-view sets end in terms of screen size, features, and price. The cheapest rear projection model usually costs in the $1,000 to $2,000 range, whereas high-quality, front-projection models can cost up to $20,000 or $30,000 for the projector alone (not to mention the costs of the screen, and professional installation, alignment, and focusing).

In both the short and long terms, we believe that these models will remain popular for use in home-theater rooms, but probably won't be widely used anywhere else in the home.

Hang your TV on the wall: Flat-screen TVs

The really hot item in the TV world today is without a doubt the flat-screen TV. Rather like the screen of a notebook computer stretched to previously unimagined proportions, these new TVs use computer technologies like liquid crystal diode (LCD) and plasma display systems to provide a large-screen television system that is usually only four or five inches deep. Several models of these TVs are on the market now. You can find them at the bigger home electronics stores in your area, but these first models are super expensive, somewhat experimental products — more a plaything for people who absolutely *need* to be the first to have the new technology (and who have the $12,000 or $15,000 to spend on it).

These first-generation flat-screen TVs are really, really neat, but you're much better off waiting a few years before plunking down a big stack of your own money on a flat-screen TV. The flat-screen TV's picture quality and features are at best no better than those of standard TVs selling for a quarter or less of the price.

Don't get us wrong, though. In due time, flat-screen TVs (and flat-screen displays of all sorts) will become an essential part of just about every home. After prices come down — and they will — the added convenience and flexibility of installing these systems (you can just hang them on a wall like a picture), along with their high image quality (they'll soon be suitable for high-definition TV and computer usage), means that a flat-screen in every room is quite likely.

Video source components

Video source components are the magical black boxes that let you record or watch movies, play games, watch the baby, or even surf the Web on your home's televisions. A huge number of these products are on the market (and probably already in your home), including the following:

- Videocassette recorders (VCRs)
- Laserdisc players
- DVD players (digital versatile disc, or alternately, digital video disc) — the new CD-sized discs for playing movies
- In-home video devices like doorbell cameras or video baby monitors
- Video game machines
- WebTVs (a television that can surf the Web)

Most folks tend to view these kinds of video source devices as dedicated, one-room components. If you want to watch a movie on the VCR, for example, you go to the room the VCR is in and sit down. In a properly networked home, however, you can connect your video source devices to your video network and use them from any TV in the house (see Chapter 6 for more information).

Stereo Systems

Today's audio systems are designed to reproduce audio signals in *high fidelity*. In other words, the equipment should re-create the music so that it actually sounds like it did in the studio or concert hall where your favorite recordings were made.

A high-fidelity sound system has several components:

- **Source component:** This component can be a CD player, cassette deck, radio tuner, or the audio portion of a video source like a VCR, laserdisc, or DVD. The source component produces a low-level audio signal — called a *line-level signal* — that is transmitted over an RCA cable.

✔ **Preamplifier or control amplifier:** This device amplifies (or increases the power of) the line-level signal, and also serves as a switching device to allow you to select from different source components. The preamplifier also contains, at a minimum, a volume control, which determines exactly how much the signal is amplified. The control amplifier connects, via another interconnect cable (or via internal wiring if you are using an integrated amplifier), to the next stage in the sound reproduction process.

✔ **Power amplifier:** This unit adds more power to the audio signal — enough power to make your audio signal audible through the speakers.

Note: A preamplifier and power amplifier integrated into one component is known as an *integrated amplifier.* Add a radio tuner to this box, and you have a *receiver.*

✔ **Loudspeakers:** Connected to the amplifier by speaker cables (what else?), the speakers use electromagnets to move speakers — the famous "woofer" and "tweeter" — back and forth. This movement, which corresponds with the audio signal coming from the amplifier, pushes the air in front of the drivers rhythmically, creating the sound waves that you hear. Loudspeakers can range from a full, surround sound five- or seven-speaker home entertainment center, to remote speakers in your kitchen or dining room, to the intercom speakers throughout your house. If you plan correctly, any of these are viable outputs of your Hi-Fi system.

As audio systems expand from single to multiple rooms, a new breed of components has come onto the marketplace — the *multizone* system. Traditional audio systems have always been *single-zone,* meaning that the control portion of the preamplifier — the switches that let you select which audio source you want to listen to — only lets you select one source at a time. This is fine for a stereo system that you are using only in one room, but this solution lacks flexibility for multiple rooms.

Newer, multizone systems have control sections that let you select more than one source component at once. So if you and your spouse want to listen to a Yanni CD in the living room and your kids want to bang their heads to Nine Inch Nails in the basement, you can do so. If you want to use a multizone system, you'll also need additional amplifiers — one for each independent source that you want to play back at one time.

Intercom Systems

Unlike stereo systems, intercom systems aren't designed with the highest audio quality in mind. Their main function is to get your voice from Point A to Point B without weakening or incurring interference. That's not to say that intercoms are cheap or unsophisticated, just that they have a different mission.

Intercoms fall into two main categories:

- ✔ **Wireless systems:** These intercoms use radio *transceivers* (TRANSmitter and reCEIVER) to carry your voice signals from room to room. Just install a simple device on your desk, raise the antenna (and do the same with the other device), and you are ready to communicate. Variations on this theme include fixed wireless intercoms (which you can mount on the wall anywhere you want one), portable baby monitors, and even many cordless phones that use a speaker phone on the base station to create a simple, point-to-point intercom system.

- ✔ **Wired systems:** As the name implies, these intercoms are wired together and send your voice as an electrical audio signal between rooms. Wired intercom systems run the gamut from simple voice systems to advanced audio systems that can also carry radio and other audio signals. Figure 5-4 shows a typical wired intercom system.

Intercoms can be a useful feature (though phone networks can serve a similar function), and many find them handy. Danny finds his intercom useful in his four-story house. The Fisher Price monitor that he and his wife used with

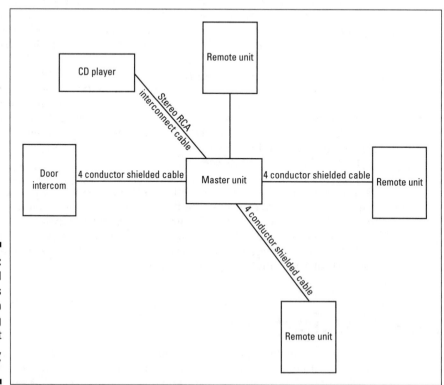

Figure 5-4: "Calling all stations, this is Mom in the living room, get down here, NOW!"

the first set of twins has been replaced with a simple press of the Monitor button on the Nursery intercom unit. The babies' cries can now be heard all over the house. (Wait, is that good?!)

Most decent intercom systems have an *Audio In* source option, too, whereby you can plug your home entertainment system into your intercom system. By tying the two together, you save yourself money.

As you map your wiring runs, keep in mind that many intercom manufacturers void your warranty if you don't use their proprietary wiring systems. However, using their wiring (which, admittedly, is designed specifically for their systems) is more expensive and goes against the idea of a uniform backbone over which all communications travel. (If you're a real risk-taker, we talk about ways to wire audio systems in Chapter 9.)

TV Connections from the Outside World

An important part of television is its ability to bring programming into your home from the world beyond. Like televisions themselves, these connections to the outside world are undergoing a series of major changes. New ways of receiving programming are becoming common, and established methods are revamping themselves for a digital world.

Broadcast TV

In spite of the proliferation of cable and satellite television and compact discs, "old" media like broadcast television and radio are still very much alive and kicking.

In fact, increasing consumer acceptance of DBS satellite television systems has caused somewhat of a renaissance in the market for run-of-the-mill television antennas, because in most instances these systems don't carry programming from the big networks — and they don't carry any local stations at all. With this system, you either need to keep some level of cable television service or buy an antenna if you still want to watch the local news or get the local weather report.

Luckily, television antennas have improved, so without spending too much money, you can avoid the nightmare of fine-tuning a set of rabbit ears on top of your television.

You can divide television antennas into two general categories:

 ✔ **Indoor:** These antennas sit on or near your television.

 ✔ **Outdoor:** These antennas mount on your roof — or in the case of some of the newer ones, right alongside your DBS satellite dish.

Whether your television antenna is outside or inside, you have to connect it to the TV somehow. Most modern antennas use the same coaxial cable that cable television and DBS satellite systems do. (See Chapter 7 for strategies for wiring antennas into your video network.)

Cable TV

The prevalence of cable service nationwide makes it an important part of any home-networking strategy — both for you and future owners of your home. And with the wide range of services coming from the cable companies, you may be surprised at what you'll be buying from them in the future (things like Internet access and even telephone service, for example).

The cable system operates in a pretty straightforward manner. Central offices, or *head end sites,* (sort of like the central offices the telephone company has), receive television signals from various sources (mainly from satellite feeds, as well as local over-the-air broadcasts). The companies then assign the signals to specific channels and distribute them over a combination of fiber-optic and coaxial cables (which, coincidentally, always make up the final portion of the network that enters your home).

The channel system that cable systems use is slightly different from those of over-the-air broadcast television. So, the frequency of Channel 20 on a cable system is likely different than Channel 20 in a broadcast environment.

What this difference means to a you as a homeowner is that you can't plug your cable TV feed into the back of any old television and expect it to work. Instead, you have two options:

Has cable TV passed you by?

You're probably familiar with cable television. In fact, you probably already have cable TV, or at least have it available to you.

Studies show that cable television service is available to about 90 percent of American homes, and of those homes, about 80 percent use the service.

You may hear cable companies talk about *homes passed* — meaning that cable is running down a given street — as an indication of their service area and the present number of potential customers. A cable company won't run the cable from the street to a house until someone actually wants to buy the service. Over time, as homes turn over, more and more homes have the cable run to the building. Because the cable is never removed, the cable company can quickly activate more homes for any sort of cable service.

✔ **A *cable-ready* television set or VCR:** These models let you select a cable mode and then use their internal television tuner to decode and display the television signals. Most TVs made in the last few years are cable-ready, so all you have to do is plug the coaxial cable into the back of the TV and you're set (after you run through the set-up routines to set the time, add the channels, and so forth).

Note: Cable-ready TVs do have a couple of disadvantages. First, most of these sets can only receive a limited number of channels, which may be an increasing, future concern for cable systems. Second, with a cable-ready set, you probably can't take advantage of special services from the cable company like premium movie channels and pay-per-view programs.

✔ **A set-top box (or *converter*):** These devices take the cable television signals and feed them to your television by using a single broadcast channel (usually either Channel 3 or 4). With your television tuned to that single channel, you channel-surf stations through the box.

These set-top boxes, which your cable service provider furnishes for a fee, are becoming increasingly sophisticated. In fact, some allow two-way communications, which can be a bonus in a multi-TV household.

Running cable TV service to six different rooms in your house gets expensive if each TV needs its own set-top box. You may prefer to bring the signal into one point, and then let multiple rooms subscribe to that signal. For instance, in our houses, the signal in the master bedroom comes from the output of the VCR in the living room. A low-cost, wireless, infrared device that is connected to the living room system allows us to change channels from the bedroom (see Chapter 8 for more information). The only time this setup doesn't work is when two people want to watch different shows on different sets at the same time.

Satellite TV

As common as cable TV service is, a growing number of homeowners are cutting the cord and installing satellite TV receivers. Satellite TV, especially the new, small-dish varieties, can provide high-quality video programming — with more channels than all but a handful of cable systems — to homes just about anywhere in the world.

Direct broadcast satellite TV (DBS)

If you look around your neighborhood, you've no doubt noticed a profusion of small (eighteen inch to be exact), white or gray satellite dishes popping up on many housetops. These are receiving dishes for the DBS television.

Literally millions of consumers have adopted DBS as an alternative to cable television. What do you get when you choose DBS?

- ✔ **Channels galore:** Depending on which service and service level you choose to buy, you can get hundreds of channels.

- ✔ **Digital quality:** The DBS system uses a computer digital video standard called MPEG (which stands for *Motion Pictures Experts Group* — the people who developed the standard) to digitize and compress the video and audio signals it sends to you. Being digital means that the system is generally higher in quality and less susceptible to interference. Most cable systems are still analog! *Note:* Not all of the satellite systems use MPEG — DSS and Echostar, however, do.

- ✔ **Audio channels:** Plug into your stereo or home theater for audio-only programming.

- ✔ **Easy-to-use graphical interfaces, with telephone-line access to providers for pay-per-view programming.**

As with everything, DBS has some downsides:

- ✔ **You don't get local programming:** You still need a broadcast antenna or basic cable television service to see local channels and news — not to mention broadcast network (in other words, FOX, ABC, NBC, and CBS) programs. Some of the DBS networks don't carry a UPN station yet — the most major downside we see as *Star Trek Voyager* fans.

- ✔ **You need a receiver:** The receiver acts like a cable converter box, and converts the digital television signals from the satellite to signals that your television can understand. If you have more than one television, you need additional receivers for each TV because, like a cable converter box, the receiver only puts out one channel at a time.

- ✔ **You need to have a free telephone line:** The receiver must be plugged into a telephone line to communicate with the DBS provider's headquarters for billing and service provisioning.

- ✔ **You can't live in Canada:** Even though the satellites cover Canadian territory, regulations keep these U.S.-based companies from offering services to consumers in Canada. You may also have a hard time getting a satellite signal if you live in areas far away from the satellites' orbits. If you live in upstate Maine, for instance, you may have more problems getting an Echostar signal than a DirecTV signal, because of the satellite's physical location. (In some cases, the dish is so low to the horizon that mountains and atmospheric clutter can get in the way.)

- ✔ **You have to install the system:** This system is not hard to install, and installation kits are available. But something about getting up on your roof conjures up visions of back surgery. Of course, you can mount the dish on the side of your house or put it in the yard. One company even makes nifty large fake rocks that cover the dish and keep your neighbors happy. And a growing number of installers nationwide will do the installation for you if you like.

Three competing DBS systems are currently on the market. Each offers relatively similar services, so you just have to compare prices and services and choose the one you like best.

✔ **DSS:** DSS uses an 18-inch dish and sends its audio and video signals by using the digital MPEG system. A variety of different companies manufacture the widely available DSS hardware — the most popular of the three systems. DirecTV and USSB, the two service providers in the DSS system, offer consumers various service packages. If you go with DSS, you'll probably buy both DirecTV and USSB because most of the premium movie channels (such as HBO and Showtime) are on USSB. Keep in mind that dealing with two companies for what seems like one service can get sort of messy.

✔ **Primestar:** Another popular service, Primestar differs from its competitors in two main ways. First, you don't have to buy the satellite dish — instead you rent it as a part of your monthly service fee. Second, the dish is a bit larger, measuring between 27 and 36 inches. Primestar is digital, like the other DBS systems, but uses a different encoding system, called DigiCipher, instead of MPEG. Also, its user interface is not as user friendly and flexible as DirecTV and Echostar.

✔ **Echostar:** The newest entrant in this marketplace, Echostar (also called the DISH network) service is very similar to DSS, using an 18-inch disc and digital MPEG encoding technology to transmit its video and audio. Because the Echostar system has a remote control that transmits in the

The great DBS/HDTV debate

DBS systems are generally digital in nature, but is Digital TV the same as the forthcoming HDTV system? The short answer is no. In most cases, the MPEG system that DBS systems use is higher quality than standard over-the-air or analog cable television broadcasts. However, it's not up to the highest quality standards of HDTV, and it doesn't offer HDTV's widescreen aspect ratio.

When HDTV programming becomes available and as HDTV sets become popular, DBS service providers may offer some HDTV programming — either by using the high-speed data output port found on many DBS receivers, or by using a new generation of receivers. Most likely, not all channels will be available in this format, however, because a single HDTV channel uses as much bandwidth as four or five of today's channels. Service providers will probably choose to offer a larger number of lower-quality channels and just a few full HDTV channels in their limited amount of bandwidth.

UHF frequency range, the remote control will work a few rooms away, allowing the system to drive two TV sets. To have the same capability with the other systems, you need an infrared remote-control extender.

C Band

The grandfather of today's DBS satellite television systems is the C Band satellite system — those huge satellite dishes that used to sprout up like monstrous mushrooms. At about 7 feet across, the average C Band dish is expensive and difficult to place. Zoning restrictions keep C Band dishes out of many suburban areas, so you tend to see them only in rural areas. Still, in the early 1980s, having one of these dishes in your backyard meant that you could pick up all sorts of channels from all over the world. Unfortunately, many of the channels that C Band systems once picked up for free are now encrypted (like those channels on your cable system that you don't subscribe to) and require that you subscribe to a service to receive them.

The advent of DBS and almost universal access to cable television has severely limited the growth of the consumer C Band marketplace. These days, most C Band users are either satellite hobbyists or businesses, like hotels. Many television networks and cable systems also use C Band systems to distribute programming.

The name C Band refers to the chunk of frequency spectrum allocated to these services. In case you were curious, DBS satellite systems use the Ku band — though only hard-core satellite techie types call them Ku band systems.

Satellites and your home

Millions of people are installing satellite dishes for a multitude of reasons. Satellite dishes are low-cost, easy to install, and provide several services including high-quality video programming, Internet access, and so on. Many people find that satellite dishes are a quick solution to a messy problem, especially when they live in areas where cable service is not available or in rural locations where the local telephone company doesn't have a local telephone switch. The service is highly reliable and very effective, so be sure to take a look at these options alongside cable and other offerings.

If you decide to go with a satellite dish, be sure that no zoning restrictions apply to satellite dishes in your area. Just because everyone else has one does not mean that they are necessarily legal. Some towns only pursue enforcement when too many people get the dishes, especially in historic districts.

Chapter 6

Getting Video Where You Want It

• •

In This Chapter

▶ Choosing between base or broad

▶ Going the distance

▶ Getting the most with coaxial cable

▶ Doing the modulate thing

• •

*Y*ou can wire gobs of capabilities into a video network — a much greater variety of choices than is possible in most other networks we discuss (such as data networks or phone networks). That's the good news. The bad news is that we have to hold the number of pages in this book under the *Encyclopaedia Britannica,* so we can't go into them all. On second thought, maybe that's good news, too, because rather than confusing you with a laundry list of all the different video possibilities and boring you with technical drivel on this super-video whatsit and that video-switching doodad, we concentrate on showing you how to wire the most common video network features, including

✔ Coaxial video outlets in all rooms that may one day contain a television

✔ Return video connections in rooms that may contain video sources — ranging from VCRs to baby-monitor cameras

✔ Inputs for cable television and/or a broadcast TV antenna

✔ Provisions made for the inclusion of a DBS satellite system into the network

✔ A central distribution node tying all of this good stuff together

The network we lay out for you uses *broadband RF video distribution* (whew!), which means that special devices called *video modulators* send the signals from video sources such as VCRs or security cameras through the wires in your walls and broadcast them on TV channels not used by your local TV stations. Just tune into the right channel and you can watch these sources anywhere in your house. In this chapter, we take you systematically through the process of wiring such a home video network.

Distance Counts in Video Signals

You can get video signals from place to place in two basic ways: *baseband distribution* and *broadband distribution*. The difference between these two methods is in the amount of information that the cable can carry. Baseband cable only has enough capacity to carry a single channel of video, so you generally use baseband cable for the connections between your video components, such as your VCR and TV. Generally, baseband cables are short. Broadband cable (such as coaxial cable), on the other hand, has enough capacity to carry many video channels over greater distances.

If you've read Chapter 5, then you know that we are going to concentrate on a broadband video-distribution network, but actually, you find elements of both methods within just about any video network. In the most general terms, you use baseband connections for short video connections, like plugging your DVD player into the TV next to it. You use broadband connections for longer connections, like the cable that runs from an antenna on the roof to a television.

Cabling between components (baseband)

Baseband video is the distribution of a single channel or program over a cable. The *Video Out* port on the back of VCRs, cable converters, satellite receivers, DVD and laserdisc players and camcorders are all baseband video signals, as are the *S video* ports of the same devices (we discuss S video in more detail in the following bullets). Generally speaking, baseband video distribution is best suited for short distance connections, such as between components in the same room. Baseband video uses video patch cables to connect components in a system and requires audio patch cables to carry the corresponding audio signals (because you need both sets of cables, we refer to this set of cables as *A/V interconnect cables*).

Home systems commonly use three different types of baseband video connections (which we list from least sophisticated to most sophisticated):

- **Composite video:** You find this connection system on all video source devices. Composite video carries all the various components of an NTSC (the standard U.S. television system discussed in the previous chapter) video signal over a single wire, and uses standard RCA or phono plugs to connect devices — the same kind of plugs used for connecting stereo components like CD players and amplifiers together.

- **S video:** You find S video on more sophisticated VCRs and on DVD players, DSS dishes, and many laserdisc players. This method uses a single cable with multiple conductors to carry the brightness and color parts of a video signal separately, resulting in better picture quality.

✔ **Component video:** Only a few DVD players and new top-of-the-line televisions use component connections, making them a relative rarity. (You won't find component video on any sources other than DVD players right now, although it may be used for digital TV set-top boxes in the future.) Component video actually breaks down the video signal into three separate parts, each carried on a separate cable. This breakdown lets you avoid much of the internal circuitry in both your DVD player and your TV, so you get a better picture. At least that's what all of the videophiles we know tell us.

When you're making a baseband video connection, and you have more than one of these options available to you, always choose the most sophisticated first. If your source and TV both have component video, use that. Your next step down in quality is S video, with composite video coming in third. Most of these source devices also have a modulated RF output that works on Channel 3 or 4 of your TV, but consider this choice only as a last resort because the video quality will most likely be lower than one of the baseband connections.

Cabling the video-distribution network (broadband)

A broadband video-distribution system combines many different video signals — and their corresponding audio signals — onto a single cable by *modulating* the signals onto different radio frequencies or channels. In simplest terms, modulation means that the total available bandwidth of a cable is divided up into equal parts, and each signal (or channel) uses one of those parts of the bandwidth. The frequencies correspond with the standard channels on your television, which has an internal tuner that demodulates the signal and displays it on the screen. Figure 6-1 shows how different program signals are assigned by the broadcasters or cable service providers to different frequencies (channels) and are sent over the same cable.

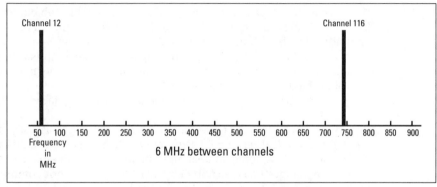

Figure 6-1: Modulating multiple channels onto different radio frequencies.

Broadcast and cable networks modulate multiple channels; modulation is also how DBS programming is sent from the satellite to your dish and receiver. Just about all video source devices also include a broadband output — usually switchable between Channel 3 and Channel 4. An internal modulator provides this signal and allows you to connect the source to older televisions that don't have any baseband video inputs.

Coaxial Video Networks

Although technologies exist that allow you to create video networks without running cables (we describe these in Chapter 7), in almost all cases, running cables for your network gives you better performance, flexibility, and capacity. Wireless alternatives are usually more expensive than their cabled partners, and they do less. Bottom line: Anytime you can build a video network by running the wires, we recommend that you do so.

The wired version of a video network is one that distributes video signals (separated into different channels) over coaxial cable to each television in your home. If you've had cable TV, you've had a network similar to what we describe, except that the cable TV network is a paltry, one-way video network in comparison to the two-way video distribution system that we describe.

Note: New cable modem services are coming out that run on coaxial cable — the same coaxial cable that we're talking about here. Our design covers this development to some degree. You can also use cable modems in conjunction with telephone/computer wiring in your home to distribute the data signals around the house. (See Chapter 7 for more detail about how cable modems fit into your network.)

Coaxial cable

Coaxial cable — usually just called *coax* — is a metallic cable most often used for transmitting radio frequency (RF) signals like broadband television video and radio signals. Coaxial cable contains two conductors — or *axes* — to carry data. A layer of dielectric insulating material surrounds a single, center conductor. The other conductor is a metal shield — usually made of some sort of braided metallic wiring — that goes around the dielectric (insulating) layer. The outermost layer of coax cable is an insulating jacket.

Coaxial cables are rated by their *impedance* — which is basically the AC version of electrical resistance. Different applications require different impedances. In the home, almost all systems that require coaxial cable use 75 ohm impedance coax, although some LAN systems (not commonly found in the home) use 50 ohm coax (in case you're not familiar with ohm, it's the unit of measurement for impedance).

You find three main types of coaxial cable within the home. These cables are shown in Table 6-1.

Table 6-1		Video Coaxial Cable Grades	
Coaxial Cable Type	*Cost*	*Use*	*Comments*
Unrated 75 ohm coax	Lowest	Older cable TV installations and aerial antenna-to-TV connections	This low grade of coaxial cable suffers from high resistance to the video signal and provides generally poor picture quality. Not recommended for video networks.
RG-59 coax	Medium	Cable TV and antenna-to-TV connections	This is the standard grade of coaxial cable found in most existing installations, suitable for standard cable TV and broadcast antenna use.
RG6 coax	Highest	Cable TV, DSS, and cable-modem connections	The highest grade of coaxial cable found in the home, provides the best resistance from interference and the least amount of signal degradation, required for DSS and cable-modem installations, and recommended for all new installations.

Note: You may encounter coaxial cables labeled RG6QS or RG6 Quad Shield, which means that the cable has additional shielding beneath the cable jacket — four layers, as the name implies. These layers provide additional protection from interference from external sources.

You can think of the difference between RG-59 and RG6 as similar to the difference between the CAT-3 and CAT-5 UTP cables, which we discuss in Chapters 11 and 15. They look pretty much the same, and they do just about the same thing, but the higher-rated cable is slightly more capable of carrying your signals cleanly — and for longer distances. The price difference is minimal, and we strongly recommend that you choose RG6 for your coaxial cabling needs — the small extra cost is worth ensuring that your wiring will be able to handle the future needs of your network. In fact, some applications, like DSS, require RG6 and specifically tell you not to use RG-59.

Coax connectors

Coaxial cables utilize standardized connectors (as does just about all of the network cabling we cover). Only one type of connector — the *F connector* — is really used in residential applications. If you have cable television, then you're already familiar with the F connector; Figure 6-2 shows this screw or push-on connector.

Like most connectors, F connectors come in two "genders" — male and female. Generally speaking, you find female connectors on video equipment and wall outlets; male connectors are used to attach the cables to these outlets.

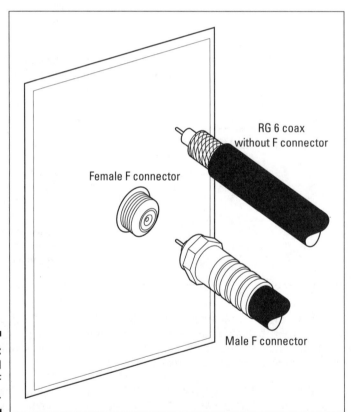

RG 6 coax
without F connector

Female F connector

Male F connector

Figure 6-2:
RG6 coaxial
cable and F
connectors.

Components

The cable and connectors are the permanent parts of your video-network infrastructure — the parts that you put in your walls and expect to keep there for 20 years or so. The other components that your video network

Coax — what's it used for?

Coax cable is useful stuff, and you may find it in places other than just video networks. Specifically, the following applications use coaxial cable:

✔ **Cable television:** Cable TV uses 75 ohm coax, typically RG-59 rated cable.

✔ **Broadcast television antennas:** These systems also require 75 ohm coaxial cable, again RG-59 rated cable is the minimum grade used.

✔ **FM radio antennas:** Like television antennas, many external FM antennas use RG-59 coaxial cable.

✔ **DBS satellite systems:** The downlink from your dish's LNB output to the back of your DBS receiver requires RG6 cabling.

✔ **10Base2 (Thinnet) Ethernet data networks:** These computer local area networks use RG-58 cable.

needs, things like distribution panels and modulators, are probably going to be slightly less permanent members of your household electronic family. Over time your network needs may change, and new technologies like digital television will become available, precipitating changes in some of your network components. These changes will cost you some money perhaps (the price of progress?), but the main part of your investment — namely the materials and labor used in installing the coaxial cabling in your walls — will remain intact and useful.

Outlets

If you're anything like us, you won't want to have your coaxial cables and F connectors dangling out of gaping holes in the wall. Luckily you can find a huge assortment of coaxial cable in-wall outlets that fit into standard electrical junction boxes and use standard faceplates, just like your electrical outlets and light switches do.

Dozens of companies manufacture these outlets, which come in an amazing number of combinations and sizes. If your budget allows, we recommend running two RG6 cables to each room in your home. One coaxial cable allows you to receive video signals from an external source like cable TV; two let you share devices like VCRs and DVD players with the rest of the home as well. You may not run two cables to every single spot in your home, but certain areas will require that you do.

A coaxial outlet for this cabling consists of two female F connectors, one above the other, in a compact, single-gang junction box. Single-gang means that the Dalton boys don't ride with Jesse James. Okay, actually, gang simply refers to the size of the box and cover. For reference, a single-gang junction box is the same size as a typical two-receptacle electrical outlet or a single, switch-toggle light switch. Many of these twin coaxial outlets have relatively large faceplate openings and use a standard-sized faceplate called a Leviton Decora. (These are the same faceplates that you see in the large light switches in many newer homes.)

As you design your home networks, you may find that you want to put several different kinds of outlets together on a wall — speaker connections for an audio network, a phone line or two, and your coaxial outlets, for example. In these cases, consider using a larger double- or triple-gang junction box and install a multipurpose outlet that can terminate all of these cables in one place. Most of the major outlet manufacturers make all sorts of these combinations outlets, and some even make modular ones so you can pick and choose what goes where.

Low-voltage signals like coaxial video networks don't get along all that well with AC power lines. You should ideally keep at least three feet between the two to avoid noise and interference. Never try to connect your coaxial lines and powerlines in the same junction box — the result is a real mess.

Distribution panels

The key component in your video network is the distribution panel. This device is the central node for your video network — all coaxial lines to the various rooms of your house begin here. A distribution panel has several functions:

- ✔ It accepts one (or more optimally) coaxial, broadband, video signal inputs.

- ✔ It combines these input signals together into one unified broadband output.

- ✔ It splits this output to feed *multiple video endpoints* (in other words, televisions).

- ✔ It amplifies the outgoing signals to make them stronger (because splitting the signal weakens it).

Figure 6-3 shows a typical video-distribution panel.

When you're shopping for a video-distribution panel, look for the following:

- ✔ **Number of inputs:** Choose a unit that has at least two — preferably more — inputs. Doing so allows you to take local video sources (like DVD players) and distribute their signals throughout your home, instead of to the nearest TV.

- ✔ **Number of outputs:** Each television that you want to connect to your video network needs its own output on the distribution panel. These panels are engineered to maintain the proper signal strength and quality when used in a "one television per outlet" way. If you try to cheat and use a coaxial splitter to connect an extra television to a single output, you're throwing away all of the design and engineering expertise that went into the panel — and you probably won't be happy with the results (besides cheaters never win). Most panels on the market have anywhere from 5 to 12 outputs, so you should be able to satisfy your home's needs without having to install a second panel.

Distribution panels are often described as 3-x-8 or 5-x-12. The first number is the number of inputs, the second the number of outputs.

✔ **Amplification:** In order to maintain a signal that is strong enough to result in good picture quality on your televisions, you need to amplify it. Most distribution panels have built-in amplifiers that take care of this for you. In fact, the more sophisticated models have different levels of amplification built in so that some of the outputs are optimally amplified for your shorter cable runs, while others are optimized for longer runs.

Why different levels of amplification? Because overamplifying a signal is almost as bad as underamplifying it. Panels that have different tiers of amplification typically have several outputs designated for short distances (0–50 feet, for example) and some for longer runs (perhaps for 50–150 feet). Models with several outputs (like the 5-x -12 panels) may even have a middle tier of distance ranges.

More than you ever wanted to know about modulators

After the RG6 cabling and multiple-input distribution panel is in place, you have the makings of a two-way, whole-home video network. Now you just need an easy way to select the source you want to watch. That's where modulators come in. A modulator takes the baseband video and audio signals from a source and translates them into a standard TV RF channel — just like the ones that broadcast and cable companies send you. So that they don't interfere with existing channels, modulators need to be *frequency agile.* In other words, you need to be able to select what frequency (TV channel) modulators will send their signals over so that you can pick an unused one.

You may not be aware of it, but you probably have several modulators in your house already: in your VCR, DVD player, laserdisc player, or DSS dish. However, these modulators only give you two choices — Channel 3 or Channel 4 — which gives you little flexibility; their sole purpose is to provide a means of connecting these devices to televisions that don't have separate, baseband A/V inputs on the back. In most television networks, Channels 3 and 4 are almost never unoccupied, so these modulators make use of an internal switch (the VCR/TV button on your VCR's remote) that disconnects the antenna or cable feed to the TV, preventing interference with existing channels.

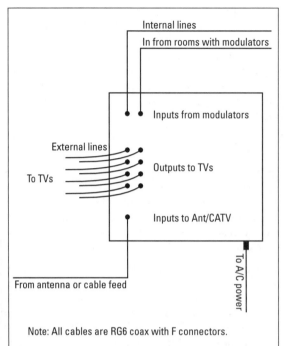

Internal lines

In from rooms with modulators

Inputs from modulators

External lines

Outputs to TVs

To TVs

Inputs to Ant/CATV

To A/C power

Figure 6-3:
The center
of a video
network, the
distribution
panel.

From antenna or cable feed

Note: All cables are RG6 coax with F connectors.

These Channel 3/4 modulators are not suitable for distributing video through-out the home because of the existing channels (we've yet to find a VCR/TV button for the whole house!). Even in the unlikely event that you don't have any existing channels on Channels 3 or 4, building a Channel 3/4 modulator into a source device won't do much for a whole-home network because you can only add one source device for the entire house.

Think about the following when you're choosing a modulator:

- ✔ **Digital or analog:** Analog modulators are much cheaper than digital ones, but they usually aren't as flexible in the frequencies you can choose from, so you have to buy a modulator that is factory-set to the channel you have available. Analog models tend to "drift" off stations just like those old dial radios did, requiring frequent readjustment. Digital models, though more expensive, are much more reliable and accurate — you basically set them once and forget them.

- ✔ **Single or multichannel:** You can buy modulators that translate a single video source onto a single television channel, or ones that will do the task for up to four separate sources on four different channels. A multi-channel unit may better serve your needs for two reasons:

- A multichannel unit allows you to distribute several video sources in one location (such as a home-theater room) throughout your whole house.

- With a multichannel modulator, you eliminate the confusion and complexity of using coaxial splitters to increase the number of internal video inputs on your distribution panel.

✔ **Mono, stereo, or no audio:** Most modulators will take the audio output of your source device and transmit it as *monaural audio* — no stereo separation, no surround sound, just mono (the same thing out of both speakers). Even if they have two inputs (for left and right channel audio) they're probably mono. You can buy modulators that transmit *MTS* (the stereo system that TVs use), but they cost significantly more. If you're installing a modulator that will be carrying the video from something like a surveillance camera, you can save yourself some money by purchasing a modulator that has no sound input at all.

If you're building a whole-home audio system but don't want to spend huge amounts on MTS-capable monitors, you may want to utilize mono modulators in your network, and use the audio network to carry high-fidelity sounds around the house.

✔ **Shape and size:** Modulators don't come in a standard shape and size, so you do have a few options to choose from:

- **Black box:** These modulators don't look particularly pretty, but they will fit in with the rest of the stuff on your A/V equipment shelf.

- **Wall outlet size:** A newer variation — and much less obtrusive — are modulators that actually fit into a standard wall outlet gang box. The same size as a light switch (or a coaxial outlet, for that matter), these miracles of miniaturization make sense for use in places like bedrooms where you don't have a huge rack of video equipment already in place.

- **Distribution panels:** You can get modulators out of the room entirely by purchasing an all-in-one distribution panel that has a modulator or two built right into the same box. This option does limit you because your source devices must be close to the distribution panel — so that VCR on the fourth floor is out of luck!

✔ **Loop through ability:** Many modulators offer something called an *A/V loop through*. Most source devices — except for some DSS receivers — only have one set of baseband video and audio outputs. If you plug these into a modulator, you don't have any way to make a baseband A/V connection to the local TV — you have to use the source's built-in Channel 3/4 modulator instead. The loop through provides an extra set of baseband video and audio out on the back of the modulator so you can connect to the local TV this way instead.

You need to keep a couple of things in mind when you're using a modulator system to create your own TV channels in your home:

✔ **Install a signal amplifier between your antenna and the distribution panel/modulators:** When you create your own TV channel, you're doing pretty much the same thing in your house that cable companies and broadcasters do at their headend offices and stations. If you are using an antenna feed to receive broadcast TV stations, you could end up sending your video out your antenna and over the airwaves (and into your neighbor's TV perhaps!). The FCC doesn't like this idea too much, so it requires you to install a signal amplifier between your antenna and the distribution panel/modulators. Amplifiers are inherently one-way — signals don't pass back through them — and they help pick up those distant stations better.

✔ **Skip channels between modulated channels:** Most modulator manufacturers recommend that you skip at least one channel between modulated channels to avoid any possible interference.

✔ **Be aware of signal interference:** Channels that your TV can't really pick up may still be strong enough to interfere with your internal channels — often the case in the higher, UHF band for broadcast TV. The same can apply to cable TV — just because you don't subscribe to a particular channel doesn't mean that its signal isn't taking up bandwidth space on your coax. If this problem occurs for you, you need to adjust the modulator to a different channel.

✔ **Make sure that you have free channel space:** Channel space isn't too much of a problem if you use an antenna — even the most crowded urban areas have plenty of unused channels. However, cable service providers in many areas are beginning to saturate their available channels with programming. They're also using TV channels for other services like cable modems and audio services. So if you're planning on modulating several channels onto your network, do your homework first and make sure that you'll be able to find open channels. You can do this by physically looking at channels you think are unused on one of you televisions (making sure there's not a scrambled signal there) and also by checking the complete listing of channels provided by your cable service provider.

Blocking existing channels to make room for your internal TV stations is neither practical nor economically feasible. You'll have to consider either changing your outside TV connection from cable to broadcast or satellite (or both), or look for an alternative method of distributing internal video signals throughout the home, like using a wireless video-distribution system.

Chapter 7

Wiring a Video Network

· ·

· ·

*I*n Chapter 5, we spend a fair amount of time talking about all the pieces and parts that fit into a home video-distribution network. That's important stuff to know — but it doesn't do you much good if you don't have everything connected together properly. So in this chapter, we tell you about the model that you use in setting up your network. The technical words for this model are the *topology* or *network architecture,* but don't be intimidated. These words just mean a way of thinking about your network so you know what to connect where.

In this chapter, we tell you how to get the right cables in the walls (and infrastructure devices, too) to create a futureproof, two-way video network. Maybe you don't plan to install all the equipment that we describe in Chapters 5 and 6 (such as modulators) right away. No problem. As long as you get your wires in place, the general network model that we describe in this chapter will serve you well in the future as your needs change and grow.

Connecting Your Video Network

After you have a good idea of the components that go into making a video network and what they do (see Chapter 6), you're ready to actually run the cables and make the connections. We provide you with the steps here. Note, however, that we don't tell you how to tear your walls apart, drill holes in your floor, or shut off your power at the power main. Consult a home remodeling book such as *Home Improvement For Dummies,* by Katie Hamilton, Gene Hamilton, and the Editors of HouseNet (IDG Books Worldwide, Inc.), for that kind of information.

Don't feel like you have to wire a video network (or any network) yourself. If you're the least bit squeamish about drilling holes and running cables through your walls, do yourself a favor and hire a professional. Having a professional install your network saves you a ton of aggravation.

We recommend that you build your whole-home video network with two segments of RG6 coaxial cable connected to each video outlet you install in your major rooms — one cable that brings video into the TV and one cable that allows you to distribute video source devices (such as VCRs) through the network. Specifically, you should have at each location:

- ✔ **An *external* video connection:** This connection carries video signals from your distribution panel to your television. Think of external as outbound.

- ✔ **An *internal* video connection:** This connection carries video signals from any source devices in the room back to the distribution panel, where they can be combined with your external video source (cable or broadcast TV) and sent back out on the outbound lines. Think of internal as inbound.

Note: We use the words *external* and *internal* in reference to the central hub of the video network, the video distribution panel. *External,* or *outbound,* means away from the video distribution panel, and *internal,* or *inbound,* means toward the video distribution panel. If you start feeling confused, just remember that your point of reference is the distribution panel.

Running one outbound coaxial cable allows you to receive signals in that room and may be sufficient for rooms where you don't intend to send any video sources back through the network. However, figuring out which rooms fall into that category is very hard to predict. Who, five years ago, would have predicted $49 cable modem service for the Internet? Who would have suggested that you think about putting in a video camera to watch your nanny? New uses like these are hard to predict.

Figure 7-1 shows the layout of a typical centrally-homed coaxial video network. In the next sections, we walk you through the network step by step, from a single room back to the distribution panel.

Step 1: Running the cables

The first part of wiring a video-distribution network is running two RG6 coaxial cables between the distribution panel and each area of the house where you want to have video. You may want to hire a professional cable installer to run this cable for you. For an attractive appearance, the cables should connect to wall-mounted female coaxial connectors, as we describe in Chapter 6.

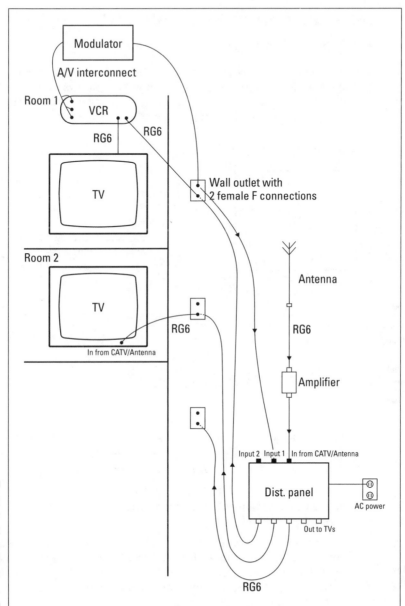

Figure 7-1:
A video net-
work that
runs to a
central
distribution
panel.

To make things easier for connection and future system changes, make sure that all your RG6 cables are well labeled. At a minimum, you need to know which room the cable is coming from and whether it is the internal or external line. We recommend that you buy your RG6 cable in two different colors (it usually comes in white or black); use one color for all internal runs and the other for all external runs.

Step 2: Making connections in the TV rooms

This section covers how you connect to the network in the rooms where the TVs and the video source devices live. Figure 7-2 shows typical *in-room* video connections. Assuming that you're finished making your cable runs between the rooms and the distribution panel, just follow these steps:

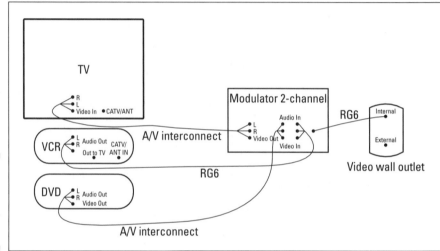

Figure 7-2:
Plugging
video
equipment
together.

1. **Connect each video source device (such as a VCR, DVD player, or camcorder) that you want to distribute to other areas of the house to a** *modulator,* **using an RCA cable or other component patch cord.**

   Modulators allow you to broadcast a device's video signal around your house using an unused TV channel. We explain modulators and RCA cables in detail in Chapter 6.

   If you have several video source devices in the same room (such as your home-theater room with a VCR and a DVD player), you can use a *multichannel modulator* to broadcast multiple audio and video signals onto unused channels. Using a multichannel modulator may save you some money.

2. **Run a length of RG6 coaxial cable with male connectors on both ends from the output jack of your modulator to the** *internal* **female coaxial connector jack in your wall.**

Remember that your point of reference for internal is inbound to the distribution panel. So when you're standing in the room with the TV, the internal jack runs *out* of the room toward the distribution panel. If you think about it too long, you get a headache.

3. **Connect another length of RG6 cable with male connectors between your TV (or the input of your VCR if you have one) and the *external* connector on your coaxial outlet.**

   If you are using a VCR, you can then connect it to your television with either an RG6 coaxial cable connected between the coaxial connector jacks in the VCR and TV, or you can connect RCA cables from the Audio and Video Out jacks of the VCR to the Audio and Video In jacks on the TV. Figure 7-3 shows the signal path for watching a VCR in another room.

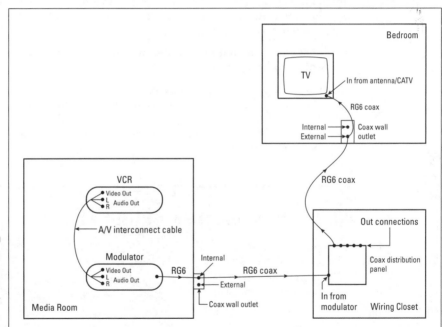

Figure 7-3:
Watching a VCR in another room.

If your VCR is connected to a modulator that has a loop through connection (see Chapter 6), you can use these outlets and RCA cords to connect your VCR to your TV.

4. **Perform Steps 1 through 3 for each room and pair of coaxial cables in your network. Lather, rinse, and repeat as desired.**

Step 3: Making connections at the distribution panel

If you do everything right when completing the steps in the preceding section, you should have a gob of cables running into a central point, which we call the central wiring closet. This section tells you how to connect these wires to your distribution panel to complete your network.

1. **Connect each external RG6 coaxial cable to one of the distribution panel's outputs.**

   If your distribution panel comes with multiple levels of amplification, take the time now to double-check the amplification levels. Each of your meticulously labeled cables should be connected to outputs with amplification levels that correspond to the distance of each cable run. (See Chapter 6 for more information.)

2. **Connect each internal RG6 cable into one of the modulator inputs on your distribution panel.**

   You may find that you have more internal video cables in your wiring closet than you have inputs (remember that most panels have five or fewer inputs). If you don't currently have any video sources connected to a particular cable, you can leave it disconnected — but well labeled — until you need it.

Where does the new digital TV fit in?

High Definition TV (HDTV). The mere words make us smile. Widescreen TV images with film quality. Is your video network going to be ready for it?

There's no simple answer, mainly because there's still a lot of controversy over how these digital TV signals will get into your home. The first source of HDTV and other flavors of DTV *(digital TV)* will be broadcast television stations. In this case, the video-distribution network that we describe in this chapter should work pretty well. The DTV signal will be carried over a broadband RF signal just like today's analog TV signals are, so your RG6 coaxial network will be able to handle it. The amplifiers in today's distribution panels are a cause of some concern — they may need to be optimized to work their best with a large number of HDTV stations. So when

DTV becomes a reality, you may need to replace your panel.

Modulators are in a predicament of their own. They are designed to work with today's NTSC (National Television Standards Committee) analog TV standard. Luckily, future digital TVs will be able to decode and display NTSC pictures as well as the higher-quality pictures of the new standard, so you won't have to throw your existing modulators away when they are used with your current video source devices. However, as new video source devices (like digital VCRs) are developed to record or display HDTV/DTV pictures, your existing modulators won't be able to do anything with those signals. In the long-term, you'll probably need to replace your modulators.

If you *still* don't have enough inputs on your panel, you can use a good quality splitter/combiner to connect two or more internal cables to a single panel input. If you choose this option, don't try to save a few bucks on a cheap splitter/combiner — the 99-cent specials from your local discount store are worth exactly what they cost (next to nothing). Spend $15 or $20 on a high-quality model from a manufacturer like ChannelPlus or ChannelVision.

3. **Connect the RG6 cable from your antenna or cable TV feed to the Antenna/CATV input on the distribution panel.**

If you're using modulators and an antenna to pull in local broadcast stations, you need to install an amplifier between the antenna and the distribution panel so that you don't broadcast to your neighbors and upset them (and the FCC!). Most manufacturers of distribution panels also make these signal amplifiers — use the amplifier that they recommend to go along with your distribution panel.

You can't simply plug the output of your DSS satellite system into your distribution panel's Antenna/CATV input. Although DSS signals are a kind of RF modulated broadband video signal, they are in many ways a different beast altogether, and video distribution panels won't work with them. Read the section "Special Needs of Satellite Systems," later in this chapter, for more info on this unfortunate phenomenon.

Most distribution panels (except for those without any signal amplification built in) need electrical power to do their job. The majority use a small *wall wart* AC/DC power adapter like those used by cordless phones, modems, and tons of other small electrical appliances.

If you have completed the steps in this section, you have a whole-home video network up and running now! Your work isn't completely done, however; you still need to program each of your modulators to unused channels. We're not going to give you step-by-step instructions on this task because each manufacturer's model is different. For the most part, however, digital modulators are pretty easy to tune in — it's just a matter of pressing a program button a few times. Many models even have LCD or LED digital displays so you can't mess up. We like those displays — otherwise you have to remember things like "Did I press that button five times or six times?"

As we mention before, if all this two-way video sounds like something that you'll never, ever want to get involved with, you *can* build a very similar video distribution network that forgoes the second RG6 cable to each outlet. Just follow the same basic architecture guidelines — all outlets individually wired with a length of RG6 cable running back to your central distribution node — and skip the second cable run. At the risk of being repetitive, we think that this kind of abbreviated network is probably a false economy — we like the flexibility the second cable gives — but it is a perfectly valid way of constructing a home video network. If you set up your network this way, we

---

You don't need an extinguisher for FireWire

A new technology for carrying digital video signals is beginning to get a lot of attention — FireWire (also know as IEEE 1394, which is the name of the international standard for the system). FireWire is a snazzy new networking/interconnection system that provides superfast throughput (400 or 800 Mbps today, more in the future) for digital signals of all kinds. Right now, FireWire is most common in the personal computer world, where it is used to connect items like video cameras and even hard drives. It is also being adopted as the standard way of connecting a cable TV DTV set-top decoder box to a digital HDTV monitor/TV. This connection is local — you'll still use an RF signal to get from the cable system feed to the set-top decoder.

So far so good for your coaxial network, but there's a *but*. Many consumer electronics companies like Matsushita want to use FireWire as the backbone for a whole-home entertainment network that carries your video signals, digital audio signals, and perhaps other stuff like computer LAN data. There's no clear indication at this time how a FireWire network will be physically carried throughout your home. Current local FireWire connections like those used for PCs utilize a special copper FireWire cable, but this cabling isn't really suitable for the long distances found in the home.

What will this potential whole-home FireWire network use for cabling? There are many possibilities — some pundits prefer inexpensive plastic optical fiber (POF), others say it should use CAT-5 cabling like that used for Ethernet LANs, and still others want a wireless FireWire system to be developed. Will it use coaxial cable? The industry really has not decided yet, but we do know this: No one knows whether FireWire home networks will really happen, but your coaxial video network will remain useful for quite some time.

---

strongly recommend that you at least run a second cable to the room containing your home theater/media center. Chances are that's where you'll have all the fun source devices, and having a second cable there at least gives you the opportunity to share those sources throughout the home at a future date.

If you are considering installing a cable modem in your home to get high-speed Internet access, you should be aware that you can't plug a cable modem into any outlet in your video network. That's because cable modems send data two ways over a single cable, and most distribution panels and amplifiers block the signals heading back to the Internet from your computer. See Chapter 13 for some advice on how to integrate a cable modem into your network.

Special Needs of Satellite Systems

DSS (Digital Satellite System) and DBS (Direct Broadcast Satellite) small-dish satellite systems are a great way to receive TV programming, but they're sort of a pain in the rear end to integrate into your video network. Because the frequencies that satellite systems use and the way that coaxial cables carry the signal are different from standard TV signals, you can't connect your satellite to your video distribution panel's Antenna In or Cable In connector and distribute it through your house. You have to be a bit devious to integrate your satellite into your network. In this section, we tell you how.

Big-dish, C Band satellite systems have very similar networking requirements as the small-dish satellites we describe here, but the systems aren't identical. If you're going to get involved with one of these systems (and we think they're great if you have room for the dish), find a good professional installer to walk you through the ins and outs of big dishdom.

We provide you with two methods of running your DBS- or DSS-satellite signal across your video network. The difference between them depends on whether you want a two-way network that can bring video back from various rooms.

Running a one-way satellite network

You may be thinking to yourself, "Heck, I've got this dish, so I don't need cable." And we have just the solution. You can build a video network for your DSS system that will carry the outputs from a DBS dish to multiple receivers throughout the home by using a *multiswitch* instead of a distribution panel. The downside to using a multiswitch, however, is that the satellite network is one-way. You still have to install a distribution panel if you want to share video sources across the network as we describe in the section "Connecting Your Video Network," earlier in this chapter. If you want a two-way network in conjunction with a satellite, check out the following section on a hybrid video network.

To run your satellite picture to different receivers around your home, you need to replace the distribution panel with a special device known as a *multiswitch* or *voltage switch*. The multiswitch connects to both of the outputs of a dual LNB (*low noise block*) dish and provides coaxial connections for up to four separate receivers. To hook one up, you simply use RG6 coaxial cable to connect each of the LNB outputs to your multiswitch and then run individual lengths of RG6 to each receiver.

You can't (except in rare instances that, due to some new FCC rulings, are becoming rarer) get any of the broadcast networks like FOX, NBC, CBS, and ABC over a DBS system. Nor can you get any local independent channels. You have to hook up an aerial antenna to get these stations. (Cable also brings in these stations, but cable doesn't work with a multiswitch or voltage switch.) As an aside, we doubt that we're alone in thinking that having to rely on an antenna to get broadcast network signals is a real pain in the tush. Maybe we should start a massive consumer backlash and petition the FCC to overturn the rules that make this so!

If you're interested in running an aerial TV antenna to pick up local stations, buy multiswitches that accept the output from a broadcast TV antenna and carry it over the same RG6 cables to your DBS receivers and televisions. Some of these multiswitches also include a device called a *diplexer* (check out the sidebar "What if I just want DSS and none of that fancy stuff?"), which lets you integrate both the satellite and local TV signals onto the same RG6 coaxial cable.

Creating a hybrid satellite/video network

The drawback to using a multiswitch as the hub of your video network (as we describe in the preceding section) is that it creates a one-way network — from the satellite dish to the TV. If you want to be able to watch video in one room that's sent from a device in another room (whether from a VCR, a DVD player, or a video camera in your baby's room), you need to use a separate distribution panel for the return signal (or use alternate technologies like wireless and telephone line systems — which we describe later in the chapter).

You have a couple of options if you want to get the best of both worlds in a hybrid two-way satellite/video network:

- **Build a separate video network for your satellite.** Build a video-distribution network for your DBS or DSS dish, with independent runs of coaxial RG6 cable from the dish to each location that will have a satellite receiver. With a multiswitch connected to the outputs of your satellite dish, you can connect up to four separate receivers to a dish. You can then build a video-distribution network using a distribution panel to handle the return signals.

  The benefit of this system is that it gives you the ability to watch up to four DBS or DSS channels on four different TVs simultaneously, while still allowing you the benefit of being able to watch in your bedroom a tape playing in a VCR in the home-theater room. The drawback of this system is the added expense and complexity of building a separate network — more cable to run, more equipment to buy, and more money to spend.

- **Treat your DSS receivers as *source* devices — just like VCRs or DVD players.** You still need separate RG6 cabling runs from the dish to the receivers (we don't have any magic pill that takes away that requirement), but you can then use modulators to send the output of these receivers to every television in the house. Just install receivers in your two favorite watching areas and modulate them onto different channels for viewing from other TVs in the house.

This solution has the benefit of adding only moderate cost (you only
have extra runs to the receivers) and limited complexity. The drawback
is that without using a multiswitch or voltage switch, you can only
watch two DSS stations simultaneously (assuming that you have a *dual-
LNB satellite* that allows you to run two coaxial lines from your receiver.
With a single-LNB receiver, you can only watch one station). ***Note:*** You
can however, use a device called a multiswitch with a dual-LNB satellite
to increase the number of receivers you can watch simultaneously to
four. We discuss multiswitches in the next section.

A few builders of video distribution panels — AMP's OnQ system is one —
make panels that have DSS pass-through ports. In this case, you can run your
dual RG6 cables from the dish location to whatever location you choose for
your distribution panel and then run an additional RG6 cable from the central
node of your video network to the two locations where you want to place
your DSS receivers. This cable is electrically separate from the cables that
make up the rest of your video-distribution network — so you actually have
three cables running to the locations that contain your DSS receivers (one to
carry the satellite feed, one to carry signals from the distribution panel to
your TV, and the third to carry signals from video source devices in the room
back to the distribution panel). When it comes time to go the DBS route, you
need to install your dish, of course, and then connect each of the RG6 cables
that you've already run to one of the LNB outlets on the base of the dish.

They're getting to be rare, but some dishes out there still have just one coaxial cable connection (LNB). Avoid these dishes like the plague if you have
even the slightest inkling that you'll ever want to connect more than one
receiver to your DSS system. No amount of magic pixie dust lets these dishes
get beyond the one-receiver limit. A *dual LNB* dish is what you need, what
you want, and what you should get.

Making satellite connections

After running a satellite network, you should have a DSS input coaxial connector in each room. Depending on whether you opted for a hybrid system,
you may or may not also have internal and external video jacks.

To complete the installation, simply connect the satellite receiver to the jack
on the wall that carries a short RG6 patch cable. Doing so brings the satellite
signal from the wall to the satellite receiver. After connecting the receiver to
your television, you should see crystal-clear satellite television.

If you want to distribute your DSS receiver's signals throughout the house,
connect the receiver's outputs to a modulator (using one of the sets of
audio/video connectors on the back of the DSS receiver), set the modulator

to an unused TV channel, and run another RG6 patch cable from the modulator to the F connector on your wall that leads back to your video-distribution network. Presto, shazam — you can now watch the programming from this receiver on any TV in the house by tuning to the correct channel.

Here are a few more tips on DSS systems that are important to remember:

- ✔ **You need a phone line in every room that has a DSS receiver.** The DSS service provider uses this phone line to authenticate your box and provide stuff like pay-per-view movies and ACC basketball games. You can get by without a phone line on the second receiver, but you lose some convenience features like easy pay-per-view for that receiver. (You may also have to pay more for the second receiver's programming if you don't have it attached to a phone line.)

- ✔ **You can use a so-called *wireless phone jack* to run the phone line across your electrical cables.** They're not really wireless, because they use electrical cabling, but they save you from stringing a phone line across the room like a trip wire. Plug in the wireless phone jack in the outlet nearest your phone jack and run a phone line between them. Now plug a terminating wireless jack at an electrical outlet near your satellite receiver and run a phone line from the wireless phone jack into your satellite receiver. You have a phone connection for your DSS receiver!

- ✔ **You should install special *inline amplifiers* if the distance between the dish and a receiver is longer than 100 feet.** These amplifiers boost signal strength for long cable runs and are pretty cheap (between $25 and $100, depending upon the level of amplification). They draw their power over the coaxial cable from the receiver, so they're easy to install — just cut the cable and connect the amplifier between them.

- ✔ **You may want to install coaxial surge protectors on the RG6 runs from your dish.** Doing so prevents lightning strikes on your roof from destroying your DSS receivers. Be careful when you choose a surge protector, though, because the standard cable TV models available in most electronics stores don't pass the entire DSS signal. You need to buy special-purpose surge protectors that specifically support DSS.

- ✔ **You can run lines for up to four receivers in your house if you use a multiswitch.** You may even want to run an extra length of RG6 coax to your home theater/media room and put two receivers there — if you have a multichannel modulator there, you can use a spare channel for the second receiver.

You can get a second remote control that looks exactly like the one that comes with your system. We highly recommend this tip for marital bliss.

We don't tell you in this chapter how to remotely control all this video equipment from other rooms. We haven't forgotten; in fact, we have a long description of how to remotely control video (and audio!) network components in Chapters 19 and 20.

What if I just want DSS and none of that fancy stuff?

If you decide that you really don't need or want a full-fledged two-way video network and you're going to use just DSS and local channels in your video network, you need to get familiar with the *diplexer*. The diplexer looks just like the splitter/combiner but is designed especially for the purpose of combining broadcast or cable TV signals with the output of a DSS dish on a single length of RG6 cabling.

Diplexers *must* be used in pairs — one near your DSS dish where the antenna/cable feed is combined with the output of your LNB, and another at the far end of your RG6 cabling, immediately before the cable plugs into your DSS receiver. The first diplexer takes the two cable feeds and combines them onto a single RG6 cable; the second splits this signal back into

two separate signals — one connects to your receiver's LNB input, the other to the Antenna/CATV input on the back of the receiver.

If you feed two DSS receivers from a dual LNB dish and you want to add in your local channels from cable or antenna, you need four diplexers. If you use a multiswitch to send the output of your dish to more than two receivers, you need to buy a multiswitch with a diplexer built in and then use another diplexer at each receiver.

Warning: Even though they look pretty much the same, diplexers and regular splitter/combiners are two different devices. Don't try to save $20 by using any old splitter in your system: It won't work.

Cut the Cord: Wireless Alternatives for Video Distribution

Phones and data networks aren't the only things in your home that can benefit from advances in wireless networking. A few products that use wireless technologies work well for your home entertainment network if all you need to do is to add a device (for example, one TV or one set of speakers), rather than take care of your entire whole-home networking needs.

Wireless video-distribution systems are designed to accept the video and audio outputs of a video source — like a VCR, DBS satellite receiver, or DVD player — and send them somewhere else in the home by using an RF wireless link. These systems basically consist of two small units, each containing an antenna. The transmitter unit attaches to your video source via standard RCA-type audio and video connectors, while the receiver unit usually offers both an RCA and an RF output to connect to the television on the far end. Figure 7-4 shows a typical layout of a wireless video network.

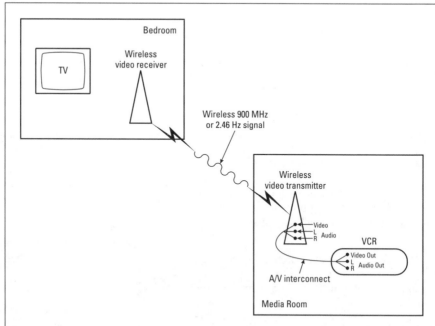

Figure 7-4:
Wireless
video
network.

Note: These systems accept and distribute *baseband* video signals (which carry only a single channel at a time), not broadband signals (the signals that can carry many or all channels) — an important difference if you're thinking about using one of these systems with a DBS satellite system. You can't use a wireless video-distribution system to send your dish's output to a second satellite receiver; you can only use it to distribute the output of the first receiver (in other words, you see the same program on television two that you would see on television one — you can't use this setup to watch two different channels at once).

If you're looking into a wireless video system, here's what you should keep in mind:

- ✔ **What frequency spectrum does it use?** Some of these systems utilize the 900 MHz frequency band, while others use the higher 2.4 GHz band. In general, the 2.4 GHz systems perform better because these higher-frequency RF signals run more cleanly with less interference from other systems and pass through walls and ceilings better. Additionally, 2.4 GHz systems provide more available bandwidth to carry the video signals.

- ✔ **Does the system transmit audio in mono or stereo?** If your video source includes high-quality sound, you probably want to spend a bit more to get the stereo audio.

IR in control

The home entertainment remote controls that let you change channels, turn on your VCR, and turn the volume up and down — among other chores — usually use beams of infrared light to do their job. Infrared (or IR) works really well in this role and is a cheap, well-proven method of enabling remote control. It does have one major drawback, however: IR beams, like all light beams, don't pass through solid objects very well. Stuff like doors, walls, floors, and even large dogs can interfere with an IR signal, rendering your remote useless.

IR beam interference typically isn't a problem when you're dealing with a single-room system, but when you move into the whole-home video realm, it suddenly becomes a salient point. When you can put a movie in the DVD player in the home theater and watch it upstairs in the bedroom, the DVD player's remote doesn't do the trick. You have to find a way of getting that IR signal from the remote back down to the DVD player.

Two ways of getting the IR signal to the right place are described in more detail in Chapter 20. Here's the lowdown:

✔ You can carry the IR signal over RF waves (which pass through walls and floors and fairly large dogs) back to an IR emitter located near the source device.

✔ You can install IR targets in the walls throughout your house. These targets convert the IR signal from your remote into electrical signals and carry them either over your coaxial cable or over special-purpose IR wiring back to an emitter installed at the source device.

✔ You can skip the remote control altogether and install in-wall keypads that are wired back to a central point. These keypads contain most of the controls that a universal remote does and send electrical signals to IR emitters that control your source devices.

✔ **Does the system carry IR (infrared) control signals?** Some do, and it sure is handy to be able to do things like pause, rewind, or change channels while watching a program in the bedroom without having to walk to the living room. This feature seems like a must have to us unless you already have an IR control network built into your home — but if you have an IR network installed, we're pretty sure you want to have a coaxial video-distribution network as well, so you won't be needing the wireless system.

Use What You've Already Got: Phone Line Alternatives for Video Distribution

While most of the action in developing home-networking systems that run on existing phone wires is in the data-networking field, some companies are beginning to look into ways for using these phone lines for home entertainment systems. Like the phone line data-networking systems, these products utilize digital signal processing to carry the entertainment signals on completely different frequencies than those used by telephone service — meaning that they can be used simultaneously with the telephone equipment connected to the network.

These systems use different frequencies than do analog telephone systems, but there's no guarantee that they use different frequencies than the phone line data-networking systems do. That means interference could be a major problem if you try to use both of these systems in your home — in fact, we strongly recommend against it. Single-purpose wiring eliminates these kinds of conflicts, which is why we think it's the best way to go.

Terk Technologies is a major manufacturer of antennas and home-theater accessories. The HomeNetwork by Terk is a device — or rather a pair of devices — that transmits video and/or audio signals from a source device (like a DSS receiver or VCR) to a remote location over existing phone lines. The transmitter half of the pair connects to the RF or line-level video and audio outputs of the source unit and plugs into a standard RJ-11 phone jack. At the remote end, the receiver also plugs into an RJ-11 phone jack and connects to the RF or line-level audio and video inputs of the remote television or audio system. The HomeNetwork also carries infrared control signals over your phone lines, so you can carry your remote with you to the room containing the receiver and do all the pausing, freeze-framing, fast-forwarding through commercials, and channel-changing you like, without running back and forth.

Chapter 8

Planning to Bring Music to You

In This Chapter

▶ Getting the sound around (the house, that is)

▶ Getting into the zone

▶ Understanding various pieces and parts

*L*ike the video systems we discuss in the previous two chapters, home audio systems are increasingly becoming *whole*-home audio systems. Wiring your home to provide music everywhere and anywhere from a central set of source components is both convenient and a true money saver.

This chapter looks at many of the cabling issues in creating a whole-home audio network.

Zoning Out: Single-Zone versus Multizone Systems

In a *single-zone audio system,* you only have one audio source that you distribute across the network. You can turn various sets of speakers on or off, but you don't have the ability to listen to different audio sources in different parts of your house at the same time. A *multizone system,* on the other hand, allows one family member to listen to a CD while another person listens to the audio channel of a VCR. Single-zone systems have a few advantages:

✔ **They're inexpensive:** A single zone can utilize the smallest number of components to get up and running, and the components themselves are the least expensive to purchase.

✔ **They're easy to set up:** In the simplest case, a single-zone system can consist of a single source — like a CD player — connected to one amplifier, and then through an *impedance-matching system* to several sets of speakers (we discuss impedance matching in the section entitled "Matching impedance," later in this chapter).

✔ **They're upgradable:** The hardest part about building an audio network is getting the right wires into the walls in the right places. Once you do that, you can easily switch from a single zone to a multizone system by simply upgrading a few components and swapping out a few connections.

Multizone systems, on the other hand, provide the following benefits:

✔ **Multiple audio sources:** Multizone systems allow different members of your family to listen to different audio sources in different areas. For example, you can send the output from your CD player to one room and the output from your AM/FM radio tuner to another. This feature tends to increase the domestic tranquility, just as our Founding Fathers recommended.

✔ **Video-network integration:** Multizone systems integrate better with your video-distribution system. The video-distribution network that we describe in Chapters 5 and 6 brings audio and video to each television in your house. With a multizoned audio network, however, you can take that one step further to send the stereo audio portion of any video program to a set of speakers near your remote TVs. This feature is appealing for two reasons: Stereo video modulators are pretty darn expensive, and separate speakers usually sound much better than those inside your TV.

The trouble with multichannel audio networks

The stereo audio standard, in which sound is separated into a left and right channel, still dominates music production. However, just a bit beyond our crystal ball's range, is the possibility of producing music according to a new multichannel method. This proposed audio standard will use speakers in front of you, behind you, and possibly alongside you to re-create the spatial dynamics of the concert hall in your home (at least that's how fancy stereo magazines describe it).

You can already buy an audio system that supports a home-theater standard that uses a multichannel system to create all sorts of neat sound effects. Movie soundtracks and some TV shows (in a limited fashion) come through speakers in front of you, behind you, and beside you. These multichannel systems also sometimes support subwoofers (which give you the really deep bass sounds), floor-shaking transducers (devices which mount in the floor and literally shake it, so you can really feel that explosion in the movie), a special-effects channel, and other wild-and-wooly add ons.

We recommend that you don't add multichannel capabilities to your whole-home audio network, at least not right now. Although you can build an audio network that goes beyond the two channel (stereo) limit, the network quickly becomes extremely complicated and prohibitively expensive.

By all means, go ahead and set up a special multichannel amplifier, a surround sound decoder, and surround sound speakers, but set these up in your home theater or home entertainment room. When you run your whole-home audio network, however — at least for the foreseeable future — stick with good-old stereo.

Regardless of whether you choose to install a single-zone or multizone system in your house, the basic wiring infrastructure is very similar (see Chapter 9), so you can start with something very simple and make it more sophisticated in the future.

Audio Connections (In the Short Run and the Long Run)

The wires that connect the various pieces and parts of audio systems can be divided into two groups — the wires that run between components like CD players and amplifiers, and the wires that connect amplifiers to speakers. In this section, we delve into these cables in a bit of detail.

Your audio system generally carries audio signals between components in one of two ways:

- **Line-level signals:** These are the low-power electrical signals that contain an analog, electrical representation of the musical sound wave, but not the electrical power to actually move your speaker diaphragms and create sound. Everything in an audio system up to the power amplifier uses line-level signals — the CD player, the tape deck, the audio outputs of a VCR or DVD player, to name just a few. These are usually short-run connections between components.

- **Speaker-level signals:** These are the higher-powered signals that come out of your amplifier (or receiver, if you don't have separate components) and actually drive your speakers — that is, they cause the electromagnets in your speakers to move, creating the sound you hear. These are generally the long-haul connections that run through your walls and around your house.

We'd be remiss if we didn't tell you that you actually *can* run line-level signal cables between rooms. Doing so, however, exposes you to some problems that you don't face with speaker-level signals. Low-level signals are more susceptible to loss of audio information over long distances and interference from other wires — meaning that the quality of the audio may not be as good as if you had run speaker-level signals. Moreover, if you run low-level signal cables through your walls, you still have to amplify them before the signals can be output from speakers, meaning that you have to have an audio amplifier in every room in which you want to hear your audio network.

Some digital audio devices — such as CD players and DVD players — let you carry a digital signal (rather than analog) between the component and the amplification system. To use such a function, you need a digital-to-analog converter built into the amplifier or receiver to convert this digital signal to an analog signal that can drive your speakers. (If your amplifier or receiver supports this function, you should see a Digital In jack on the back somewhere.) There are several different types of cables used for this kind of connection, including fiber-optic cable and coaxial cable with a standard RCA jack on each end (which one you use depends upon what kind of connections your equipment manufacturer chose to install on its equipment — there's not a single standard). At the present time, digital signal transmission is an uncommon method of distributing audio, but we expect it to become more common in the future. (See Chapter 9 for more information.)

Line level (for the short haul)

Cables called *line-level interconnects* carry *line-level signals,* the unamplified signals that move between audio components. Any cable with this type of jack is generically called an *RCA cable* (because RCA first created it). Although not a requirement, interconnect cables are usually shielded wires. They typically come in *stereo pairs* (two separate wires bound together in a left and right channel configuration).

The rise of multichannel audio in the home theater has lead many manufacturers to create interconnects with odd numbers of cables and connectors — five, for example, to connect the two front, two rear, and single center channels, or single cables to connect subwoofers to the receiver.

The sheer number of choices you'll find in the interconnect marketplace can be bewildering. Go to a stereo store, and you'll find interconnects ranging from freebies thrown in with a stereo system to $1,000-a-foot (literally) cables wired with precious metals — silver or gold or copper mined by old-world artisans at the purest mine in the world, somewhere in Bolivia (or so the typical advertising pitch goes). Whether or not these super-expensive cables make any difference at all is always a matter of intense debate among audio aficionados — go check out one of the audio newsgroups on the Internet (like `rec.audio.opinion`) if you want to see some people really slugging it out on the subject.

You probably get what you pay for with the really, really cheap (or free) cables. You may want to seek out a knowledgeable and trustworthy expert if you haven't made up your mind on what to buy.

Speaker level (for the long haul)

The wires that connect your speakers to your amplifier are by necessity quite a bit beefier than those that carry delicate line-level signals. Like interconnects, an amazingly huge range of speaker-cable designs are available, but generally speaking, all cables consist of two conductors (either a solid wire or a set of smaller wires stranded together) within a common outerjacket or insulator.

In a whole-home audio system, you can run speaker wire in two places:

- **Through the walls:** You use special in-wall speaker cabling to connect your centrally located amplifier or amplifiers to remote outlets or in-wall speakers throughout your home. (We talk about what to look for when you choose this in-wall cabling in just a moment.)

- **From the wall to the speaker (patch cabling):** This speaker wire connects your stand-alone speakers to speaker outlets that you install in your walls. You can use the same cable you have in your walls if you'd like, or you can run down to the stereo shop and pick up some shorter lengths of pre-cut and pre-connectorized standard speaker cable for this job.

    The only reason not to use the same wire that's in your walls is aesthetic, really. The wire in your walls is usually covered with lots of silk-screened writing and labeling that stands out like a sore thumb against your powder blue walls. You can buy speaker patch cables that are easier to hide than the in-wall stuff, and you can even paint some brands to match your walls.

 If you read high-end stereo magazines, you may run into alternate speaker wiring configurations like *biwiring* (where you run two sets of speaker cables from the amp to each speaker) or *biamping* (where you run a separate speaker cable from two different amps to each speaker). Both of these approaches have their proponents, but they aren't really necessary in our opinion. If your audio system is sophisticated enough to take advantage of these kinds of speaker connections, we suggest that you get some expert advice from your dealer and audiophile friends to decide whether this capability is worth the added expense and complexity.

Cables and Components

Like any other network in your home, variations abound in how you may create a home audio network — you can make it as simple or complicated as you'd like. However, you should be familiar with a few basic components that are common to just about every home audio network.

Control systems

A *control system* is the switch that allows you to select from among your audio sources, such as your CD, tuner, or cassette deck. The control system matches up the audio source device that you want to listen to with the amplifier that powers your speakers. (We're not talking here about the *remote-control networks* that allow you to switch from your CD to your tuner *from another room.* Check out Chapter 20 for more information about remote-control networks).

The preamplifier or control amplifier that is installed in your audio system — or the one built into your integrated amplifier or receiver if you aren't using separate components — performs the source-switching function for a single-zone, single-amplifier system.

Single-zone control systems

If you are creating a single-zone distribution system but want to use multiple amplifiers, you have to get around a specific obstacle. As a general rule, audio source devices like CD players have only one set of line-level outputs, so you can't just plug one device into two separate amplifiers. You can choose from a couple of strategies for distributing your audio signal. Each uses a different piece of audio equipment:

- ✓ **Multi-room integrated amplifier:** This special amplifier accepts the stereo line-level input from a source device and amplifies *the same signal* into several pairs of stereo speaker outputs (these amplifiers usually feed up to four or six pairs of speakers).

   Don't confuse a multi-room amplifier with the *multichannel amplifiers* you find in surround sound systems for home theaters. In a home theater, each of the speakers (the front, center, surround, and subwoofer) receives a different audio signal — for example, a five-channel amplifier has five separate line-level inputs from your surround sound decoder. Multi-room integrated amplifiers take a single stereo pair of line-level inputs and internally sends this signal to more than one pair of amplifiers — in other words, it accepts the input of a source device like a CD player, and basically clones it, so that each pair of amplifiers built into the unit receives the same signal. Each of these pairs of amplifiers is then connected to your remote speakers with in-wall speaker cable.

- ✓ **Signal distribution amplifier:** This device takes the output of a source device, splits it into multiple outputs, and then amplifies these outputs to ensure that your signal is not degraded (if you just split the signal up without amplifying it, it would be too weak, and would cause distortion that you would be able to hear as a background noise or hiss). You can then connect these outputs to individual stereo amplifiers — one for each pair of speakers.

Multizone control systems

Multizone systems require the use of specially built control systems that can take the output of several different source devices and independently route these line-level signals to multiple amplifiers (one for each zone, remember).

You can choose from two ways to step up a multizone audio system:

- ✔ Buy a high-end preamplifier or receiver that has built-in multizone capabilities (most of these systems are limited to two zones).

- ✔ Purchase a separate multizone control system that can feed any of your audio source component's signals to a specific zone's amplifiers (these systems usually allow more zones — often up to eight or more).

Do not attempt to put in a multizone system unless you have access to an audio geek. The documentation is usually awful to read, and it requires adept handling of a remote-control device.

Because of the increased costs, you may decide *not* to install a multizone audio system in your home right away. By following some of our guidelines throughout this book, however, we feel that you can indeed get a multizone treatment without breaking your bank account. No matter what decision you make, you should (and we tell you how in Chapter 9) install the proper wiring infrastructure in your house ahead of time.

Amplifier and speakers

The basic job of an audio amplifier is to increase the power of an audio signal enough to let the speaker re-create sound. Just how loud those speakers get (and if you're anything like us, you want it loud!) depends on two factors:

My wattage is bigger than your wattage!

We often hear people (usually in macho, bragging voices) boasting of how many watts their speakers are rated for — and therefore how loud their stereos can go. Don't believe them. Speaker wattage ratings have nothing to do with how loud an audio system is. Rather, they are simply recommendations for the minimum amplifier wattage a given speaker requires (which is a factor of the speaker's sensitivity), and the maximum amplifier wattage the speakers can handle without melting down or ripping into shreds. A speaker's wattage rating is usually found in the owner's manual or on the back of the speaker itself, and will say something like *20 Watts minimum, 100 Watts maximum*.

✔ **The power of the amplifier:** How many watts of head-banging power the amplifier pumps out

✔ **The sensitivity of the speakers:** How many decibels of loudness the speaker produces when a given number of watts come from the amplifier

Amplifiers are one of the largest issues you confront when putting together a multi-room home entertainment system, so be sure to put adequate time into researching your options. Don't make the mistake of assuming that you can just run speaker wire all over the house and then use your present amplifier. The salesperson at your local stereo store should be able to help you figure out all your amplifier needs. In order to get the best help from the stereo-store techie, we recommend that you draw a picture of your house, literally and quite accurately, and note where you want each device and speaker to go, along with accurate distances and likely conduit paths. This way, she can help you calculate your exact needs based on the equipment that store carries. Try a few stores, compare differences in approaches and pricing, and make a decision.

Impedance matters

When making the match between an amplifier and speakers, you need to take into account the speakers' *impedance.* Impedance is the force that the current coming from your amplifier pushes against. About all you need to know about impedance is that if you don't have enough, you may damage your amplifier! That's because lower-impedance speakers may cause an amplifier to overheat — which is never a good thing for a piece of electrical equipment.

The impedance rating of your speakers and your amplifier need to match. Most speakers are rated at 8 ohms impedance, but some are rated at 4 ohms. Lower-impedance loudspeakers (like the 4 ohm models) are more difficult for amplifiers to power — in fact, many inexpensive amplifiers aren't capable of powering 4 ohm speakers and may overheat or just plain not work if you try to combine them.

Wiring more than one speaker to an individual amplifier channel greatly decreases the overall impedance presented to the amplifier by the speakers. So even if you have an amp rated for 8 ohm impedance and speakers that are rated at 8 ohms as well, if you wire two speakers to the same output (in different rooms, for example), you effectively halve the impedance — to 4 ohms. Drat. Adding more speakers lowers the impedance even more. Double drat. Pretty soon you're going to cause damage to your amplifier.

Matching impedance

After the first two sets, adding speakers to an amplifier may cause the amplifier to malfunction, because you lower the impedance on the amplifier.

You can avoid this impedance problem a couple of ways:

- ✔ **Use separate amplifiers for each extra pair of speakers:** If you use a separate amplifier for each set of speakers, you won't need to worry about impedance matching. You can blithely skip this section.

- ✔ **Use an *impedance-matching device:*** This device lets you connect multiple speakers to an individual amplifier channel without causing impedance problems — though it does decrease the amount of power that each speaker receives (and therefore the speaker's maximum loudness).

You may be tempted to hook several speakers up to one central unit, but overall, the more amplifier power you have, the better. So, if you can afford additional amplifiers — they're relatively inexpensive — go ahead and get them. The more speakers you hang from your amplifier, the lower the power driving your speakers, which can ultimately do damage to your speakers and amplifier.

If you decide to go with a single amplifier for your home audio network, you need to get some sort of impedance-matching device into your system. You have a couple of choices:

- ✔ **A central impedance-matching transformer system:** This device is a small box that accepts a single stereo pair of speaker-wire connections and has several sets of speaker outlets. The internal transformer matches the impedance, so even if you have several pairs of speakers simultaneously connected to the amplifier, the amplifier functions correctly. Many of these transformer boxes also double as speaker selector switches, on/off switches for your speakers, so you can control which speakers are actually playing music, and which are blessedly silent.

- ✔ **An impedance-matching transformer built into an in-wall volume control:** These volume controls, which you place in each room with speakers, perform the same function as a central matching transformer, plus they let you easily adjust the volume without using a remote control. Some of these devices even have built-in on/off switches, so you can completely disable the speakers in the room — a nice feature to have in a single-zone system when you don't want to be disturbed.

If your audio network is going to be rather limited in scope — feeding only two rooms, for example — you can probably get away without any impedance-matching system at all. Just be sure to choose an amplifier or receiver that has two sets of speaker outlets, and make sure that it can handle the impedance load that your speakers put upon it. After you get beyond two sets of speakers, though, we highly recommend that you install an impedance-matching system. Skipping this step is not worth the risk of damaging expensive equipment.

Speaker cable

The main backbone of your home audio network is the speaker cable that you install in your walls. You can't just pick up any old speaker cable for this job — you need to use cabling that is specially designed for in-wall use. Look for the following when choosing cable:

- **Gauge:** Gauge is the actual thickness of the conductors within your speaker wire, measured in units known as AWG (American Wire Gauge). AWG works on an inverse scale — meaning that lower numbers denote thicker cables. Most audio experts recommend that you choose in-wall wiring that is a minimum of 16 gauge in size (a recommendation with which we agree). (Many people choose to go with 14 or even 12 AWG wires, which is probably overkill; these heavy gauge cables are really thick — and hard to pull through the house.)

- **UL listing:** Underwriter's Laboratories (UL) rate in-wall cables for safety and quality. Look for wires that are rated at least Class Two (UL CL2) or Class Three (UL CL3). The class rating is usually silk-screened on the wire jacket or rated wires.

Always check with your electrician or local building inspector to confirm the cable rating that your town requires. Although there is a *national electric code,* which lays out minimum standards for in-wall wiring, many municipalities have their own more stringent requirements. In fact, there's a bewildering array of such requirements, and not meeting them could cause your local building or electrical inspector to make you rip out your wiring and start over again.

- **Extra features:** Some wire manufacturers design their speaker cables with extra features like super-slippery cable jackets that slide through your wall more easily, length markers silk-screened on the jacket, and easy-to-remove insulation for terminating the wires — the kind of stuff that makes installers happy.

One particularly neat feature we've seen is a line of cables from Monster Cable that have additional wires for a wired IR control system wrapped up in the same jacket as the speaker cables. This feature makes good sense, because you'll probably want to have IR controllers in the same places that you have speakers — allowing you to install IR receivers or keypads in the wall to remotely control your audio system (we talk about this in greater detail in Chapter 20).

- **Wire quality:** Manufacturers of speaker wires tend to market them with the same sort of hyperbole that they use in the interconnect marketplace (not surprising, as the same companies tend to make both). So beyond objective stuff like gauge and UL category, you'll hear about things like the alignment of the copper molecules in the wire strands — again we recommend that you go with a good name brand and seek the advice of a trustworthy audio expert.

Audio connectors

Unlike video cables (and most of the other wires and cables we discuss throughout the book), no standard, one-size-fits-all family of connectors exists for speaker wires. In fact, you can terminate speaker wires in many different ways, leaving enough options to make the whole matter confusing.

Ways of connecting the speaker wires themselves include the following:

- **Bare wire:** Many people choose not to get too fancy and just strip off the insulation and use the bare wire ends to terminate their speaker wires. We don't like this method because the exposed copper wiring tends to corrode over time. Also, having exposed wire ends increases your chances of accidentally short-circuiting the wires. Neither of these possible outcomes is a good thing.

- **Pins:** Many manufacturers install (or sell for you to install) gold-plated pins that you can crimp or solder onto the ends of your wires. These pins make hookup much simpler, and they look neater, too (in case your neighbors are snooping around the back of your speakers). Hardcore audiophiles tend not to prefer this method of terminating speaker wires, but we think that it's a very good, reliable, and flexible choice.

- **Banana plugs:** No fruit is actually harmed in the manufacture of these speaker terminations — they are so named because these cylindrically shaped pins bend outward in the middle and roughly approximate the shape of a rather portly banana. Banana connectors come in both single and double varieties. In other words, you can have a single banana on both the positive and negative conductors of your speaker wire, or you can connect both wires to a double banana. The double bananas are spaced apart by a standardized distance, so they fit correctly into the banana connectors on your amplifier, speaker, or speaker outlet. We really like banana plugs because they are so easy to plug in and the outward bend in the middle of the plug ensures a nice, tight connection.

- **Spades:** Hard-core audiophiles (the people who live and breathe audio equipment and have a stack of dog-eared stereo magazines next to the bed) believe that these connectors offer the most secure, airtight connections. Spade connectors are U-shaped, and fit over standard, screw-type binding posts — allowing you to get in there with a wrench or strong pair of fingers and tighten things down really well. We agree with the audio types, spades are the best connection method if you can use them.

Any of the last three speaker-wire terminations is better than using just bare wire ends, and which one you choose will probably be driven by the device and connection to which you are connecting it. For example, many lower-priced amplifiers and receivers have spring-loaded connectors that only accept bare wires and pin connectors, so you can forget about using banana or spade connectors.

You find the following connectors on typical amplifiers, speakers, and wall outlets:

- ✓ **Spring-loaded clips:** These are the simple connectors with a spring-loaded clip that you push down to accept a thin, bare wire or pin connector. When you release the spring, it holds the wire or pin in place. You find these on most older audio systems and on less expensive current models.

- ✓ **Banana-plug receptacles:** Some speakers and amplifiers accept only banana plugs. Be sure to check that your banana receptacles are designed to accept double bananas before you terminate your speaker wires. (Double bananas do have a standard, but some audio equipment — mainly from Europe — is not built to this standard and requires you to use two single bananas on your speaker wire.)

- ✓ **Five-way binding posts:** This speaker connector is the most flexible, because it can accept single and double bananas, bare wire, pins, and spades. These connectors consist of a pair of metal posts with a couple of holes — one running parallel to the length of the posts to accept bananas, and one running through the posts at a 90-degree angle to accept bare wires or pins. Spade connectors simply slide over the posts, like a well-thrown horseshoe wrapping around a metal pole. Five-way binding posts also have plastic, screw-down caps on the posts, which you use to tighten the connection on bare wire, pins, and spades.

Speaker outlets

A whole-home audio system distributes music throughout your home by means of speaker-wire connections — that is to say, you run speaker wires through your walls to each room that is part of your network.

Because you probably don't want to have speaker wires dangling out of holes in your walls, you'll need to find some sort of finished outlets for ending runs of in-wall speaker cable. Look in any good home electronics store or catalog, and you'll find a host of speaker outlets. Like the video outlets we discuss in Chapter 6, these outlets are designed to fit into standard single-, double-, or triple-gang electrical junction boxes, and they come in all sorts of neat combinations. For example, you can buy a double-gang-sized outlet that contains two RG6 video cable outlets and a pair of five-way speaker binding posts, which allows you to make your audio and video connections right next to each other.

When you purchase speaker outlets, do yourself a favor and skip right over any that have those spring-loaded, clip-style connections and go right for the banana or five-way binding post types. The spring-loaded clips won't accept the expensive speaker cables with the huge, gold-plated spade connectors. Besides, they're pretty flimsy as well.

In-wall speakers

When you are considering a whole-home audio system, you need to know about a subcategory of speakers — speakers that can be flush mounted in your walls or ceiling. (See Chapter 5 for information on woofers and tweeters and that kind of stuff.)

In-wall speakers are appealing to many homeowners because they greatly increase the neatness of your installation, and give you that cool, custom look. Just imagine — no outlets, no exposed wires, no ungainly speakers to put on stands or bookshelves. Definitely a great way to go!

In-wall speakers, like conventional models, come in all sizes and shapes, but you should look for a few specifics:

- **Check the speaker size:** Make sure that whatever speakers you choose are going to fit into your walls without major modifications. Most of the common, rectangular wall models are designed to fit between standard stud spacings (16 inches), but all the same, go ahead and double-check your walls and your preferred speakers ahead of time.

- **Check the speaker depth:** You probably don't want your in-wall speakers sticking out a few inches. Again, most in-wall designs take into account the average depth of your wall, but double-check before you start cutting holes.

- **Think upward:** The walls aren't the only place to stick a speaker — ceilings are appropriate locations as well, especially in locations where your audio system serves primarily as background music. In those situations, you won't be quite as concerned about having some geometrically perfect speaker arrangement that allows you every nuance of the stereo music experience. If keeping your sound out of sight is a priority, you can even find round, in-ceiling speakers that look just like light fixtures.

- **Listen to them:** Unlike standard models, in-wall speakers require a commitment — namely a big hole in your wall. Always listen to your speakers in a reputable stereo store before you take the leap. You'll be glad you did.

- **Check out the speaker grill's design:** Many models have paintable grills, so you can make them match the walls around them — or make them stand out if you like that kind of design statement. Most speaker grills are pretty innocuous in design (some even claim to be invisible when installed), but variations do exist, and we won't fault you if looks are just as important as sound quality.

If you really want to hide your speakers, check out the speakers sold by a company called Gekko (www.artgekko.com). These speakers don't go inside the walls — instead they hang on them, like a picture. They're very, very thin, and you can actually outfit them with digitally printed art work; they're not only the same size and shape as pictures mounted on the wall, they are pictures hanging on the wall!

Chapter 9

Running Audio Here, There, and Everywhere

• •

In This Chapter

▶ Becoming a star-network architect

▶ Looking at single-amp and multi-amp single-zone systems

▶ Going for the gusto: the multizone system

▶ Peeking ahead at the digital future

▶ Choosing to go wireless

▶ Integrating an intercom system

• •

*I*n Chapter 8, we describe the various pieces and parts that fit into a whole-home audio network. In this chapter, our goal is to tell you how to hook all these pieces together.

Although you can choose to run line-level cables between different amplifiers located in each room, we prefer to run speaker wires to different sets of speakers to build a home audio network. Using line-level wiring complicates the network and makes it more susceptible to interference. The network architecture we describe in this chapter is designed around the assumption that you have speaker wire distributed to speaker locations throughout the home.

In this chapter, we begin with a description of the simplest whole-home audio network — a single-zone system that provides a single audio source simultaneously to each room — and then move on to a brief description of more sophisticated, multizone audio systems, which let you listen to different audio programs in different parts of the house. We also discuss some wireless alternatives to a home audio network, and how to utilize an intercom system for distributing audio.

Reaching for a Star

The audio network that we recommend you design into your home is similar to the video network — and, incidentally, most of the other networks we talk about throughout the book — a centrally-distributed star configuration. All the audio sources, amplification, and control systems are located in one place, and speaker cables are distributed in a star fashion, with individual runs going to each speaker location. As is the case with your video network (but not with the other networks we describe), you probably want to use your home-theater room (or media room) as the central distribution point for your audio network. We describe the media room in Chapter 2.

The audio network is different from the other networks in one major way — it's a one-way network. That is to say, all the audio source devices are located at the central distribution point. This type of network doesn't easily lend itself to a two-way architecture, in which remote source devices can send signals back to the central distribution point.

You can distribute an audio source that's located in a room other than your media room if you really need to do so, but it's a bit difficult. You can accomplish this trick by connecting a long run of line-level component cable (line-level cables are those that typically connect components like a CD player and a receiver) from the remote audio source back to your central amplifier control point. We don't address this option specifically in our basic network architecture, so if you need to do this, we recommend that you consult with a knowledgeable installer to help you choose a good, shielded interconnect cable to make this connection.

The best way to distribute line-level audio signals over long distances is to use something called a *balanced* line-level cable. It's what the pros use in recording studios. The problem with trying to set up this kind of audio distribution on a consumer level is that only a very small percentage of home audio equipment is outfitted with these kinds of connectors (only the really expensive stuff, for the most part). A few manufacturers sell soup-to-nuts, integrated, whole-home audio systems using this method of audio distribution — all the pieces, including cables, from the same manufacturer. Although nothing's wrong with these systems — in fact, they typically work great — you'll probably be locked into that manufacturer when you need to replace, repair, or upgrade components. Generally, lack of choices means more money.

Single-Zone Simplicity

The simplest and most inexpensive way to move into whole-home audio is to build a *single-zone audio network,* which is a network that allows you to send an audio source to speakers in different rooms (although you can't listen to different audio sources in different rooms). We tell you about the functions of the individual components of such a network in Chapter 8; in this section, we can tell you how to hook this network together.

Whole-home audio networks have a ton of variations, even simple, single-zone audio networks like this one. Your personal preferences, budget, and existing audio components all play a big role in shaping your network. For example, you can choose between an all-in-one receiver or integrated amp to handle the control and amplification roles, or you can use separate components. You can decide to use a single amplifier with impedance-matching devices, or you can set up separate amplifiers in your media room for each pair of speakers. You can choose in-wall speakers or conventional models.

Regardless of what you decide, the basic network architecture remains the same — pairs of speaker cable run in a star wiring configuration from a central amplification point to each speaker location in the house.

Installing a single-zone, single-amplifier system

Here's a general layout for a single-zone, single-amplifier system:

1. **The starting points of an audio network are your source devices. Using pairs of line-level audio interconnect cables, connect these devices to the inputs of your preamplifier (also known as the *control amplifier*).**

2. **Connect your amplifier to your power amplifier with a pair of RCA cables.**

   If you're using a receiver (or integrated amplifier) instead of separate components, you can skip this step. Instead, connect your audio source components directly to the receiver.

   You've now reached a decision point in your network layout. How you proceed from this point depends upon which impedance-matching system you choose.

3a. **If you decide to use multiple impedance-matching transformer/volume controls in each room, connect the main speaker outputs from your amplifier or receiver to a *parallel connecting block* with a short length of speaker wire.**

   The parallel connecting block splits a single audio output into multiple audio outputs — like an audio cloning device.

3b. **If you choose to use a single impedance-matching/speaker-selector device that resides in the media room, connect the impedance-matching device to your amplifier's speaker output with a short length of speaker wire.**

The impedance-matching/speaker-selector device both matches impedance and acts a central selector for turning speakers on or off.

4. **Connect the speaker outputs of your connecting block (3a) or speaker-selector device (3b) to individual runs of speaker wire for distribution throughout the house.**

5. **Run pairs (left and right speaker) of speaker wire through your walls to the desired locations.**

6. **If you're going with multiple impedance-matching volume control units in each room, connect the speaker wires to the inputs of the wall-mounted, impedance-matching volume control.**

The impedance-matching volume control units usually fit in a standard, single-gang junction box, which can be mounted just like a light switch in a convenient spot on the wall. (We explain junction-box sizes in Chapter 7.)

If you're using a central impedance-matching/speaker-selector switch instead, just blithely ignore this step and continue to Step 7.

7. **Terminate your speaker-wire runs (or a shorter run of speaker wire leading from the impedance-matching volume control's outputs, if you went that route) in one of two places:**

   • If you decide to use external, stand-alone speakers in this room, connect the ends of your speaker wires to a speaker-connector wall plate (we prefer the kind with banana jacks or five-way binding posts).

   • If you're installing in-wall speakers, connect the ends of the speaker wires to each speaker's inputs.

8. **For each set of speakers in your home, repeat Steps 4 through 7.**

A wiring layout for a single-zone audio system is shown in Figure 9-1.

When you're finished, we recommend that you put on your favorite CD, pour your favorite beverage, and sit back for a little listening break.

You may decide to start small, with speakers in only a few select rooms of the house. That's a fine way of setting up this kind of network, but go ahead and install runs of speaker cabling to other rooms now — while you have the walls open — in case you want to expand your audio network in the future. You can put a blank cover on the outlet box so you don't have wires hanging out of your walls.

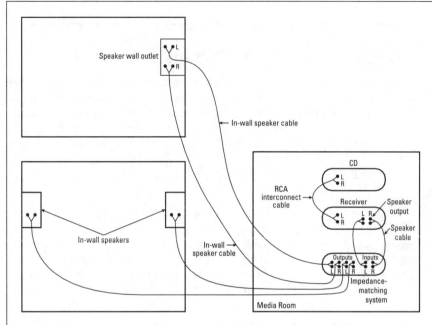

Speaker wall outlet

L

R

In-wall speaker cable

CD

L
R

RCA
interconnect →
cable

Receiver   Speaker
output

L   L R
R   Speaker
cable

In-wall speakers

In-wall →
speaker cable

Outputs   Inputs
L R L R   L R

Impedance-
matching
system

Media Room

Figure 9-1:
A typical
single-zone
audio net-
work layout.

Implementing a single-zone, multi-amplifier system

A single-zone, multi-amplifier system uses separate amplifiers in the media
room for each set of speakers in the audio network. This network eliminates
the need for an impedance-matching system and provides more power to
each set of speakers.

The process for installing a single-zone, multi-amplifier network is very much
the same as the one we delineated in the preceding section. The two main differences are

✔ You don't need the impedance-matching system anymore — because
   each speaker has its very own amplifier powering it.

✔ You need to split the audio signals from your source components — a
   single stereo pair of outputs — to several pairs of amplifier channels.
   Doing so can be a bit of a sticking point. You have three options:

   • If you're installing speakers in only two different locations, you can
      probably just use a Y-connector cable that takes a single pair of
      line-level outputs and splits the signal into two pairs of connectors.

Phase matters

One important thing to keep in mind when you're playing around with speaker wires is the concept of *phase*. All speaker-level inputs and outputs are color-coded, usually with a red and black connector. It's really important to make sure that you maintain consistency when you connect speaker wires, so that both speakers in a stereo pair have their wires connected to the amplifier in the same way. If you cross a pair of wires (red to red and black to black on one speaker, but red to black and black to red on the other speaker, for example), you won't blow up anything or start a nuclear meltdown at your local power plant. You will, however, have degraded sound, with decreased bass and a totally messed up stereo image.

It doesn't matter (except to a few audiophiles) which wire from the amp goes to which terminal on the speaker — just that you do the same

connection on both speakers in a pair. So you can be contrary and hook all the red amp connections to black speaker connections and vice versa. Just so long as you do it that way throughout the system.

Most speaker wires are well marked, with different colors of wire in the pair or with markings on one of the conductors, so you can figure out which is which.

If you really can't tell or remember what's connected to what, test CDs that help you put your system through its paces to make sure you've hooked it up correctly are available. Pat has one from *Stereophile* magazine (www.stereophile.com) that prominently features "Ralph the barking dog," who woofs from both speakers in and out of phase so you can hear the difference.

- You can buy a *distribution amplifier* that accepts the line-level input and provides multiple pairs of outputs (sort of an audio cloning device). This device also amplifies the signal (which gets weaker as its reproduced) so that each power amplifier has the signal strength it needs.

- You can buy an integrated amplifier specifically designed for a multi-room system. This amp internally splits your source device signals amongst its amplifier channels, so you don't have to sweat this detail.

Mega-Multizoning

The basic steps for installing a multizone audio system (which is capable of sending different music sources to different rooms in your house simultaneously) in your home are pretty similar to those needed to install a single-zone system. At least they are in a high-level overview.

As long as you get the right wires in the wall, you can change from a single-zone system to a multizone system later, by changing the components of your audio system and how some wires are connected in your media room.

The devil, however, is in the details when you start setting up one of these systems, especially when you try to get the control system set up (we talk about how to remotely control audio systems in Chapter 20). The routing of the audio signals themselves isn't too difficult to figure out, but equipment variations keep us from giving too many specifics.

Multizone audio systems can become nightmarishly complicated. Not only does the setup depend on marrying components from different manufacturers that may have strange quirks and weird setup routines, but when you get to *controlling* the zone audio with your remote control, it gets deadly. The goal is to be able to accomplish certain things regardless of which zone you're in — such as select a CD and play it (you probably can't play CD #189 in zone 3 and CD #190 in zone 4 at the same time on the same CD player!), but to accomplish other things *only* in your current zone (such as turn up the volume or select the VCR audio as the input source). Whether something can be done from all zones or just from the current zone depends on how you hook up the wires from the IR network and how you set up the multizone amplifier. Believe us, getting all this stuff to work seemlessly is a major hassle that increases as you add to the number of zones.

How do your audio and video systems work together?

How your audio and video systems complement each other is a confusing subject, no doubt. After all, your video network (by the very nature of the programming it carries) also distributes audio signals around the house. So why have two networks?

The answer is this — the coaxial network that carries TV signals around your home isn't suited to carrying the audio signals from other sources like CD players, and the audio network is similarly unable to carry video signals. In the future, when all audio and video signals that run between components are fully digital, you probably will be able to use a single network to carry both, but for now, if you want both audio and video, you need to build two networks.

That's not to say that these two networks can't work together. For example, most television programming uses a system called MTS to provide stereo sound. The modulators that connect things like VCRs and DVD players to a home video network are usually mono — the MTS ones are much more expensive. So unless you spend more, you end up with only mono audio at remote locations. But if you feed the audio output of your video sources into your audio network, you can use your remote speakers to get stereo sound for your remote TVs.

If you're going to jump right into multizone audio and you're not a real gear-head type, we really, really recommend that you have a professional installer do the job for you. Single-zone systems aren't hard to install and set up, but a multizone system can be a real nightmare for the uninitiated.

The basic layout of a multizone system is as follows:

1. **Connect source devices to a multizone controller using standard RCA cables.**

   The multizone controller contains all the electronics to switch each incoming source to different amps and zones.

2. **If the controller doesn't have built-in amplification — and many don't — you need to connect its outputs (one stereo pair per zone) to a multichannel amplifier with interconnect cables.**

3. **Connect the amplifier outputs to pairs of speaker wire (one pair per zone).**

4. **Run the speaker wires through your walls to each speaker outlet or in-wall speaker location, as shown in Figure 9-2.**

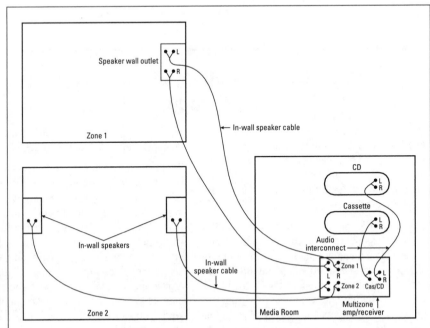

Figure 9-2:
A simple,
multizone
audio
system.

The digital future of audio networks

FireWire. Optical Fiber. Digital audio over coaxial cable or CAT-5. All of these things are possible, but none are yet widespread or practical. Many audio source devices found in the home today are digital — CD players and DVD players are the most common, although Digital Audio tapes (DAT) and MiniDisc (MD) are somewhat common as well — but these digital systems almost always convert the audio signals from digital to analog internally and use an analog connection to the amplifier or receiver.

Distribution of audio signals will change in the future. Many companies are looking into ways of distributing audio signals around the home entirely in the digital domain. In this model, the signal from an audio source like a CD or DVD player will be transmitted onto a digital wiring backbone of some sort (and there's no clear consensus yet as to what this wiring will look like) and will be available to remote systems that will decode this signal to an analog one, amplify it, and drive speakers.

An interesting aspect of a system like this is the fact that it could change not only how audio is sent around your house, but also how you get it in the first place. Right now, if you want a new CD, you run down to the local record shop and buy it. With a digital audio distribution system like the one we are describing here, there's no reason why you couldn't just purchase your new *album* from a Web site and download the actual bits and bytes over your Net connection. In fact, you can already do this, in a limited way, using a system called MP3 — but currently MP3 gets the music to your computer's hard drive and no further, unless you have the capability to make your own CDs.

In the future, as digital audio distribution systems become available, your computer will become a source component in its own right — connected to the digital backbone, downloading music from the Web, and playing it back throughout the home.

It sounds pretty simple, doesn't it? And it is, from our 40,000-foot perch here, looking down. But getting all the pieces and parts actually put together and working in sync can be a bit of a pain in the rear. That's why we recommend some professional help (if you avoid it, you may end up seeking professional help of another sort, to deal with your anxiety problems).

Other Ways to Send Audio

Not everyone is going to want to build a whole-home audio network. For some folks, it's just not something that's up there on the priority list — especially when it's ranked against telephones, television, and computers. Other people simply don't have the opportunity to run wires while the walls are unfinished.

So, for whatever reason, you may not build a whole-home audio network. But you may still want to get sound from your stereo system to some other place in the house. Luckily, a couple of alternatives to wired audio networks let you do just that. Like some of the alternative methods of distributing video that we talk about in Chapter 7, these systems are more useful for a point-to-point connection — getting audio from one specific room to another — than they are for trying to connect every room. But that's okay, as long as you are aware of the limitations.

Wireless systems

The most popular way of getting audio around the house without a dedicated network is to utilize an RF wireless system. These come in two main flavors:

- **Wireless speaker systems** connect to the line-level outputs of a source device or preamplifier and send the signal over a 900 MHz or 2.4 GHz channel to a pair of self-amplified stereo speakers.

- **Wireless line-level distribution systems** hook up to your source components in the same fashion, but send their signal to a receiver that hooks into your own amplifier and speakers on the far end.

One major potential difficulty with this sort of wireless system is that it uses a line-level input — something that most source devices have only one of. So you may run into trouble hooking up a CD player, for example, to both a receiver (or amp) for local listening and to one of these devices for remote listening. Luckily, many of these units also accept the output of your receiver or amp's headphone jack, so you can avoid this problem if you have a headphone jack available. This connection method has the added advantage of letting you select from several source devices using the receiver's built-in preamplifier.

Prices for these wireless systems range from about $200 to $500. Major manufacturers include:

- Recoton (www.recoton.com)
- Paradox (www.paradoxllc.com)
- RF Link (www.rflinktech.com)

Another wireless product that we've seen utilizes a home's electrical powerline wiring to transmit stereo audio signals. The Elcom (www.elecomtech.com) ezAudio system accepts either line-level or speaker-level inputs from a stereo system and uses powerline transmission to a matching receiver anywhere in your home. The receiver even has a built-in low-power amplifier, so you can plug it right into a pair of speakers, or you can use the receiver's line-level outputs to hook it up to your own amplifier.

Intercom systems

We explain a bit about intercom systems in Chapter 5, and we have mixed emotions about them. On one hand, they're very valuable tools for listening to the baby, giving the teenagers a little motivation when they're lagging behind their morning schedules, or for talking to your spouse from two floors away. On the other hand, between sophisticated telephone systems and whole-home audio networks, many people with smart homes just aren't bothering to install them. Whether you install an intercom system is really a matter of personal preference. We're 50/50: Danny has one, and Pat doesn't.

If you decide to go the intercom route in your house, it may be a good way to let you get music around the house without wiring a separate whole-home audio network. You need to keep a few things in mind when choosing an intercom system to do double duty as a music distribution system:

- **Is it stereo?** Many intercom units are mono only, which isn't optimal for hi-fi audio.

- **What kinds of media can it play?** Some intercom units have only a built-in AM/FM radio, while others have built-in cassette or CD players.

- **Does it have inputs for your own source devices?** You may want to connect your own CD player to the master station or maybe even connect the audio outputs of a TV. Not all intercoms accept inputs from other audio components — in fact, most don't.

The components of an intercom system are really quite simple to figure out — they number only a few:

- **The master station:** This is the central control unit of your home's intercom system, usually mounted (on a wall) in a common area of the home, like the kitchen. Any built-in audio sources, such as radios, CD players, and connections for external audio sources, are located here at the master station.

- **Remote stations:** These are the smaller consoles mounted everywhere else in the home that allow two-way communications with the master station (and other remotes). Remote stations come in a few varieties:

  - *Indoor remotes* can be mounted in bedrooms, family rooms, and so on.

  - *Outdoor remotes* let you extend your intercom to patios and decks.

  - *Doorbell remotes* let you check who's at the door without answering it.

The majority of intercom systems use the same kind of star wiring configuration that is used for audio and video networks — and just about every other network in the home. The master station serves as the *hub* of the star, and each remote station is served by its own set of wires radiating out from the hub.

The wiring for an intercom system varies rather widely, both from brand to brand and also among different models from the same manufacturer. Many manufacturers not only sell the intercom master stations and remote units themselves, but also their own wiring. A few actually *require* you to use their proprietary wire. Not doing so imperils your warranty coverage should anything ever go wrong.

Generally speaking, most intercoms that we've run across use four-pair, shielded wire for each of the two-way runs between master station and remote. It's really important to use the exact wire specified by the manufacturer of your intercom system (whether or not it requires you to use its own wire), because intercom systems can be extremely susceptible to picking up *hum* from your home's AC powerline wiring.

Choosing an intercom system, if you desire to have one, is something you really need to do early on in your home building or renovating process. Because so many variations exist in wiring requirements among different systems, you can't easily prewire your home and then just plug an intercom system into the wiring, like you can with many other home networks.

Part III
Now We're Communicating!

The 5th Wave   By Rich Tennant

30 years ago today...

Bill and Irwin Fuzzo, two plumbers from Eugene, Ore., developed the first hydro-pneumatic PC. It could be connected to an average garden hose, and response time was increased by simply "...squeezing the hose a little bit." Software was to be developed by a local manufacturer of squirt guns — 30 years ago today!!

In this part . . .

The key to a great home phone system is the flexibility to have many different types of endpoints hanging out of a good solid base infrastructure. By the pool, you may want waterproof phones. In the office, a good conference capability. In the kitchen, a cordless option. You may also need to be able to transfer calls, intercom people, use Caller ID, and so on, wherever you are in your smart home.

In this part, we tell you all about how to create your telephony backbone in your house. We discuss all the major elements of a whole-home telephone network and describe the advantages of connecting all the telephone pieces and parts together. We talk about all the different communications equipment and services available, as well as some tips and tricks for ensuring the success of your telephone system.

Chapter 10

Planning a Phone System for Your Home

Most people take their telephone service for granted. Plug your phone into the wall jack, pay your monthly bill to your area's telephone monopoly, and, as Donnie Brasco might say, *fuggitaboudit*. As life becomes increasingly wired, however, you may want to do things that require a more sophisticated phone system than the trusty AT&T model you bought back in the 70s when you switched over to Touch-Tone. For example, you may want to send faxes, transfer calls within your home, use your phone system as an intercom, and so on.

Not only are our telephone needs more complicated than in the past, but we are also about to face a plethora of choices in how we get phone service delivered to our homes. Thanks to deregulation by Congress and the Federal Communications Commission, a whole host of companies — some familiar, some not — are getting ready to offer competitive local phone services to residential customers.

In this chapter, we tell you about all the various pieces that comprise a phone network and give you some advice in making choices for your phone networking needs.

Selecting Equipment for Your Phone Network

When you are considering any home network system, one of the big questions you need to ask yourself is "What will plug into it?" After all, why build a highway if it doesn't go anywhere?

You may be surprised at the number of choices you have about what you can plug into your home phone network — much more than just phones. We don't even consider stuff like computer modems and network appliances here, just standard telephony equipment that lets you talk and otherwise communicate with the outside world.

Plug and play the old-fashioned way

The most common category of telephone equipment found in a home network is that of analog, POTS-compatible (POTS is a telephone industry term meaning *Plain Old Telephone Service*) devices. Often called "wireline" phones, because they are corded, all these devices plug into your "network" of wall jacks, using the standard modular phone plug (called an *RJ-11 connector,* which we describe in Chapter 11) or the four-prong plugs in older homes.

Note: The RJ-11 connector family has several variations, which depend on how many telephone lines are wired to an individual jack. For simplicity's sake, we use the term RJ-11 here generically — to describe the one-, two-, and three-line versions of these connectors.

The most basic and common of analog telephone devices is the standard corded telephone. This is the trusty old telephone that we've all known and loved for decades and decades. Little has changed in corded phones for quite some time, although many features have been added to the phones over the years — like hold and speed-dialer buttons, speakers for hands-free talking, and liquid crystal display (LCD) screens.

Besides cool new features, the biggest difference among various corded telephones is their capacity to connect to multiple phone lines. Although most telephones are still single-line phones, a growing number can be simultaneously connected to two or, in some cases, three telephone lines at the same time. As more people install multiple phone lines for home offices, "teen lines," and other uses, multiple-line telephones are becoming increasingly common — and necessary.

If your telephone needs run to several lines, you may want to consider a telephone system that gives you more control over your lines and enables you to do things like transfer calls between phones within your home. To take advantage of these features, you need something beyond a standard phone. Later in the chapter (in the section "Key phones can be key"), we go into more detail about these systems — the key telephone system unit (KSU) and sophisticated KSU-less multiline phone systems.

Wireless phones

Wireline phones are great, but sometimes you really just don't want to get up from the couch to answer the phone. So it should be no surprise that cordless phones are now found in nearly 90 percent of all homes. These phones consist of two main components:

- ✔ **A base station** that consists of a battery charger and a radio transceiver, which plugs into an RJ-11 phone jack just like a wireline phone

- ✔ **The cordless handset** that communicates with the base station and carries your phone conversation over radio waves

Features, features, and more features

The basic design and functionality of corded telephones hasn't really changed much over the years. With the exception of the transition from pulse to Touch-Tone dialing 15 or 20 years ago, the way corded telephones work has remained remarkably constant for generations.

What has changed is the number of additional features that the decreasing cost (and increasing power) of computer chips has enabled manufacturers to put into low-cost consumer telephones. For example, you can now buy — for not too much money — telephones that include:

- ✔ **Speed dialing:** This feature allows you to press one button to dial a preprogrammed number that you call often.

- ✔ **LCD displays:** These displays tell you the number you called and how long you've been on the call.

- ✔ **Built-in phone directories:** These directories can store hundreds of names and numbers and display them on an LCD screen.

- ✔ **Speakerphones:** These phones, which let you talk hands-free, come in two types: *half duplex* models, which let you either talk or listen (but not both) at one time, and more sophisticated *full duplex* models that let you do both at once. Full duplex phones are immeasurably better, in our opinion, because you can carry on a hands-free conversation naturally, without choppiness or lost words.

- ✔ **Caller ID displays:** This feature shows you the phone number and, in some cases, the name of the person who is calling you. Caller ID requires both the hardware on your end — either built into the phone or a stand-alone display unit — and a subscription to Caller ID service from your local telephone company.

You can choose from four main types of cordless phones (which, like wireline phones, are available in both single- and multiple-line versions):

- ✔ **46/49 MHz phones:** These are the traditional cordless phones that have been widely available for many years. They send your phone signals over the 46 and 49 MHz radio channels in an analog form. 46/49 MHz phones are the cheapest available and generally have the shortest range.

- ✔ **900 MHz analog phones:** These cordless phones are very similar to 46/49 MHz phones, except for the fact that they use a higher-frequency radio channel to carry your phone signals. These higher-frequency radio waves have a longer range and are also a little less susceptible to interference.

- ✔ **900 MHz digital phones:** A step up in price from the analog models, these phones convert your phone signal into a digital format before sending it over the airwaves. These digital signals are less likely to suffer from interference and signal degradation, so you should end up with a clearer phone conversation with less static and noise.

- ✔ **900 MHz digital spread spectrum phones:** The most sophisticated — and expensive — cordless phones, these models take the digital radio signal and send it over a large number of different radio frequencies in rapid succession. This *frequency hopping* decreases the likelihood that you pick up unwanted radio signals — like your neighbor's cordless telephone — and also increases security (because it's much more difficult for someone with a radio scanner to tune into very much of your conversation as you switch frequencies).

You may want to look into these new wrinkles to cordless phones that may soon be available in the marketplace:

- ✔ **Multiple-handset cordless phones.** These models, which use multiple handsets with a single base station, make it easy to add additional phones: You need to plug only the one base station into an RJ-11 phone jack. The additional handsets require only a battery charger station — which plugs into your electrical power lines — so you don't need a separate RJ-11 phone jack for each additional phone.

- ✔ **Dual-mode cordless phones.** These phones' handsets have both cordless phone and cellular (or PCS) phone circuitry built in. When you're within range of your home base station, phone calls are carried over your standard telephone lines. If you take the handset outside your home, the phone automatically switches to its cellular mode, and phone calls are carried over the cellular phone network.

While we love cordless phones and use them constantly, you need to be aware of a couple of drawbacks associated with them:

✔ **Quality:** No matter how expensive — and no matter what the ads may try to tell you — the quality of your phone signal on a cordless phone isn't as good as a wireline phone.

✔ **Security:** Your phone conversation is less secure and confidential on a cordless phone than it is on a wireline telephone. Although digital phones — especially spread spectrum models — do offer increased security, any phone conversation that you have on a wireless system is potentially susceptible to interception by unscrupulous folks with radio scanners. We don't think this is a major problem for most folks, but you should be aware that the possibility exists. Some cordless phone manufacturers offer phones with a secure encrypted mode to lessen this potential hazard.

Fax machines

Although traditionally an office device, facsimile machines (fax machines) are becoming increasingly common in the home. Fax machines scan printed material and transmit the scanned data over a standard phone line to a remote fax machine, which then prints out the printed material on the far end. Fax machines fall into two main types:

✔ **Thermal paper fax:** These models use long rolls of thermal paper to print incoming faxes. Although inexpensive, these models have the distinct disadvantage of using the thermal paper that makes them so cheap — the quality of the incoming fax is usually rather low, the paper tends to curl up, and the image disintegrates over time. But these machines are fine for occasional use.

✔ **Plain paper fax:** These fax machines use a mechanism similar to that found on an inkjet or laser computer printer to print out incoming faxes on individual sheets of — you guessed it — plain paper. These models are more expensive than thermal paper fax machines, but they offer significantly higher print quality. An even better plus is the fact that your faxes don't roll up on themselves and end up in a tightly wound scroll on your desk. We recommend that you splurge for the plain paper fax machine.

Many fax manufacturers — and computer printer makers, as well — are beginning to combine fax machines, printers, telephones and even copiers into a single, "all-in-one" home office machine, sometimes referred to as a *multifunctional device* (MFD). These devices can be pretty handy and are usually less expensive than buying all the components separately (not to mention that they take up less desk space in your home office).

Multifunction devices usually provide lower-quality output than separately purchased components. Generally, getting a great deal of functionality into one box at a reasonable price dictates compromises in the quality of the components. You generally have to sacrifice a bit of quality in exchange for the cost savings.

The newest trend in fax machines is to build some Internet capabilities into the machine. Internet-enabled fax machines, which are just beginning to come onto the market, let you send and receive faxes the standard way — over analog POTS telephone lines — but they also let you send them for free over the Internet. Most of these machines send the fax messages as attachments to e-mail messages. That means you can save money on sending the fax and — equally importantly — send faxes as e-mail to people who don't have their own fax machines on the other end. We think that this Internet functionality will become a standard feature on almost all fax machines within the next few years. It will be pretty cool, too.

Answering machines

Remember *The Rockford Files*? The title sequence of that show prominently featured the lead character's answering machine taking an incoming call — a rare event back then (in the 1970s) when answering machines were huge, ungainly, and expensive.

The computer revolution has touched upon these devices in the intervening decades, and now answering machines are compact, inexpensive, and — as you no doubt already know — everywhere.

The least expensive answering machines you can find are those based upon the same technology found in that old Rockford machine. A cassette tape — or in most cases, a smaller microcassette tape — records both your outgoing greeting message and incoming messages from your callers. A bit clunky, but these machines usually work pretty well, and they typically cost next to nothing.

Newer answering machines use digital technology to record your voice and that of your incoming callers as digital data stored on a computer memory chip. These "tapeless" answering machines generally have a higher voice quality and — because they don't have a tape or moving parts to wear out — aren't as susceptible to catastrophic mechanical failures (so a broken tape won't cause you to miss that message from your mom or your boss or the one telling you that you've won the lottery).

The most expensive digital answering machines often behave rather like voice-mail systems found in businesses, offering features like multiple mailboxes (so incoming messages can be directed to specific individuals in the household), multiple-line capabilities, and remote operation (which allows you to check your messages when you are away from home).

Many answering machines are not stand-alone devices. Instead, they often include a corded or cordless phone as part of the same device.

Although answering machines have become increasingly sophisticated and capable, we've become proponents of the voice-mail services offered by most local telephone companies. These services basically offer you an "answering machine" in the telephone network, where that answering machine is really a giant computer that many subscribers share. You typically find out that you have a message when you pick up your phone and hear a "stutter" dial tone; small light attachments also blink when you have a message. These services have become quite inexpensive and convenient. Before you spend a bundle on a fancy digital answering machine, we recommend that you explore the voice-mail service available in your area and see how the features and price stack up.

External ringers/lights

If you've ever hung around an auto repair shop (Pat likes to do that — don't ask why, he couldn't possibly explain), you may have noticed that when the phone rings in the main office, bells and whistles seem to sound everywhere. Those are external ringers — stand-alone devices that alert you to incoming calls when you're not near the phone.

You don't need to be an automotive technician to appreciate one of these devices. You may just have a big, noisy house (if you read our bios, you know that Danny has four young children!) or spend time in the backyard far from the phone. Many hearing-impaired telephone users have attached to their telephone networks special visual indicators that light up when the phone rings. Such external indicators are cheap and easy to install — just plug them into an RJ-11 jack and — in some cases — AC power. You can find external ringers that let you choose what the ring sounds like, ringers that ring differently for different phone lines, and even ringers that give you a silent, visual indication of a telephone call.

TDD devices

A TDD, or Telecommunications Device for the Deaf, is a text device that enables hearing-impaired folks to communicate over telephone lines. Consisting of a display screen and a keyboard, it works rather like a computer chat system — without the computer.

Many telephone companies offer a service that lets non-TDD users connect with folks who are on a TDD. In these cases, an operator from the phone company gets in the middle of the conversation and types to the person with the TDD and speaks to the one without.

Key phones can be key

Key phones allow you to make a telephone network in your home that has many of the same capabilities as a business phone network. With a key phone system, you can

✔ **Make a call on a free line while other lines are in use.**

✔ **Transfer calls from one extension to another.**

✔ **Connect several lines together for a conference call.**

✔ **Use your phones as an intercom system, paging between different rooms or using the phone's speaker systems for hands-free intercom use.**

✔ **Dedicate a specific extension for all fax or modem calls and let the key system automatically route incoming calls.**

✔ **Pipe in music for people who are on hold (we find that old Spike Jones hits really make for conversation starters).**

A key phone system is a good answer if you plan to install multiple phone lines into your home, because key phone systems offer greater flexibility and sophistication when dealing with a multiple-line phone network. If you don't plan to install multiple phone lines (usually a minimum of three phone lines), a key phone system isn't the answer for you.

Key phone systems fall into two major categories:

✔ **Key telephone system units (KSU):** These systems are based upon a central control unit (the KSU), which performs all the transferring, paging, and other functions. Each telephone extension is wired to the KSU.

✔ **Multiline KSU-less phone systems:** In a KSU-less system, the intelligence of the central control unit is actually built right into the extension phone itself. There is no central unit, just independent, intelligent phones that communicate with each other rather than with a separate control device.

KSUs

A KSU telephone system consists of a central control unit (the KSU) and a series of extension phones that the KSU controls. Your incoming telephone-company phone lines connect into the KSU, which in turn connects to each individual extension phone by a single phone line.

Every phone connected to the KSU system has access to all the external phone lines — usually by simply pressing a line button on the phone.

A KSU system has both advantages and disadvantages (like just about everything else). The advantages include

✔ **The greatest capacity:** KSU systems that can handle four or more incoming phone lines are available.

✔ **More extensions:** KSU systems can often connect 16 or more extension
phones — so if you have a large house with many rooms, you don't have
to worry about limitations on the number of phones you install.

✔ **More features:** Although KSU and KSU-less systems share many
features — like call transfer, paging, and intercom — typical KSU systems let you add additional features like automatic routing of fax calls to
the correct extension, sophisticated hold functions (like foisting your
musical tastes on people you put on hold), and even high-capacity, mul-
tiple-mailbox voice-mail systems.

The disadvantages to a KSU system include

✔ **A higher price tag:** Base-model KSU systems start off near $800, and the
price can skyrocket as you add additional features.

✔ **More complicated installation:** Although KSU-less systems are more or
less plug and play, a KSU system requires a more involved installation
and setup procedure.

✔ **Special phone equipment:** Some — though not all — KSU systems
require you to buy a special key telephone for each extension, which can
be an expensive proposition. A few systems even have very specific
requirements regarding the kind of telephone wiring you need to connect extensions to the central unit.

KSU-less phone systems

While a KSU system requires a rather large up-front expenditure to get up and
running, a KSU-less phone system provides many of the same features for less
money. These systems — which are usually designed for three or four phone
lines — connect to the standard RJ-11 phone jack that you already use for your
stand-alone phone systems. Where they differ from standard phones is in their
internal intelligence. Built into each of these phones is an electronic brain that
performs many of the same functions that are found in a central KSU system.

Choosing a KSU-less phone system over a KSU system offers some advantages, including:

✔ **The price tag is initially lower:** These systems usually range in cost
from $200 to $300 per phone.

✔ **You can start off small:** All you need to get started are two KSU-less
phones — you can add more as your needs or budget grows.

- ✓ **Installation is simpler:** Basically, all you need to do is plug the phone into one or more RJ-11 wall jacks, and you're up and running. Some systems require you to set some small switches to assign an extension number to each phone.

- ✓ **Wiring requirements are less stringent:** KSU-less phone systems work in just about any kind of telephone wiring architecture — unlike KSU systems, which require a specific wiring *topology*. We explain all about topologies, architectures, and other important-sounding words dealing with phone systems in Chapter 11.

KSU-less systems have their share of disadvantages as well, including the following:

- ✓ **Less system capacity:** Most KSU-less systems don't let you handle more than four phone lines, and the total number of extensions is limited as well (most handle up to eight extensions), so if your needs go beyond these limits, you need to opt for a full-fledged KSU system.

- ✓ **Fewer features:** Compared to KSU systems, KSU-less systems typically have fewer features. Additionally, although most KSU systems are modular, meaning that you can add additional functionality to the system by plugging in components to the KSU, KSU-less systems have all the functionality in the handsets, so you have to replace all of them to upgrade.

- ✓ **The price increases as your network expands:** Although the initial price is lower than that of a KSU system, you may find that installing a network of many of these phones is actually more expensive than installing a KSU system. That's because you need one of these phones at each location to take advantage of the networking capabilities of the system. If you decide you want to install six or more of these phones in your home, you could well find that it would be cheaper to install a KSU system — especially if you choose one that can use inexpensive, standard telephones as extensions.

Deciding on a Phone Service

In the old days, you had no choice when it came to ordering phone service for your home. If you wanted phone service, you had to go to the phone company, and you took the service that the company had to offer. In this section, we talk about the growing number of phone options to consider — both in terms of which company you buy service from and what kind of service you actually receive.

Changes in regulations in the United States are allowing other companies to go after your local phone business — everyone from cable television companies to wireless PCS (Personal Communications Systems) operators. Despite entry of these new competitors, however, the vast majority of homes in the United States still receive phone service from the traditional local monopoly.

Regardless of who provides these services, however, you're basically offered the same options:

- ✔ **Analog telephone service:** Usually called *POTS* (for *Plain Old Telephone Service* — no, we didn't make that up). This is the service we all know and love.

- ✔ **Digital telephone service:** ISDN (Integrated Services Digital Network) has been the "next big thing" for a long time, but it's really never caught on. In a few areas of the country, ISDN is very inexpensive and available

Making the most of the phone lines you have

We want to make sure that you are aware of the many service options available from your telephone company that can make your telephone lines do more work for you. These services may not make a single phone line satisfy all your telephone needs — the combination of an analog modem and a teenager can pretty much eliminate free time on a line, for example — but they may help you get the most out of the lines that you do have and decrease your need to get extra lines installed.

The fancy new digital switches that are installed in just about every telephone office in North America allow services like:

- ✔ **Distinctive ringing:** This feature allows you to assign a different ring signal to a dozen or so numbers from which you routinely receive calls — so you can know in advance, for instance, if an incoming call is from the office (and you can ignore it after 5 p.m.). Some fax machines can also be programmed to utilize this feature so that they automatically answer calls from known fax numbers without your having to push the Start button.

- ✔ **Caller ID:** With the appropriate telephone or separate display screen, this service can let you see the name and phone number of most incoming callers (some telephone companies — like Pacific Bell in California — are required by law to allow people to block the sending of their name and number if they choose to do so).

- ✔ **Call waiting:** This service keeps your incoming callers from ever receiving a busy signal — if you're on the phone, a tone alerts you to the presence of another incoming call. This feature can usually be combined with Caller ID, so you can stay on your current call and check the screen to see who else is calling you.

- ✔ **3-way conference calling:** This service allows you to use a single phone line to make a three-party conference call. The phone company's network handles the bridging of the lines — your involvement in the process is limited to dialing the numbers of the other people and pressing the hang-up button on your phone a few times.

Availability of these and other services — usually called *custom calling services* — varies from location to location, but most places now have them.

in many places. But that's not the case in most areas, where expensive ISDN service has scared off many would-be buyers. We talk about the flop of ISDN in the section "Digital phone lines (ISDN)," later in this chapter.

✔ **Wireless services:** Cellular and Personal Communications Services (or PCS, if you're in the know), are growing in popularity (we've seen figures saying that up to 25 percent of Americans have one or the other, and the number is much higher elsewhere). We believe that these services will soon be a viable alternative to traditional wired telephone services.

POTS (not used for cooking)

The common denominator in telephone services is the analog voice connection (provided over copper wires) known as POTS. When you call the telephone company and ask the service folks to install a telephone line to your home, you usually get a POTS line. In this section, we briefly describe how the telephone network connects to your home.

With POTS service, an analog, copper phone line connects your house to the telephone network. The local *telco* (telephone company) has a huge network of local "central offices" — each serving individual towns or even neighborhoods, as shown in Figure 10-1. These central offices contain digital switches (usually) that connect phone calls onto the public telephone network. A call travels through the PSTN (Public Switched Telephone Network — the telephone network we are all connected to) to another telephone somewhere.

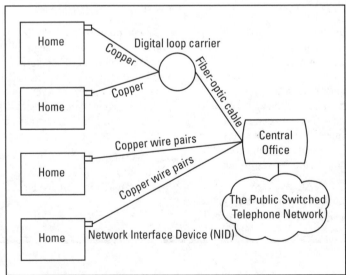

Figure 10-1: The traditional telephone network.

The gauge and number of wires running to your house varies from telco to telco and from installation to installation (depending on when your phone service was first set up). Generally, you find what's called a *quad wire,* consisting of two separate pairs of copper wire in a single sheath. POTS telephone service requires only a single pair of wires, so most people find that they already have adequate wiring for two phone lines connected to their homes.

Digital phone lines (ISDN)

For the most part, *digital services* from your phone company are most useful for data communications — Internet access, in other words — so we cover them in more depth in Chapter 13. One digital phone service — ISDN, or Integrated Services Digital Network — has some usefulness in the voice telephone arena, so we describe it briefly here.

The big advantage of ISDN over POTS service (besides increased speed for Web surfing) is that it uses digital signal encoding to provide two telephone lines over a single connection (and a single pair of wires). So when you order an ISDN line, you automatically get two phone numbers with the service. ISDN also leverages its digital connection technology to include as standard the services that we describe in the sidebar "Making the most of the phone lines you have" (such as Caller ID and 3-way conference calling).

From the viewpoint of the telephone network, ISDN looks pretty much the same as standard POTS service. It comes to your house over the same pairs of copper wire as POTS services — although the wires sometimes need to be specially conditioned (in other words, they need to be of a certain minimum level of quality) to carry ISDN signals. The telephone company takes care of that when it installs your ISDN service.

If you install ISDN, do you need POTS lines? ISDN all by itself can carry two simultaneous phone, fax, or data calls, so what's the use of having a POTS line, too, right? Well, we can make a case for keeping that POTS line even if you go the ISDN route:

- ✔ **Cost:** Many ISDN service providers charge per minute (metered) call rates for all calls — even local calls. Conversely, most POTS local calls are covered under a flat rate plan, so for your $15 or so a month, you can make unlimited local calls.

- ✔ **Power outage tolerance:** In North America (it's different in other places), ISDN requires the use of an *NT-1* network termination device to function. The NT-1 needs electrical power, so if you have only ISDN and you lose power, your phone service goes out as well. Not good if you need to dial 911 (better hope your cell phone battery is charged up!).

The NT-1 allows multiple devices to be connected to the ISDN line. The NT-1 accepts only special ISDN versions of phones and faxes directly, so you need another box called a *Terminal Adapter,* or TA, to connect a standard phone, fax, or analog modem to an ISDN line.

Figuring out what to do with the NT-1 and TA devices in an ISDN setup is pretty complicated, but fortunately, most people use ISDN with an ISDN modem, which greatly simplifies the matter. Most ISDN modems include both the NT-1 and the TA in a single box, so all you have to do is plug the modem into the ISDN connection and then plug your computer, standard telephone, and fax machine into the modem. Sure makes things easier.

Due to its high costs, we don't really recommend that you get ISDN service just for phone calls. You can re-create just about any feature of ISDN with a couple of inexpensive POTS lines and a few custom calling services. We won't fault you, however, if you read Chapter 13 and decide that ISDN is something that you absolutely must have for connecting to the Internet.

Cellular

After television and radio broadcasts, cellular phones are probably the most common wireless communications systems found in people's homes (and cars, and purses, and shirt pockets . . .).

In North America, all sorts of cellular systems are in use by the various cellular providers. Some of these are analog; some are digital. Analog wireless systems are susceptible to interference and distortion, and they make it easier for unscrupulous individuals to eavesdrop on your conversation. Their biggest flaw, however, is that they don't use the limited bandwidth allocated to cellular systems by the FCC very efficiently. This inefficiency limits the number of calls the systems can handle at any one time and makes providing services more expensive than digital systems (meaning you pay more).

We're not totally down on cellular, though. Cellular services have several advantages over their up-and-coming PCS competitors:

✔ **Cellular is everywhere.** You can take your phone anyplace and use it without too much trouble because cellular areas overlap, as shown in Figure 10-2.

✔ **Cellular companies are going digital.** Many service providers are adding digital services, offering most of the same advantages we mention in the following section.

✔ **Cellular providers are beginning to offer data services.** Called *CDPD,* or Cellular Digital Packet Data, this service enables you to hook up your cell phone to a computer and access the Internet or other data networks. You can even get special new phones that display e-mail and Web pages on their built-in screens.

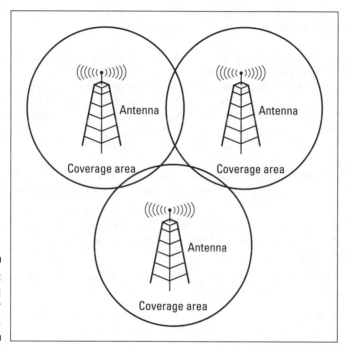

Figure 10-2:
Overlapping
Cellular
Areas.

PCS

PCS, or Personal Communications System, is the newest version of mobile wireless communications — complementing and expanding upon the services offered by the cellular phone system. Although PCS services are roughly comparable to cellular in price right now, the long-term hope is that prices will come down — way down — until they are almost as low as POTS wireline phone services. With more licenses available for each service area (six, compared to two for cellular), the FCC hopes that the additional competition will lead to lower prices.

In Europe, for example, PCS-like services have been available for several years and are quite inexpensive. Studies show that many consumers turn to PCS in lieu of a second phone line and, in some cases, use PCS as their primary phone system. Proposed pricing plans for PCS that charge standard wireline telephone rates for calls made within the area immediately surrounding your home and more when you are away from home may lead to a similar trend in the United States.

Under development are PCS phones that work in conjunction with wireline phone services. In and around your home, they act like cordless telephones, communicating with a wireline base station and sending calls over the POTS telephone network. When you get out of range of your base station, the phone switches to its PCS mode — and to higher rates.

PCS operates at a different frequency range than cellular systems — in the 1,900 MHz range versus the 800 MHz range used by some of the analog cellular systems (we're talking about the United States here, by the way — European systems use entirely different frequency bands). Unlike the vast majority of cellular systems, PCS systems are digital, and they leverage this fact to improve the service they can provide you. Compared to standard analog cellular services, digital PCS services can

- ✔ Offer higher-quality voice connections — because the digital streams of 0s and 1s that they send are less susceptible to interference and distortion

- ✔ Provide additional functions like paging, alphanumeric messaging, and data broadcasts of things like stock prices and sports scores — all displayed on your phone's screen

- ✔ Avoid "network busy" signals, because digital systems can carry more phone calls at the same time

- ✔ Provide digital data services that allow you to connect to the Internet, check e-mail, and log into your company's network

- ✔ Use encryption to keep your conversations safe from prying ears with scanners and to reduce *cloning,* a phone hacker's practice of stealing your phone number and calling Bavaria (or another far-off place) on your phone bill, and other kinds of fraud.

Two digital systems are competing for PCS supremacy (and for the cellular networks that convert to digital standards):

- ✔ **GSM:** GSM stands for Global System for Mobile Communications and is the digital system in use throughout most of the world — especially in Europe. GSM uses a digital encoding technology called TDMA, or Time Division Multiple Access, to squeeze more calls into the limited bandwidth allocated to each service provider. Some of the carriers using this technology include Pacific Bell Wireless and Omnipoint.

- ✔ **CDMA:** Code Division Multiple Access is a newer, and potentially more efficient, way of carrying digital calls over the airwaves. Most American PCS providers are using CDMA in their networks, although a significant minority is using GSM. Sprint PCS is the major provider of this technology in America, and many cellular companies are beginning to use it for their digital services.

GSM or CDMA? Which to choose? That really depends, actually. They both work very well, so you should base your decision on which service provider in your area has pricing and service that's right for you. The biggest concern to keep in mind is that neither of these systems is close to being deployed nationwide, so if you travel frequently, make sure that the phone you choose will work in your destination as well as in your home region. You may want to choose a service that provides dual-mode phones that also work in standard analog cellular networks — they're just about everywhere, so you won't be stranded.

Although GSM systems in the United States use the same digital system as GSM phones elsewhere in the world, they operate on a different frequency, so you can't take your PCS phone with you to Germany or France and use it.

Paging

We don't know about your neighborhood, but we think that everyone carries a pager where we live (well, everyone except us, but that's a different story). Paging services are the older — and cheaper — sibling to cellular and PCS telephone systems. Like these other systems, pagers are compact and designed for mobile use.

Generally speaking, paging systems come in two varieties:

- ✔ **Numeric pagers** simply display a short series of numbers (typically telephone numbers, though some people devise elaborate code schemes to relay messages over these systems).

- ✔ **Alphanumeric pagers** can display several lines of text in addition to phone numbers.

Additionally, paging services can also be categorized as follows:

- ✔ **One-way systems** broadcast a page over the airwaves to your pager. If you happen to be deep in a coal mine when your page is sent, you may not ever get it, which can be considered a disadvantage.

- ✔ **Two-way systems** confirm your receipt of an incoming page — or keep sending the page until you receive it. The more advanced systems even allow you to send a brief reply to an incoming message.

The really hot new function of paging systems — and the area where they may become important to a home networker — is the emergence of Internet interfaces to paging systems. Many paging service providers now let you use Internet e-mail or a Web browser to send a message to someone's pager.

If you really know what you're doing, you can even automate sending a page over the Web. For example, Pat has a network administrator friend who set up a new system in his office to e-mail a message to his pager every time a network error occurred. While you may not want to set up this kind of automatic messaging on your pager — it tends to limit your actual time away from work — you may want your home-automation or security system to page you every time a certain condition (like water in the basement) occurs.

Connecting in New Ways

Traditional telephone service and cellular phones are, for most of us, the only real options when it comes to getting telephone service. That's about to change — and soon — as companies that have had nothing to do with local telephone service take advantage of FCC deregulation and enter the local telephone marketplace.

The cable squawk box

If you were to walk down to the local office of your cable company and say, "I want cable phone service," they'd probably cast a sideways glance at you and call security, because in most areas, cable telephony just doesn't exist yet. That doesn't mean cable companies aren't thinking about it, though, and technically speaking, it wouldn't be all that hard to squeeze the bandwidth equivalent of a telephone line or two (per customer) onto the cable system and offer the equivalent of your current local telephone service.

Manufacturers of cable-modem equipment have boxes on the shelf (or at least on the drawing board) that split off telephone signals and send them to your home's telephone network. Issues like infrastructure (connecting the cable system to the POTS telephone network), finances (paying for the infrastructure), and regulation (getting permission to offer the service) may take a few years to sort out, but we think it won't be too long before your cable company fills your mailbox with offers for phone service.

When this kind of service becomes available in your neighborhood, you won't have to worry about figuring out how to plug your telephones into the cable outlet. Instead, cable telephony systems will typically include a small device called a *splitter*. This small "black box" will be installed right at the point where your cable connection enters the home and will separate the telephone signals from the rest of the cable signals (television, audio, and cable modem). The telephone signals will then be connected to your home's standard telephone wiring (in place of the connection you now have with the local telephone company), while the rest of the cable signals will be carried over your home's cable network.

That's not the only way cable companies are thinking about offering telephone services, or *voice services,* as they're called in the business (and by *the business,* we mean, of course, the industry). Another thing called *voice over IP* (as in *Internet Protocol,* the language of the Net) is getting the cable companies a bit excited. We got excited, too, so we wrote a book about it called *Internet Telephony For Dummies* (published by IDG Books Worldwide, Inc.).

In the voice-over-IP scenario, the cable company will carry your telephone calls as bits and bytes of IP data through your cable-modem Internet connection. That means you'll be able to make calls through your PC or even through the set-top box on your TV, *and* you'll also be able to plug your existing phones into an interface on your cable modem and make these Net calls with a regular phone. On their end, the cable companies will install a magical black box (well, they're not always black, but they are rather magical) called a *voice-over-IP gateway* that will allow your calls to be carried to regular phones on the POTS telephone network. Figure 10-3 shows such an arrangement.

With voice over IP becoming a viable way of delivering telephone services, in addition to cable-modem service providers vying to sell you phone services, many Internet service providers are also investigating ways to offer telephone service using IP telephony. Voice over IP may open up all sorts of different ways to connect your home to the Internet, such as DSL modems, wireless systems, and even electrical power lines.

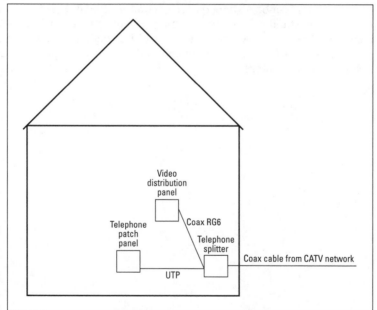

Figure 10-3:
A voice-over-IP network

Fixed wireless telephone service

In addition to the usual mobile cellular service that everyone is accustomed to, other systems offer wireless telephone services for nonmobile telephones called *fixed wireless services.* These services are based on the notion of using wireless service as the main telephone system in the house.

Fixed wireless services that are available right now, however, are generally offered by cellular or PCS companies. These services generally cost the same as mobile cellular or PCS services, which is to say, more than wired telephone services. The target markets for current offerings are, therefore, not homeowners but businesses, for use in remote locations — like construction sites — that can't be economically wired to conventional wired telephone services.

Homeowners may soon begin to see fixed wireless services from companies trying to enter the competitive marketplace for telephone services. Instead of leasing and reselling copper local lines from incumbent telephone companies (the most common way of offering competitive telephone services), a few companies — most notably AT&T — are considering offering a fixed wireless service instead.

Services such as the one that AT&T has proposed — based on a system by Lucent Technologies — will provide homeowners with the wireless equivalent of ISDN digital telephone service. With this system, homeowners will mount a flat, pizza-box–shaped antenna on the side of their homes and connect it to the standard telephone wiring already in place inside the house. Like ISDN, the service will provide two 64 Kbps digital lines, which can be used for standard voice and fax telephone services or to provide data connections for computers.

Chapter 11

Making the Phone Connection

As we tell you in the Chapter 10, a ton of stuff fits into a home phone net-work. A plethora of phone devices and multiplicity of lines can add up to a big headache if you don't wire your house properly for phone service. This chapter tells you how to avoid such headaches, as well as headaches that may come up if you have your house wired in a way that doesn't allow you to take advantage of tomorrow's technologies.

For example, although the cables that telephone companies run throughout your house are fine for most of today's uses, tomorrow you may be talking over data networks like the Internet. By running data-grade cabling to all your telephone and data outlets, you can futureproof your home.

With futureproofing your phone system firmly in mind, we tell you what kind of wiring to buy for your phone network and then discuss how to lay your network out.

Although we concentrate primarily on how to create a phone network that relies on wires — the way that most people's phone systems work — some very good whole-home wireless options are coming to market as we write. We describe some of these options toward the end of the chapter.

Going Every Which Way — What to Run Where

A good way to start planning a phone network is to create a quick list of places where you may need phone outlets. The phone network we describe here has the capacity to support up to four lines at each outlet station; you should be able to handle several devices at each outlet without any capacity problems.

As part of your plan, determine each room's minimum phone communications requirements:

- **Living room:** Depending on your home layout and your plans regarding an entertainment center/home theater, your living room can be very simple or very complex. We recommend that you put a single telephone outlet next to your favorite seat and another multiline outlet where you plan to have your television entertainment area.

- **Dining room:** A single outlet should suffice in your dining room. However, if you work at home your dining-room may double as your conference room. In that case, think about adding both phone and data access to this room. If you intend to use the dining-room table as the place to put your gear, consider a floor mount in the middle of the room (but recognize that to do so you have to cut a hole in your floor covering, which can be rough on antique Oriental rugs).

- **Family room:** Again, your phone requirements here depend on where your main entertainment equipment resides. Because these rooms can be big, we usually recommend that you put one outlet on each of two facing walls. Otherwise, you may have to run 20-foot-long patch cables — which, trust us, kids and dogs have a knack for getting wrapped up in — to your telephone across the room.

- **Kitchen:** Most people spend a good deal of time in the kitchen, so at least one outlet is in order here. Many people base their answering machine or cordless phone in this room, so make sure that your phone outlet is also near a power outlet. Try to create a nook for your phone and related equipment — you don't want to spill honey on that stuff.

- **Bedrooms:** Plan for at least one multiline outlet in each bedroom. Your master bedroom may require an additional outlet on the wall opposite your bed, for your cable, DSL, or satellite set-top box access. Any bedrooms that you may eventually convert to a home office may also require a second outlet. (We highly advise against a fax machine in the master bedroom if you want to stay married, though.)

- **Home theater:** A phone jack behind your A/V component shelves gives your DSS receiver or DIVX disc player the capability to show you the movies you want to see (both of these systems may require a phone line connection to authorize pay per view or repeated viewings of movies). You may also want to include a phone jack near the seating area if you plan to have a regular telephone in this room.

✔ **Home office:** Your home office is probably a communications hub, most likely using all of your phone lines. We recommend that you install at least two multiline jacks on opposite walls to give you a bit of flexibility. If you have an assistant helping you out, you may need to add extra jacks in this room.

✔ **Other places:** Don't overlook other parts of your home when you're planning phone outlets. We recommend that you include phones in the garage, the bathroom, the basement, and the exercise room. *Note:* If you want your phone system to double as an intercom, you need to run out-lets to the places you'd like to intercom as well.

Throughout this book, we show you more and more home-network function-ality in each and every room. Much of this functionality depends on the telephone. Don't shortchange yourself for a few dollars, counting on wireless options down the road. If you have the luxury of planning in advance, a wired infrastructure has many advantages. Almost any habitable room (closets excluded — for now) should have phone access.

Choosing Cables

After electrical wiring, telephone-type wiring is probably the most common within home networks. This category of cabling, which is usually referred to as *twisted pair,* actually does much more than just carry telephone signals. In fact, twisted-pair cabling is the basis of most computer LANs, and can be used to carry other data within your home network as well.

The wiring in modern phone and LAN systems is twisted for a reason (besides the fact that colored wires woven together look pretty). Through some magical properties of physics, the physical interweaving of the wires actually protects against electrical interference. With no interference, you don't get *cross talk* — the fax transmission on Line One bleeds through into the voice call on Line Two, for example. *Note:* The conductors are twisted within the outer sheath — you can't really "see" the twisting except to note slight bumps at regular intervals in the cabling (sometimes you won't even see that much of a twist, unless you cut the wire open).

If you own an existing home, you no doubt have some kind of telephone wiring in your walls already. What you actually have varies widely depending upon how old your house is, who wired it, and a host of other variables. Older homes (and even many homes being built today), were usually wired with a flat, untwisted cable often referred to as *quad cable.* This quad cable contains two pairs of wires, sufficient for carrying two phone lines. Because they're not twisted, however, these cables are much more susceptible to interference and cross talk, and really aren't well-suited for modern, high-speed communications and networking. If you currently have this kind of wiring, our advice is to replace it.

You usually find twisted-pair phone and data wiring in a cable jacket that has no electrical shielding. Those in the know refer to it as *UTP*, or unshielded twisted pair.

Newer homes are generally wired for telephone service with a round cable (usually in a gray jacket) that contains two twisted pairs of wires (four actual conductors). This cabling is much less prone to interference problems, and most types can carry up to two POTS or ISDN phone lines (which we discuss in more detail in Chapter 10). In most cases, however, these cables are not adequate for high-speed data networks, but they are perfectly adequate if you only use them for distributing telephone and low-speed analog data service throughout your house.

Although these cables are just fine for telephone service, in most cases the architecture (network design) of existing home phone networks isn't optimal.

If you're starting from scratch, you can choose to utilize this generic four-pair, twisted phone wire for your telephone network, but we prefer higher-quality wire. Specifically, we recommend that you choose Category 3 (CAT-3) or Category 5 (CAT-5) UTP data grade wiring (see Chapter 22 for more details). This wire doesn't really cost much more than the non-rated variety, and it is better suited to the high-speed technologies that your phone lines may carry in the future — stuff like *digital subscriber line* (DSL) data connections (we discuss this high-speed phone-line technology in Chapter 13).

Either CAT-3 or CAT-5 wiring is more than adequate for most current phone applications. However, we strongly recommend that you spend the small, extra bit of money and go with CAT-5, just to be on the safe side for the future. Running CAT-5 everywhere gives you the flexibility to switch back and forth between data and telephone applications as you desire. If you're also building a computer LAN in your home, you're probably buying CAT-5 cabling in bulk anyway, so why bother with two separate crates of wire?

No matter what kind of phone wiring you choose, make sure that you install *four-pair wire* — the kind that can handle four phone lines on one cable — to give you a bit of leeway as you add lines. If you think that you'll need to access more than four incoming phone lines in your network, this cable still does the job. Of course, at that point you should really consider a key system or home PBX to route your phone lines around the house; four-pair UTP is adequate for all of the consumer systems we've ever seen.

Hardwiring a Phone Network

In the previous chapter, we discuss several different endpoint components — the stuff that you actually plug into your phone network to do your calling, faxing, videoconferencing, and pizza ordering. The wonderful thing about a phone network is that all of this stuff is inherently modular and standardized. In other words, plug it into a standard RJ-11 jack (maybe also into a power outlet), and it works. Gotta love that.

Bringing in phone-network components

Besides the cables we discuss in the preceding section, a few other components come together to make up your phone network. Like cables, these components are all pretty standard, and they enable you to build the infrastructure to tie all the endpoints (in other words, your telephones, faxes, and modems) together.

The Network Interface Device (NID)

The Network Interface Device is a small plastic box that serves as the point of demarcation between your telephone networks and your service provider's network. Incoming phone lines connect to one side of the NID, terminating within a locked portion of the box (only the phone company's techs are allowed in here). This side of the NID is electrically connected to the consumer side of the NID, where your internal phone wiring begins.

The NID is part of the standard telephone-company line installation. Its demarcation function makes the NID a significant part of a phone network. Everything on the telephone company's side of the NID (all the way back to their central telephone-switching office) is their responsibility to maintain and repair. The consumer side of the NID is your own inside wiring, and if something goes awry, you pay for its repair.

Many local telephone companies offer inexpensive inside wiring repair policies that they tack onto your phone bill every month. If something goes wrong with your inside wiring, the phone company sends someone out to troubleshoot and repair the problem for free. This service can be a good deal if you have an older house.

The patch panel

The many telephone cables that run through your house are potentially a big mess when you get back to the NID to hook up with the telephone company. Fortunately, technology has kept up with market requirements, giving you what's called a *patch panel* (sometimes called a terminal block or punchdown block) to neatly patch one line to another.

You connect your incoming telephone lines through the patch panel, which acts as the central hub for your telephone network, to centrally homed telephone cables running to jacks throughout your home. (*Centrally homed* refers to the star-wired architecture of a phone network, where each jack is individually wired back to the central hub.)

The patch panel is a wall-mounted piece of equipment that serves as a junction point for lines. Consisting of a plastic frame with several evenly spaced wire receptacles or *lugs,* the patch panel makes future changes to the phone system easier and eliminates having to reroute cables in the walls.

Depending on how much you want to spend and on whom the installer is, this patch panel can have the following interfaces:

- ✓ **Pole and nut terminal interface:** You unscrew the nut, put the wire in, and screw the nut back in.

- ✓ **RJ-style interface:** You directly plug the individual runs of phone wire into modular jacks.

- ✓ **Punchdown interface:** You use a special tool known as a *punchdown tool* to push the wire down into the receptacles. The punchdown simultaneously strips the wire of its insulation and connects it electrically to the panel.

Figure 11-1 shows a phone patch panel.

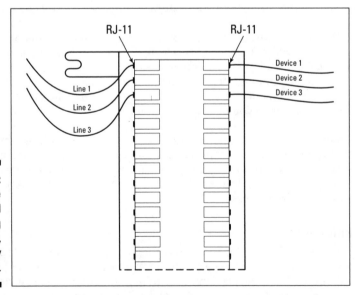

Figure 11-1:
A telephone
patch panel
isn't a thing
of beauty,
but it's very
useful.

Typical patch panels are based on standard designs (known as 66 or 110 panels), although some home-cabling companies offer their own proprietary designs. In the simplest terms, your centrally homed cables connect to one side of the patch panel and incoming phone lines from the NID connect to the other side. The patch panel is then wired internally to distribute each incoming line to multiple outlets — a process known as *bridging* or *cross connecting*.

If you use a structured prewiring system, such as Lucent's HomeStar system, the patch panels are housed within the central wiring hub (which Lucent calls their service center). For more information on structured prewire solutions, refer to Chapter 2.

Modular wall outlets

The endpoints of your telephone network are the wall outlets in each room. You can find wall plates equipped with RJ-11 modular jacks (and you can plug any of your old telephone equipment into these) in just about every configuration you can imagine. If you're running four-pair wiring, you can connect four pairs of UTP wire into four separate RJ-11 jacks, for example, or you may choose to connect two pairs into a single jack for dual-line phones or key phone systems. You may even decide to connect only one or two of the pairs into one line RJ-11 jack and leave the other pairs unused for future requirements.

When you're choosing phone wall outlets for a room, consider what other home-network outlets you're going to need in the same location. You can find many modular outlets that take up a double- or triple-gang-sized junction box (which we talk about in Chapter 7) and allow you to connect data and video networks all in one large outlet.

Accessorize your phone network

A range of other small, useful accessories are handy with your home phone network, including the following:

- ✔ **1-to-2 splitter jacks:** These jacks take a single RJ-14 connection (which has two-pair) and split it into two single-pair RJ-11 connections so you can connect two devices.

- ✔ **2-jack modular adapter:** These adapters take a single RJ-14 connection and split it into two RJ-14 connections, allowing you to have two, two-line phones sharing the same

wall jack, for instance. You can readily find three- and five-jack versions as well.

- ✔ **Inline coupler:** This accessory connects two four-wire phone cords together, which is great when you have to run an extra long distance across the room. For example, you can use an inline coupler to connect two six-foot telephone cords together to get one 12-foot cord.

These gadgets offer more flexibility when you find that your wired network doesn't quite give you exactly what you want. Grab a handful and keep them in your toolbox — you'll need them.

Jacks and plugs for everyone

For the past 20 years or so, telephone wires have been using standardized modular connectors — plugs and jacks — to connect equipment to the wiring infrastructure.

These modular connectors come in three physical variants, which all look basically the same but come in varying widths to accommodate more wires (or positions):

- ✔ **Four-position jacks and plugs:** Used to connect handsets to telephones.

- ✔ **Six-position jacks and plugs:** Can handle one to three lines, meaning that either two, four or six wires actually terminate in the jack.

- ✔ **Eight-position jacks and plugs:** Not normally used for phone purposes, these widest jacks are used for data applications like Ethernet and other computer LANs.

Businesses sometime use 25-pair jack and plugs as well, but you're not likely to need or see these in your house.

We recommend that you use these six-position jacks throughout your home. Most consumer phone equipment, whether it be one-, two-, or three-line capable, uses these standard connectors.

Beyond physical size, the communications industry also differentiates jacks by their *configuration* (how many wires are actually connected to them). You may see documentation referring to jacks and plugs as

- ✔ **RJ-11:** Two wires connected for a single-line connection

- ✔ **RJ-14:** Four wires connected for a two-line connection

- ✔ **RJ-25:** Six wires connected for a three-line connection

- ✔ **RJ-45:** Eight wires connected for data LAN purposes (wider than phone jacks)

Security systems use a special kind of RJ jack — the RJ-31X. We talk about this jack in Part V, which covers home security systems.

As you can imagine, all of this "RJ-this" and "RJ-that" talk quickly gets confusing. Even the experts can get confused, as an RJ-11 can mean different things, depending on whether you are following an old Bell Telephone standard or a Telecommunications Industry Association (TIA) standard or something else. We usually refer to four-position phone jacks as RJ-11s, regardless of how many wires are connected, and eight-position jacks as RJ-45s. That's the way most people talk, regardless of what the standards say.

This old house

If you are renovating an old house that had a home office, you're likely to see some interesting things. Totally bypass these and other artifacts on your new smart home:

✔ **Hardwired phones:** No jacks, just a line running into the wall like at a hotel. (You typically find these in hotel rooms when you really have to send an e-mail from your laptop only to discover you have no place to plug in.)

✔ **Four-prong plugs/jacks:** Four round prongs, sort of like an electrical plug, that plug into

a matching jack. These were the original standardized plugs for telephones, before todays' modular jacks were in common use.

✔ **25-pair wiring:** Some years back, the only option for a home-office telephone was to run the same type of wiring as the large office installations — 25-pair cables. These have big, thick connectors on the end that look more like printer connections than phone jacks.

Building the architecture

The *architecture* of a network refers to the logical model on which it's based. If you've ever seen one of those AT&T commercials where they show the company's switching network as red lines connecting big red dots and showing telephone calls boogying across those lines and dots, then you've seen a model. Obviously, the telephone company's switching network is much more complex than lines and connection points, but you can get an idea of how it works by thinking of it as these lines that connect at various dots.

The not-so-good daisy chain

If you have an older home, or if you are building a new one and just let the electrician or telephone company wire your home for phones without any specific instructions, chances are that you have a daisy-chained telephone network.

In this type of network model, a telephone cable (typically a quad cable — four conductors, capable of supporting two telephone lines) is connected to the telephone company's NID (Network Interface Device). This cable then runs throughout the home, from jack to jack, until it reaches the final, most-distant jack.

Phone companies and electricians often choose this method mainly because it's easy and cheap. Unfortunately, many problems come with a daisy-chain system, not the least of which are

✔ You lose your connection when more people pick up the line to take part in a conversation.

✔ You're limited to having the same outside line on each jack in the house — you won't be able to reconfigure a jack to connect to an extra phone line that you might purchase from the phone company.

Don't wire your telephone network in a daisy-chain configuration. The star architecture that we describe in the following section is much more flexible and capable than the daisy-chain architecture.

Reach for a star

In the *star architecture,* each jack runs to a wiring hub that acts as a central connection point. If you draw this system on paper, it looks like a star (or maybe a wagon wheel with the spokes all connecting at the hub).

The star architecture provides many advantages over the daisy-chain architecture we describe in the previous section. Here are a few advantages:

✔ **Reliability:** If you use a daisy-chain architecture, any physical or electrical problems in your phone cable affect all the phones farther along on that cabling system. In a star network, only the phones at the end of the individual affected cable are out of order.

✔ **Greater capacity:** Daisy-chained telephone networks are useful for only the number of lines that start out from the wiring hub, whereas a star network lets you handle as many lines as each home run carries.

✔ **Flexibility:** In a daisy-chained network, each telephone jack station is stuck with whatever phone lines its cable is connected to back at the NID. In a star network, all the cables go back to a central point, which you can patch to different incoming lines with a minimum of fuss. If you decide to convert a spare bedroom into a home office, you very simply reconfigure your connections — to connect those remote phone jacks to your incoming fax line, for example — at the network's hub.

Starting from the telephone company's incoming service feed, you build a typical star-wired telephone network as follows:

1. **The telephone company installs an incoming line or lines (called a** *feed***) from the local central office (also known as the Digital Loop Carrier or DLC).**

   Depending upon a host of factors — when your telephone company's connection was installed, which company did it, how many lines you have — the telephone cable may consist of two, three, or four pairs of

copper wire. The wire may or may not be twisted (most older installations aren't). For the most part, many recent telephone-company
installations use four-pair, UTP cable. The telephone company connects
the incoming feed to the Network Interface Device (NID) outside your
home.

2. **Connect a UTP cable from the consumer side of the NID to the patch
   panel in your home's wiring center.**

   This line is the central feed between the outside world and your home
   phone network. Attach each conductor wire within the line to the patch
   panel. (For information about choosing a location for your home's
   wiring center, beam yourself to Chapter 2.)

3. **Connect a UTP cable onto the terminal block.**

   This cable — commonly known as a *drop* — provides telephone service
   to an individual phone outlet.

   If you are planning to use four-pair UTP cabling and your phone network
   is starting off with less than four lines used at a particular jack, no problem — you can leave some of the pairs of wires within your UTP cabling
   unterminated to start off. Just make sure that you label your cables well
   so you know which room each drop serves. Leave the unused cables
   coiled up out of the way at each end (in other words, behind your future
   wall outlet and near the patch panel). And in the future, if you add additional lines, you can simply connect additional feed and drop lines to the
   patch panel (and to your modular outlets at the endpoints of your network). This quick and easy reconfigurability is one of the biggest
   advantages of a star-wired phone network that uses four-pair cables.

4. **Run a UTP drop cable from your wiring center through the walls to a
   modular outlet in a room where you want to use a phone device.**

   As we mention earlier, you have a fair amount of flexibility here — you
   can connect your UTP cabling, say, to two separate two-line outlets, four
   one-line outlets, or some combination thereof. The kind of phones and
   phone equipment you're going to connect to the outlets drives your
   cable choice.

5. **Connect *end devices* — all the neat stuff we discuss in Chapter 10,
   such as phones, faxes, and modems — to the wall outlets by using
   simple telephone patch cables.**

6. **Repeat Steps 3, 4, and 5 for each individual outlet in your phone
   network.**

Figure 11-2 shows the finished product — a star-wired telephone network.

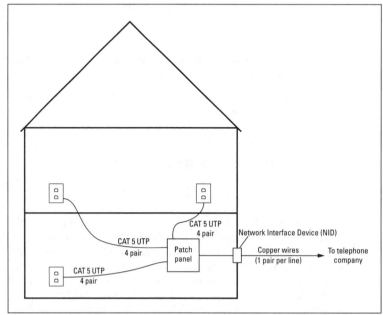

Figure 11-2:
The star of
our phone
show.

Hybrid networks

If you discover the need for an additional outlet someplace in your home (after buying a larger bed, you realize that you need a phone line on the other side of your bedroom, for instance) that you didn't wire with a star run, you can use a modified version of the daisy-chained wiring scheme. Running a daisy chain from a new outlet from the nearest star outlet is easy and acceptable when necessary.

Ideally, you want to avoid this kind of hybrid network, but adding an outlet or two to a star network by daisy chaining won't mess things up at all. Remember, however, that these new outlets lose the flexibility of runs back to a central point — they will have to be connected to the same phone lines as the star-wired outlet they are connected to, so you can't use them for different phone lines.

Plugging into a KSU

The phone network that we describe in the previous section gets you up and running. You have multiline phone service available throughout the home, which is worth a good deal all on its own. You may decide, however, that you want more.

For example, you may want the ability to transfer calls from one phone to another or the capability to use your phone as an intercom. You may even want to have some music available when you put that telemarketer on hold (ahhhh, sweet revenge). In that case, you need a KSU, or *key telephone system unit,* to control all of your phone lines.

The KSU serves as your phone system's intelligence. The phone lines plug into the KSU, which is usually located with your punchdown block. The in-home drops (the star-wired phone cables connected to each of your home's phone outlets) connect into the other side of the KSU, which allows the KSU to conference calls together, transfer calls, and to ring any extension at any time.

The marketplace offers a huge variety of key systems, each with its own particular wiring and equipment requirements. Because the vast majority of these systems require exactly what you already have installed — a star-network architecture and UTP cabling — integrating a KSU into your phone network is a pretty simple proposition.

In shopping for key systems, you hear terms like 6-x-16, which means that the system supports up to six lines and 16 extensions off those lines.

Here are a few things to keep in mind:

- ✔ **The central control unit — the KSU — installs in your wiring center between the incoming service feeds and the patch panel:** Incoming feeds use modular RJ-11 jacks to connect to the system's input side, and then additional UTP cabling connects the individual extension outputs to your service drops for each room.

- ✔ **Most KSU systems require just a single pair of UTP wiring to each extension, though a scant few require two or even three pairs:** Those requiring two or three pairs are either heavy-duty systems or are for providing extra services, like ISDN capabilities, to the extensions. You can cover all your bases by installing four-pair UTP at the outset.

- ✔ **Many KSUs have additional inputs and outputs:** The additional inputs and outputs are designed for things like door phones, music inputs, and even a printer interface for printing out *call detail reports,* which itemize the phone numbers and times that calls are made from each extension.

Low-cost home phone systems

You can find some great, low-cost home phone systems out there. One such system is Centrepoint Technologies' (`www.ctrpoint.com`) $495 Concero Switchboard. This key telephone system allows you to do all the things big companies do — things like conference calling, call transferring, putting callers on hold, acting as an intercom, and using prioritized or selective ringing.

Concero integrates one or two phone lines with six extensions for your standard phones, fax machines, answering devices, modems, PCs, and cell phones. You can dial or answer either line from any phone. Any three outside phone numbers become remote extensions (cell/PCS phones, pagers, or satellite offices, for example). So when you leave the office, you can have the calls forwarded to where you are, giving you seamless one-number service.

If you answer a ringing telephone and you hear fax tones, you merely press the fax machine's extension number and hang up. If you enable the fax tone detection feature, Switchboard automatically answers in fax mode. Switchboard also performs callbacks and call rerouting, which saves you money by letting you place long-distance calls through your home. (Ever make an international call on a cell phone? It's expensive.)

If you need more than two lines for your home telephone system, Panasonic (`www.panasonic.com`), Lucent (`www.lucent.com`), and others offer good systems. Expect to spend around $400–$600 for a 3-x-8 KSU. Phones run $100–$200 apiece, depending on whether you want a speakerphone, LCD, and so on. A 6-x-16 system is in the $600–$800 range, with phones also in the $100–$200 range.

Using KSU-less phone systems

In Chapter 10, we discuss *KSU-less phone systems* — sophisticated, multiline telephones that have a degree of networking intelligence built into each phone (as opposed to putting all of the control functionality into a central unit).

KSU-less phone systems have a price advantage over KSUs. However, the handsets themselves are rather expensive and if you install several of them, dropping the money on a KSU system up front may be financially advantageous.

KSU-less phone systems aren't nearly as picky about network architecture as a KSU system. Although, most KSU systems absolutely require the star-wiring configuration we describe earlier in this chapter, many KSU-less systems are designed to work in either a star or a daisy-chained wiring architecture. So you can utilize your existing phone wiring and still get many of the intercom, call transfer, and conference call features that KSUs provide.

This approach does come with a couple of caveats, however:

- **The ultimate capacity of a KSU-less network is less than that of a full KSU:** If you need a really big bunch of lines and extensions, you may be out of luck. You can, however, handle three or four incoming lines, and up to a dozen extensions, depending on the system you buy.

- **Utilizing this kind of system on your existing phone wiring assumes that your current wiring already provides three or four lines to each phone outlet:** If your house was wired recently, you very well may meet this requirement, but unless you are sure that you have three- or four-pair wiring connected to each outlet, you may have to run new wires after all.

Make sure that you figure out how many phone lines your current wiring will support before you decide on a KSU-less phone system. If you find that you need to run new wire anyway to get that third or fourth line installed, we highly recommend that you start at square one and build a star phone-line infrastructure. You can still use KSU-less phones if you like, but you have all of the flexibility and expansion capacity of a modern phone network in place for future needs.

Music on hold sounds good

Many KSUs have a music-on-hold port that you can use to provide soothing sounds to people who get stuck in your phone queue. The KSU itself won't give you high-quality stereo sound, but you can plug the line-level output of a CD player or radio tuner into your system for that effect.

You can also try a system specifically designed for music on hold, like the $199 PromoCast DXA by MetaSound (www.metasound.com). The PromoCast DXA uses a computer memory chip to store audio broadcasts for playback. Audio broadcasts, including promotional and informative messages and licensed music, are recorded onto a CD or cassette tape, and then loaded into the DXA via an external audio input port.

All you have to do is push the record button, adjust the sound volume, and play the broadcast into the DXA, which stores the message in digital memory. The DXA includes courtesy messages and licensed music stored in non-volatile flash memory (in 5- or 10-minute production options) — which means it keeps the information stored even if you lose power.

Additionally, the package provides a CD offering a selection of various courtesy messages (in both English and Spanish), along with a variety of music tracks, such as jazz, classical, rock, country, New Age, and so on. Customers can also subscribe to MetaSound's broadcast production services for fully customized messages for an additional price. You can also record your own messages onto the system.

Cool KSU-less phones

KSU-less phones are the multiline phones you find at office supply retail chains. You can attach other extensions and perform basic business functions like call hold and conferencing.

Nortel has a $299 Venture Multi-Telephone (www.nortel.com) that allows up to eight telephones to share three analog lines. Because each set contains system intelligence inside, Venture provides integrated Caller ID and call waiting ID right on the telephone. Other features include intercom, paging, voice messaging, Caller ID integration with voice messaging, eight memory keys, speed dial buttons, and a three-

line backlit display. Venture allows all telephones in the system to share directory and call logs, which is nice because you don't have to perform individual entries on each telephone.

Panasonic has its $199 KX-TS400-W 4-Line Phone with Speakerphone (www.panasonic.com) that offers four-line operation. Among its features are automatic line selection when you pick up the phone, three-way conferencing, speakerphone, 12-digit LCD readout with clock, mute function for privacy, full one-touch automatic dialer for up to 24 stations, auto redial, and electronic hold.

Connecting Alternatively

You also have non-wireline options for distributing phone service throughout your home. These methods don't give you the same ultimate capacity as a wireline phone network (they're limited to two or three lines at most), but you *can* get much of the same functionality with some of these alternatives.

For wireless phones to work, you have to have some kind of phone setup in your house, even if you're talking a 1937 Ma Bell wiring job.

Taking the wireless route

The simplest way to expand an existing phone network is to utilize wireless phones and phone systems. You most likely have a cordless phone of some sort, so you're already using this technology in a limited way.

Conventional cordless phones — available in one- and two-line models — do expand your network by adding a degree of mobility to your telephone devices. What they don't do, however, is offer the more sophisticated call control features like call transfer and intercom features (except between the handset and the base station). They also don't provide connectivity for other telephony devices like fax machines and analog modems — all they really do is give you another telephone handset, sans cord. However, some new wireless phone systems are now available that let you do much more.

Siemens Gigaset

Siemens, the global electronics and communications giant has just introduced a really neat new wireless phone system called the Gigaset
(`www.siemenscordless.com`) that moves beyond the standard cordless
phone and performs much of the same functions as a key phone system.

Based around a single, two-line base station, the Gigaset uses a single base
station to service up to eight cordless extension phones. For about $400
for the base station, and another $125 for the handsets, you can get
the following:

> ✔ The base station, which doubles as a two-line phone, two-line answering
>   machine, and system controller.
>
> ✔ Cordless handsets that operate in the 2.4 GHz frequency range and that
>   are also two-line capable (one handset comes with the package).

2.4 GHz is a higher frequency band that is just beginning to be used by home
wireless systems like phones and wireless computer networks. It offers less
interference and a longer range than the traditional 900 MHz or lower
frequency bands.

> ✔ A call transfer feature between any handset and/or base station.
>
> ✔ An intercom feature that lets you talk with someone else in the house
>   without tying up an outside line.
>
> ✔ Caller ID on the base station and the handsets so you can see who is
>   calling — and even who is on call waiting.
>
> ✔ Three-way conference calling.
>
> ✔ Headset capability for hands-free conversations.
>
> ✔ A four-line LCD display for programming and controlling the handsets.

Installing the Gigaset is a snap. Siemens provides you with all the cables you
need to connect into your phone jack — whether you have two one-line jacks
or one two-line jack. The remote handsets — you can install up to eight of
them, if you wish — need no additional phone network connections, just A/C
power for their recharger stations.

That's it. No complexities, just phone service by the pool, on the tractor
(need to speak up though), and in the bath (don't drop it!).

If two lines and eight extensions can cover your phone network needs — and
they probably can — the Gigaset can be a great way to get a phone network
up and running. The only major disadvantage (besides an alarming amount
of interference from Danny's microwave oven) is that this system makes no
provisions for installing other telephony devices like fax machines and

modems in remote locations in your home. You need your wireline phone network for that. If you can live with that limitation, this product is a great way to expand a phone network.

Home Wireless Networks

Another wireless solution to building a home phone network — and one that offers even more potential to supplant a wired system — is a new product from a startup company called Home Wireless Networks (`www.homewireless` `.com`). Like the Gigaset we describe in the previous section, the HWN308 is a multiline, multiple handset system that uses a single physical connection to your phone network wiring. It can support three lines and eight extensions. The HWN516 supports five lines and 16 extensions.

The big difference is that the endpoints of a Home Wireless Networks (HWN) telephone network don't have to be just handsets. One unique element of the network is a wireless phone jack component that provides a standard RJ-11, single-line interface anywhere in your house where AC power available. So your fax machines, corded phones, modems, and the like can connect anywhere in the house.

The components of a HWN network include the following:

✔ The controller, which connects to incoming phone line jacks and distributes phone signals wirelessly (over a 900 MHz frequency)

✔ The handsets, which provide mobile, two-line phone connectivity anywhere in the house

✔ The wireless phone jacks that allow you to connect standard telephone devices like modems and fax machines to the network

✔ Wireless data jacks that let Windows 95/98 PCs share an Internet connection (we talk more about this aspect of the network in Chapter 20)

HWN networks also include many of the same call-control features that you find on the Siemens Gigaset — things like Caller ID, call transfer, intercom capabilities, and conference calling. Setting up a network with HWN is a very similar process, as well. Plug the controller into AC power and connect it to your incoming phone lines. Everything else connects wirelessly to your phone network and needs only a power connection to function.

HWN's products come in two configurations (which are just beginning to ship as we write):

✔ **HWN 308:** This consumer-level product is designed to handle three incoming lines. You can connect up to eight end devices of any sort (handset, wireless phone jack, and wireless data jack). An important disclaimer about the three incoming lines: One line is dedicated to your

Internet connection, so you actually have only two lines available for telephones, faxes, and other devices. In other words, the capacity is the same as the Gigaset, with an additional line dedicated to Net connections.

✔ **HWN 516:** Designed for small business applications, this product has five incoming lines (four voice/fax/other, and one Internet line) and the capability to handle up to 16 end devices. Home users may think that this much capacity is overkill, but the extra capacity is nice to have in case your needs grow.

Pricing is $239 for the 308 central controller, $119 each for the data and phone jacks, and $139 for each handset. The 516 runs about $599 for the controller, access jacks are $149 each, and handsets run $249 each.

The data-networking element of the HWN systems is a nice added dimension to the system, as it throws a simple file and Internet sharing capability into your phone network. If you are considering this system for both its phone and data capabilities, however, keep in mind that each computer attached to the network takes away one of those 8 or 16 endpoints. So a four-computer network actually takes up half of your HWN308 telephone capacity.

Adding a jack on the cheap, without wires

If you have only very basic telephone needs and don't want to spend a pile of money, you may not want to go for an all-out phone system or expensive wireless solution. Suppose you only need a phone jack for your DSS receiver, and you don't have one anywhere near the TV location? Or perhaps you need a telephone in that unfinished attic that's now becoming a finished attic? If your current phone network is meeting the rest of your telephony needs, you may not want to spend the money on an alternative phone system.

In that case, you may want to try one of the wireless phone jacks available from RCA (www.rca.com) or Radio Shack (www.radioshack.com). These devices use your home's power lines to carry phone signals — they're not really wireless; they leverage your existing wiring. The most basic configuration consists of a pair of small devices. The $99 master unit plugs into an existing single-line phone jack and also into an AC outlet. The $49 extension unit plugs into any of your home's AC outlets and has a standard RJ-11 receptacle built in for connecting a phone device. You can buy these remote units separately and add more extension units if you need extra outlets.

These jacks aren't the end-all in sophistication — they only handle one line, and they won't work on modems faster than 14.4 Kbps — but they do allow you to plug in that DSS dish, or add a phone or fax in some location that you never anticipated.

Part IV
Livin' Off the Fat of the LAN

The 5th Wave   By Rich Tennant

"Hello, smart-home maintenance? Can you send someone out? Our den is acting really stupid."

In this part . . .

A home data network used to be a rarity. Today, you may have a second, third, or fourth computer at home, and the fights over the printer, scanner, or, more likely, the high-speed Internet access link may be causing you some grief. A home data network is not a luxury anymore; it's a necessity, if only to bring peace to the household.

Putting together a home network is getting easier and easier, particularly with the advent of new wireless and electric powerline options. By planning ahead, you can pretty much access your home data network from anywhere in the house.

In this part, we tell you all about how to create your data backbone in your home. We discuss all the major elements of a whole-home data network, and how this data network interfaces with your home telephone network — the two have a lot in common. We also tell you about all the different types of data-networking equipment and services available, as well as some advice for ensuring the success of your home data network.

Chapter 12

A Cornucopia of Computers

● ●

In This Chapter

▶ Picking an operating system and physical form for the computers on your home network

▶ Cutting out the fat with thin clients

▶ Making your television and phone work harder with WebTV and smart phones

▶ Getting an assistant — a Personal Digital Assistant, that is

▶ Perusing a plethora of peripherals

● ●

*M*ore than 40 percent of homes in North America have a home PC, and that number is going nowhere but up. Computers become cheaper and more powerful by the minute, and every year you find new ways of using your computer.

Home offices, World Wide Web surfing, e-mail, videoconferencing, computer banking — you name it, and people are doing it on their PCs right now. Even more importantly, they are doing it over a network, whether it be the Internet, America Online, a remote access connection to the office LAN, or even a home LAN between computers in the same house (an increasing number of computer owners now have more than one computer in the home).

In this chapter, we tell you about the equipment that fits into a home computer network — everything from PCs to printers to peripherals. We also discuss some devices that aren't PCs but fit into a computer network and make use of your home's Internet connection — devices like WebTV and new generations of networked computers.

Considering Computers of All Kinds

Chances are pretty good that if you're reading this book, you, too, have at least one PC in your home. So it makes sense to think about your computer networking needs as part of your total home-networking needs. Your present network may consist of only a modem that connects your PC to the outside world, or perhaps a simple A/B switch that lets two computers share a single printer, but the decreasing cost of PCs, combined with the increasing speed of Internet connection methods, makes it worthwhile to install a more sophisticated home computer network in your home.

In the environment of an office or school, computers are routinely networked together to take full advantage of their capabilities — and we think the possibilities are numerous enough to justify your thinking that way at home.

Choosing traditional PCs

We use the term *traditional PC* to differentiate the types of PCs most families have from some of the emerging forms that computers are starting to take (like the network computer or WebTV boxes). We're definitely not disparaging your Pentium III, 3-D graphics, 8-million-megahertz new PC as an obsolete clunker.

When we talk about PCs (whether they be desktop or laptop models), we're basically talking about one of two things:

- **Windows-based PCs:** These are PCs that have Intel CPUs (or similar CPUs from companies like AMD and Cyrix) and use Microsoft Windows operating systems (OS).

  Note: Some people call these *Wintel* machines — people like us, for example.

- **Macintoshes:** These are Apple computers (or Mac clones) that run the Mac OS.

More advanced readers may be using other types of computers — such as a UNIX-based computer — but if you're advanced enough to survive in the UNIX environment, you don't need us to explain what a PC is. (Hard-core UNIX users think graphical user interfaces, such as the ones that come with Wintel machines and Macs, are for wimps. They prefer to do all this stuff at the command line.)

For the most part, both Wintel and Macintosh computers fit into a home network the same way — other than a few differences in the connectors for peripherals. Which kind of PC you use is really a matter of personal preference (we both have one or more of each in our homes), and both are very capable of connecting to just about any kind of network that you might run into.

Our only caveat is this: Microsoft and Intel, along with major PC manufacturers like Compaq and IBM, spend a lot of resources to visualize how home networking and the PC can more fully integrate into the home of the future. As these research efforts start to bear fruit, the Wintel side of the fence may develop a home-networking advantage over Macs. On the other hand, Macs have had easy-to-use plug-and-play networking capabilities built into the system for years. You can build a home network with either platform over the longer term.

Although both Windows and Macintosh computers work just fine in a home network, they can't coexist on the same network without some special software. The networking software built into each operating system doesn't know how to talk to the other operating system's networking software — so Mac's AppleTalk and a Windows computer's Neighborhood Network software don't really communicate with each other. Check out MacLAN by Miramar systems or Dave by Thursby Software Systems for a solution to this problem. For more information on integrating different computers into the same home PC network, check out *Networking Home PCs For Dummies* by Kathy Ivens (IDG Books Worldwide, Inc.).

Looking at laptops, desktops, and more

You need to consider the physical form of the computers you will be adding to your home network. For instance, you can choose among the following types of computers:

- ✔ **Desktop computers:** Full-sized — and full-featured — computers that are only portable in the sense that a very strong person can move them across the room without needing a quick dose of oxygen. Desktops are big and bulky, yes, but they are also, dollar for dollar, more powerful, have larger displays, and can be more easily expanded and upgraded than laptop computers.

- ✔ **Laptop computers:** As you may infer from the name, laptops can be taken with you from room to room or town to town. The first generations of laptop computers were inferior in just about every way to desktops — except, of course, in terms of portability — but current models have enough power and functionality to do just about everything the average user needs. They do, however, cost more than an equivalent desktop computer.

- ✔ **Palmtop computers:** Take a laptop computer and shrink it down by about 50 percent, and you have a palmtop. These models — as opposed to the Personal Digital Assistants (PDAs) described later in this chapter — are full-fledged PCs, running Windows 98, but they don't normally have as much processor power, memory, or screen size as laptops or desktops.

Which one, or several, of these computers you choose for your home network is a personal decision based on your own computing needs, but it is important to make sure that the systems you choose have the capability to connect to your home network. In Chapter 15, we tell you about the various kinds of home LANs that you can install in your home, but regardless of which network type you choose to use, your PCs will require some sort of *Network Interface Card* (or NIC). The NIC is the physical interface between your PCs, internal systems and the outside network.

For desktop computers, the NIC, if it doesn't come preinstalled in the computer, generally fits into one of the internal *PCI* (Personal Computer Interface) card slots within the PC. Other slots in your computer can also accept NIC cards, but we prefer to use PCI NICs because they're a heck of a lot easier to set up. Laptop and palmtop computer NICs use an expansion device known as a *PC Card* (which looks rather like a thick credit card). Any PC built within the past three or four years has these expansion slots built right in — the only real concern is that you have one free to install the NIC.

Beyond the PC — Next-Generation Computers

Many companies are working to bring to market special-purpose *network computers* designed to cost only a few hundred dollars, plug into your TV and phone lines just like a VCR or a telephone, and (hopefully) automatically connect to a service provider and the Internet without a complicated sign-up and configuration procedure.

The term *network computer* (NC) is both a brand name for a kind of computer developed by Oracle Corporation (the database company — and the second largest software company in the world after Microsoft), and a more generic term for a new breed of computers more properly known as *thin clients.* Thin-client computers retain many of the components of regular PCs — like relatively powerful CPUs and decent amounts of RAM — while stripping away or minimizing other parts like hard drives and expansion buses.

The goals of thin-client computers are twofold:

- ✔ Reduce the cost of the computer
- ✔ Simplify use by centralizing the administration of software and data

The stripped-down nature of thin clients makes them less expensive than traditional PCs, supposedly, and allows companies to deploy more computing power in a more controlled and less confusing manner. You see, instead of doing everything themselves, these computers rely on server computers, located somewhere else in the network to which they are connected, to store data and computer programs. Like an automated teller machine that has to go fetch your bank account information from the bank, thin-client computers rely on the network to store information and software.

The biggest challenge to new network computer technologies is the rapidly decreasing cost of traditional PCs. The fastest growing segment of the PC marketplace, as we write this, is in the under-$1,000 category. Some PCs are available for less than $500. With these full-fledged PCs coming in under the magic $1,000 mark — not a whole lot higher than what some of the thin-client equipment costs — many consumers may choose to go the traditional PC route instead.

In the long term, we won't be surprised to see many homes having one (or some) of each — a powerful, full-featured PC in the home office or kid's room (for homework, not games — yeah, right) and some NC-like devices through-out the rest of the home for quick and easy Internet access. We expect to have NCs in our kitchens for off-hours and personal e-mail, for instance.

WebTV — is it for me?

The most popular thin-client computing device currently available is the WebTV box — a small, proprietary Net computer that attaches to your television screen. Although it isn't designed to replace a full-fledged computer, WebTV is a pretty useful tool that allows you to do some neat stuff, such as:

- ✔ Surf the Web
- ✔ Send and receive e-mail
- ✔ Participate in USENET newsgroups online discussions
- ✔ Print e-mail or Web pages
- ✔ Simultaneously view Web pages and TV programs using a picture-in-picture (PIP) system
- ✔ Access TV program listings and even automatically program your VCR

If you don't need to do traditional PC tasks like word processing, WebTV is a great alternative to a PC. The low price of WebTV (under $200 for the top-of-the-line model) makes it affordable enough to get for the living room even if you have a PC in the house (so the kids can stay online but off your PC while you're trying to work at home, for example).

There are a few drawbacks to the current state of the WebTV art, however:

- ✔ **WebTV uses its own proprietary Internet service provider.** So you can't add your WebTV to the same account that you use for your PCs — instead, you have to pay for two ISPs.

- ✔ **You have to connect to the Net via the built-in analog modem.** So you're limited to the speeds possible with a 56K modem, even if you have fast cable-modem, ISDN, or DSL access.

  ✔ **WebTV can't currently display Web content using multimedia technologies like Java and Macromedia Flash.** So viewing Web pages on WebTV may seem static compared to viewing them on a PC.

  ✔ **WebTV doesn't have any capability to be networked with other home computing devices.** Bummer.

Right now, WebTV is really the only choice you have for using your TV as an Internet terminal, but you may see more options becoming available in the near future, including:

  ✔ New, more capable generations of WebTV, now that Microsoft owns the company

  ✔ TVs with PCs built into them, from major computer companies like Compaq and from major television and consumer-electronics manufacturers

  ✔ Network computers based on the Oracle network computer standard (RCA already has one on the market)

  ✔ NetPCs that utilize a version of the Windows operating system

  ✔ Cable TV set-top boxes that have enough computer power to surf the Web and send e-mail and that can convert new digital television signals to a format your TV can display

In fact, one major manufacturer, Scientific Atlanta, has recently announced a deal with Microsoft to build a WebTV system — operating at cable-modem speeds — into a new generation of set-top boxes.

Information appliances

These days *convergence* is the big word in technology circles. *Convergence* means that devices that traditionally exist in their own distinct spheres — such as phones, computers, and televisions — will increasingly overlap in function and use. So you may, for example, check your e-mail on the television screen or perhaps make a voice phone call through a multimedia computer.

In the world of telephones, convergence is starting to happen with the introduction of smart telephones to the marketplace. Smart telephones typically incorporate a small display screen (most often an LCD screen), a keyboard, and a low-power processor chip that enables them to do things like send and receive Internet e-mail messages. Today, smart phones come in two varieties:

✔ **Internet e-mail phones** let you send and receive e-mail from just about any standard Internet e-mail account. These phones are convenient if you already have an Internet service provider (ISP) account — or an Internet e-mail account at work that you want to be able to access from your telephone.

✔ **Proprietary smart phones** require you to subscribe to a special service (from your local telephone company or other service provider) to send and receive e-mail. These phones usually offer additional services — things like stock quotes, weather, or sports scores — but such services require you to pay a fee each month to the service provider. Most smart phones offer a full range of additional telephone features such as Caller ID, built-in alphanumeric phone directories, and full duplex speaker phones (see Chapter 10). Some models even come with a cordless handset as part of the package.

In the near future, we think that the Internet e-mail phones — based on the open protocols of the Internet — will add additional features like Web browsing, but right now, the proprietary phones offer a richer mix of features. For example, depending upon which service provider you choose, you may be able to use your smart phone to access directory white pages, pay bills, or even order goods and services from similarly wired vendors.

Smart phones aren't the only information appliances — they're just the first (along with WebTV). As computing power and networking technologies become more widespread in the home, we're confident that the multipurpose, do-it-all PC will give way to a more decentralized system. In this new system, inexpensive, single-purpose devices located throughout the home will do a few tasks extremely well and will coexist across the home network. We're not predicting that the PC as we know it will go away, just that it will complemented by a host of other computing devices — often built into familiar things like the telephone.

PDAs, PDQ: Interfacing with Handheld Computers

PDAs (Personal Digital Assistants) are a step down in computing power from thin-client devices but a step up in portability. These portable devices range in functionality from simple electronic address books to powerful handheld computers that can send e-mail, browse the Web, and do basic word processing and spreadsheet tasks. You see business people in airports with these little devices, looking up phone numbers or checking calendars. The functionality is increasing, however, and you can use one to track your home items, like grocery lists and phone number/address books — you may even be using them to find out where you are (using a GPS receiver) and to get directions to the grandfolks' house.

PDAs come in two broad categories:

- ✔ Proprietary devices like the 3Com (formerly US Robotics) PalmPilot
- ✔ Handheld computers that utilize a scaled-down version of the Microsoft Windows operating system, called Windows CE

Within each of these two groups, the functionality of PDAs differs greatly, but the most sophisticated are capable of networking by connecting either directly to your PC to exchange data or through a modem connection to other data networks like the Internet. Most have an infrared (IR) device that allows you to print to a printer (or update internal databases) by aiming the device at a printer (or computer) — nifty huh? Figure 12-1 shows how a PDA can network with a PC using infrared networking.

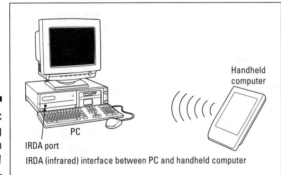

Figure 12-1:
Transferring
data with
light!

Handheld computer

PC

IRDA port

IRDA (infrared) interface between PC and handheld computer

Most infrared equipment uses a common industry standard for networking, called IRDA (Infrared Data Association).

More and more kids are getting PDAs for school. And if you think we're crazy, who would've thought five years ago that teenagers would have pagers. That ol' information age is creeping up on everyone.

Plugging in Printers and Such

Although a computer, monitor, keyboard, and mouse are all that you really need to get up and running, no computer fulfills its potential in the longer term without hooking up to all sorts of neat peripheral devices — and indeed to other computers. The number of things you can plug into a computer is almost limitless these days, including:

- ✔ **Printers** for getting your text and pictures on paper

- ✔ **Scanners** for getting text and pictures onto your hard drive

- ✔ **Modems** (including analog telephone, ISDN, xDSL, wireless, and cable modems — all of which we explain in Chapter 13)

- ✔ **Digital still cameras** that can capture still pictures and save them to your hard drive

- ✔ **Digital video cameras** that let you videoconference or record movies to your hard drive

- ✔ **Telephone management devices** (that display, for example, Caller ID information on your screen or that even open your contact management software and tell you exactly who is calling)

You can connect peripherals to a computer in two ways:

- ✔ **Connect peripherals directly to a computer using that computer's parallel, serial, SCSI, Universal Serial Bus (USB), FireWire, infrared, or other port.** These peripheral devices are called *locally connected.* If you want to know more about setting up your PC, check out *PCs For Dummies,* 6th Edition, by Dan Gookin (published by IDG Books Worldwide, Inc).

- ✔ **Connect peripherals to a computer local area network (LAN) so that you can share the peripherals among several computers.** This type of peripheral is often called a *LAN-capable* or *networkable* peripheral.

Many computer peripherals come in either a local connection or network connection variety (usually the LAN-capable version costs a bit more). Some peripherals, such as many laser printers, may come equipped with both types of connections. In an ideal world, you'd probably want to choose only peripherals that are networkable, but this standard isn't always practical.

Keep in mind that many devices that connect to a single computer may still be used remotely by other computers on that network. For example, an inkjet printer that isn't configured to plug directly into the LAN may be accessible to other computers on the network if the computer that it *is* plugged into is properly configured as a print server.

Now, this description is a little techie, and the purpose of this book is not to teach a lesson in computer hardware. Some great *...For Dummies* books do that perfectly. But the message is this: In buying hardware or trying to make use of hand-me-downs, you need to consider whether the equipment itself is networkable. Your local hardware dealer can help you determine that if you don't know. So can that neighbor kid who knows everything. Later in this book, we talk about many more issues that you need to know about, so don't try to decipher everything now.

Chapter 13

All Roads Lead to the Net

Most people think about the Internet in terms of the neat (and not-so-neat) things it allows them to do, such as send and receive e-mail, surf Web pages, and watch video clips of that annoying dancing baby. If you think of the Internet in this way, give yourself a gold star, because, most of the time, this way of thinking allows you to get the most out of your time on the Internet.

Before you do all this cool stuff on the Internet, however, you have to get connected to it. In this chapter, we tell you about the pros and cons of the many ways you can connect to the Internet.

A World of IP Devices

Today, devices that communicate on the Internet — or on private networks using IP — are basically all the same thing: computers. Personal computers, microcomputers, handheld computers, network computers, mainframe computers, and any other type of computer that you can think of (except, of course, that old Radio Shack TRS-80 that you now use as a doorstop). In fact, hundreds of millions of computers in the world are somehow, sometimes connected to the Internet. And many more will be connected in the future.

Here are a few ways that the Internet may soon play a greater part in your daily life:

> ✔ Telephone companies and data-networking service providers are realizing that using the Internet and private Internet-like networks called *intranets* is a much more efficient way to carry voice telephone traffic than the old-fashioned circuit-switched method.

✔ Independent musicians and record labels are finding that using the Net and a file format known as MP3 is a great way to get music sent to people around the world.

✔ Hundreds of companies, big and small, are finding that *electronic commerce* — using the Net to buy and sell stuff — is much cheaper and more convenient than traditional methods.

✔ Appliance and electronics manufacturers have decided that using the Internet is a great way to let future generations of *smart* products talk with each other and with service centers. Imagine a dishwasher that knows when it needs maintenance and can automatically notify the manufacturer — and even tell the technician which parts to bring for the service call.

Making the Internet Connection

All the wonders of the Internet and of the devices that speak its IP language aren't going to do any of us a darn bit of good if we're not connected. Getting connected to the Net is — in our opinion — as important as getting telephone service into your home, and is probably a higher priority for most of us than stuff like television (TV watching has never been the same since *Seinfeld* went off the air).

Not everyone shares this priority, of course — only about 40 percent of homes in the United States are connected to the Net — but the number of connected homes has grown immensely in the past few years (as if we needed to tell *you* that) and will continue to grow until every house, apartment, condo, shack, tree house, houseboat, trailer, and slow-moving sport utility vehicle has its own Internet connection. If you haven't heard this before (where have you been hiding?), please tell all your friends that we were the first to make that prediction — we like to look smart that way.

For the vast majority of residential users, access to the Net is provided the old-fashioned way — via an analog telephone modem. This arrangement won't last much longer, however, because a whole bunch of companies have decided that they can make a pretty fair chunk of change providing faster Internet access (ahh, isn't that a great phrase?) to people like us.

Analog modems

Maybe you're lucky enough to live in a city where high-speed Internet access devices like cable modems are available. If not, the primary connection between your computer — or computer network — and other computers (like all those millions of computers on the Internet) is most likely an analog modem. On a personal note, we both have high-speed connections available to us — Pat via a cable modem, and Danny via a digital subscriber line in his house in Maine — so we tend to gloat and say "nyah, nyah" to our friends who are still using analog modems.

Okay, we'll cease and desist the gloating and get back to analog modems. These devices get their name from their function — which is to *modulate* and *demodulate* the digital data coming to and from your computer into analog signals that can be carried over the standard analog telephone system.

Figure 13-1 shows the route that information takes between an analog modem and the Internet. Your phone line goes to the telephone company's central office and then to your ISP, which has a group of modems that answer several phone lines. From there, you can use some of the bandwidth of your local ISP's connection.

Figure 13-1:
How an analog modem connects to the Internet.

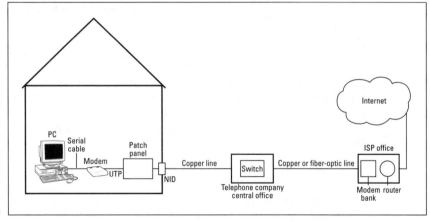

Analog modems come in many different speeds, but these two are the most common:

- **33.6 Kbps modems:** The fastest modems available just a year ago, these modems are now the base models in most manufacturers' lines — if you can still find them at all.

- **56 Kbps modems:** These modems are the utmost in analog modem technology, because manufacturers say that you can just about double your speeds from a 33.6 Kbps modem. In reality, the name is a slight misnomer, because FCC regulations force manufacturers to make these modems operate at a slightly lower ultimate speed (about 53 Kbps). 56K modems reach this high speed only in one direction — the downstream flow from your Internet service provider (ISP) to you. The upstream speed — from your computer to the Internet — is limited to 33.6 Kbps, the same as standard 33.6 Kbps modems. There's actually quite a bit to know about 56K modems, so we suggest that you take a look at the sidebar "What's up with 56K modems?" to get all the details.

Besides speed, modems can also be differentiated by their *form* factor — what they look like and how they connect to your PC. Analog modems come in three basic forms:

- ✔ **External modems:** Freestanding devices that connect to your computer's modem serial port (often called the *COM* port).

- ✔ **Internal modems:** These devices plug into an internal slot inside your PC.

- ✔ **PC Card modems:** Roughly credit-card-sized, these modems (which adhere to the PC Card, or PCMCIA — Personal Computer Modular Card Interface Adapter — standard), slide into the corresponding PC Card slot found on most notebook computers and some handheld computer devices as well.

You may also encounter modems that expand upon the basic computer-to-computer data communications function and add extra features. For example, many modems also contain circuitry that enables them — with some corresponding software on your PC — to act as fax machines. With a fax modem, you can send just about any document on your PC's hard drive to remote fax machines, and you can also receive incoming fax messages, which you can view on your screen or print out.

Other additional features often found on analog modems include:

- ✔ **Speakerphone.** A few modems come with speakerphone software that let you use your PC (with microphone and speakers) as a hands-free phone.

- ✔ **Voice mail.** Using your PC's hard drive to store messages, modems with voice mail software can handle any calls that come in when you're away (or just don't feel like answering the phone).

You can get digital Internet connections from your telephone company in a couple of different ways. ISDN, or Integrated Services Digital Network, is currently the most commonly available. It's kind of expensive — depending upon where you are and who your phone company is. ISDN can cost you anywhere from twice to ten times as much as regular analog POTS — that's POTS as in *plain old telephone service,* which really is the term the industry uses to describe it. And ISDN is not all that much faster than POTS; for example, the fastest analog POTS modems top out at around 56 Kbps — a little slower in the real world — while the fastest ISDN service available to consumers is only 128 Kbps. We think that ISDN may soon be superseded by newer services, such as xDSL, described later in this chapter.

What's up with 56K modems?

Although they've been on the market for over a year as we write this, 56K modems haven't yet taken consumers by storm. In fact, most manufacturers have found their 56K modem sales rather disappointing. Three major reasons account for this slow market:

✔ **Warring standards:** Until recently, two competing and incompatible standards have been slugging it out for the hearts and pocketbooks of 56K modem users. U.S. Robotics has been offering 56K modems using a protocol called *X2*. Competitors have mostly been offering 56K modems that adhere to a different protocol known as *56KFlex*. These protocols don't work together, so if you buy an X2 modem and your ISP decides to use 56KFlex technology — or vice versa — your modem and your ISP won't connect with each other. The good news is that manufacturers have called a truce and agreed upon a new international standard for 56K modems — known as V.90. Modems using this standard are now available in stores and catalogs, and ISPs are switching their network equipment over to the new V.90 standard.

✔ **One-directional:** The 56 Kbps speed only works in one direction — downstream from your ISP to your computer. These modems can achieve this high speed because most of the telephone network (except for the section connecting your home to the local switching office) is fully digital. So if your ISP is connected to the telephone network by a digital line — and most are — these modems can receive incoming data at a higher speed. Data coming from an analog telephone connection, however, like the data leaving your computer, is limited to a 33.6 Kbps speed limit.

✔ **Questionable speed increase:** 56 Kbps is more of a theoretical limit than a speed you'll see in real life. 56K modems have proven to be susceptible to vagaries in telephone line quality. Most testing and real-world experience have demonstrated that the maximum downstream speeds of 56K modems are often only in the high 30 to low 40 Kbps range.

Despite these shortcomings, we think that 56K modems will eventually become ubiquitous. They don't really cost much more than 33.6 Kbps modems, and even if they aren't as fast as their name implies, they do offer an appreciable increase in speed over today's 33.6 Kbps models.

 Even if your phone company provides ISDN service, you may not be able to use it with the ISP of your choice — not all ISPs offer the service. If you have a preference among ISPs, make sure that the one you like offers ISDN connections before ordering an ISDN line from your phone company.

Figure 13-2 shows how an ISDN modem connects to the Internet.

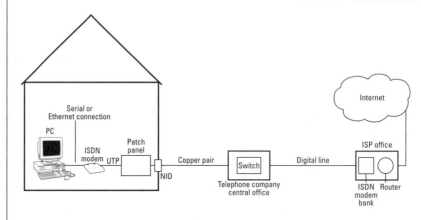

Figure 13-2:
An ISDN
Internet
connection.

In many areas today, ISDN is the best you can get. And it does have some big advantages over POTS. For example:

✔ ISDN is divided into two main channels (called *bearer* or *B* channels) that you can use for simultaneous voice, fax, or data calls — so one ISDN line basically equals two POTS lines.

✔ Your computer's ISDN modem can bond the two channels together as a single "virtual connection," giving you twice as much bandwidth. It can usually do this dynamically, so you get the extra bandwidth when you need it, but you can easily drop one of the data connections if you need a channel for a phone or fax call.

✔ ISDN uses a third, smaller channel (the *D*, or *data*, channel) to send the signals that control calls instead of stuffing them into the main channels. This setup gives you much quicker and more sophisticated call controls and saves all the available main channel bandwidth for your voice or data. The D channel can also be used for other interesting things. For example, some service providers are beginning to use the D channel as an "always on" connection that can transfer moderate amounts of data — like notifications of new e-mail. These D channel services can even automatically connect one or both of your B channels to your service provider if you have a big file to download. Pretty neat stuff.

D channels to the rescue

Although not all service providers are using it yet, the D channel of an ISDN connection has the potential to offer some pretty neat services. Unlike the B channel, which requires the computer to dial into an ISP for a connection every time you use it, the D channel is packet-switched. This means that your D channel is always on and able to send and receive packets (basically small chunks of data) all the time, without having to establish a connection.

The D channel doesn't have as much bandwidth capacity as the B channels do — about 16,000 bps versus 64,000 bps for each of the B channels — but it's perfectly capable of transmitting smaller chunks of data. The really neat part is that, with the proper software and hardware on both ends of the call, the D channel can tell when a large data file needs to be transmitted and then automatically fire up one or both of the B channels to transmit the data quickly.

So the D channel can allow you to maintain a full-time connection to an Internet service provider or to your company's corporate network without having to pay per-minute charges when you're not actually sending or receiving a lot of data.

For most folks, ISDN services come to your house over the same kind of copper wires as do analog telephone services — although the wires sometimes need to be specially conditioned (in other words, they need to be of a certain minimum level of quality) to carry ISDN signals. The telephone company takes care of that conditioning when it installs your ISDN service.

For more details and technical information related to ISDN, see Chapter 12.

xDSL

Digital subscriber line, or DSL, is an emerging way of sending data over the existing copper telephone lines that offers a quantum leap in bandwidth. Various DSL technologies are being developed, which is why we usually refer to DSL technologies as *xDSL,* with the *x* representing a range of other letters, like *A* for *asymmetrical.*

Digital subscriber lines — ADSL in particular — were initially developed as a way for telephone companies to compete with cable television providers — the high downstream speed is capable of carrying lots of digital television programming. In fact, just a year or two ago most of the major telephone companies had large divisions and joint ventures in place to jump into the cable TV market. This plan never really worked out for them, though — the trials of such services weren't such great successes that cable TV seemed like a profitable direction for these companies to move in.

But then the Internet became popular, and there was finally a new need for providing this kind of bandwidth to the home.

xDSL modems use the same single copper wire pair that POTS and ISDN services do, but their sophisticated Digital Signal Processors (DSPs) are able to make use of a whole lot more of the frequency spectrum, giving them greater bandwidth capabilities. The frequencies that xDSL devices do use are generally much higher than those used for carrying POTS phone calls, so there is no interference between the two. You can literally pick up the phone in the middle of an xDSL connection and make a phone call simultaneously without a problem.

Table 13-1 shows some of the many flavors of xDSL.

Table 13-1	Types of DSL Technology	
DSL Technology	*Downstream Speed*	*Upstream Speed*
ADSL	Up to 8 Mbps	Up to 1.2 Mbps
HDSL	2.4 Mbps	2.4 Mbps
VDSL	56 Mbps	8 Mbps
RADSL	Up to 8 Mbps	Up to 1.2 Mbps
IDSL	144 Kbps	144 Kbps

Note: Downstream speed is the speed at which data is sent to you from your service provider, while upstream speed measures the data heading back the other way.

Different service providers are beginning to offer xDSL services using just about all of the technologies shown in Table 13-1. Exactly which flavor you get isn't really important. Even though each has its own bandwidth capabilities, all are so far above what's generally available now that a bit of speed here or there won't make much difference.

Services driven by ADSL technology have the disadvantage of being *asymmetric,* which means that the upstream and downstream speeds are different. The problem with asymmetric bandwidth is that some symmetric applications that send large quantities of data both ways, such as videoconferencing (you want to see them as much as they see you!), can't take advantage of the maximum speeds available. If you have 1.5 Mbps downstream but only 64 Kbps upstream, symmetric applications run at 64 Kbps down and 64 Kbps up.

Fortunately, most applications for the Internet are very asymmetric — your request to view a page is very small, typically just the address of the page on the World Wide Web, but the page downloaded is usually quite packed with data. Most home users are incredibly happy with even 768 Kbps upstream speeds (six times faster than ISDN), and the majority of home users tend to utilize much more downstream bandwidth anyway (for things like Web browsing and downloading files).

Regardless of which xDSL variant your service provider offers, the interface is similar. The xDSL service enters your home via a standard copper telephone line that carries your POTS traffic. In order to extract the high speed xDSL data, you need an xDSL modem. Generally, you'll find two variants of these:

- ✔ **External xDSL modem:** This device looks and acts just like a souped-up version of the analog modem that you are probably familiar with, but it doesn't plug into the modem serial port (the COM port) on the back of your computer. Those modem serial ports are just too darned slow to handle the kind of speed that xDSL gives you. Instead, an xDSL modem typically has an Ethernet (10BaseT) connection running to your computer and an Ethernet Network Interface Card (NIC) inside your computer. Some modems use the faster *asynchronous transfer mode* (ATM) protocol instead of Ethernet. In these cases, the telephone company generally provides the ATM NIC card as part of the service.

- ✔ **Internal xDSL modem:** Just like an internal analog modem, this one actually plugs into a slot inside your PC — an ISA or PCI bus slot for desktop computers or a PC card for laptops. Because these internal buses are much faster than the serial port that connects standard modems, you don't need an Ethernet interface.

To split, or not to split? That is the question. . . .

You may run into another interface variation if you're lucky enough to get xDSL service into your home. Most xDSL systems use a device called a *POTS splitter* to separate the high-frequency xDSL data signals that your computer uses from the lower-frequency POTS signals that your telephone uses. The splitter helps to reduce any potential interference between data and voice calls over your phone line. Unfortunately, it also adds a bit of expense and complication to your xDSL installation, because you need to pay for and install the POTS splitter and then run a new telephone wire from the splitter to your xDSL modem.

The newest variations of xDSL, particularly one known as xDSL.Lite or Universal ADSL, are designed from the start to dispense with the POTS splitter. This makes installation cheaper and easier (just plug the modem into any phone jack in your house), but it does come at a price — splitterless xDSL systems are often a bit slower than other variants of xDSL (most max out at around 786 Kbps). Don't get too upset about this fact, though — they're still a heck of a lot faster than analog modems and ISDN.

Like the external versus internal modem decision, the choice of splitterless or conventional xDSL is probably going to be out of your hands. Your service provider offers one or the other, and in the short term at least, you probably still want to be the first on your block to get it.

For the time being, you probably don't have too much choice as to which kind of xDSL modem you can use. Like cable television set-top boxes and unlike regular modems, xDSL modems are expensive and aren't something you can run down to Joe-Bob's Electronics to buy. Instead, the service provider leases or loans you the modem as part of your monthly fee — and takes it back when you cancel the service.

When it comes to planning your home network, xDSL services will play a major role down the road for the telcos and therefore should have a major influence on your planning. xDSL services will bring a lot of bandwidth into your home, bandwidth that is likely to be shared by a lot of applications. If your spouse is watching TV in the living room, you are working in your office in the basement, and the kids are playing online games in their rooms, you all may be using the same xDSL link.

One of the neat things about an xDSL line is that you are always connected to the network, 24 hours a day. If you leave your computer on the whole time, all sorts of things are made possible. For instance, you can receive automatic software downloads while you are asleep. Or you can receive phone calls on your PC via Internet telephony. Or you can have all the major newspapers downloaded to your PC for when you wake up. An xDSL line turns a historically reactive relationship with the telecommunications networks into a proactive one.

If you want to find out even more about xDSL, check out TeleChoice, Inc.'s Web site at www.xdsl.com.

Cable modems

Cable television providers are in a frenzy to provide additional services (and charge you for them, of course) beyond just television. First and foremost among these services, for most cable companies, is cable-modem Internet access. A cable modem is basically a very fast modem that connects to the cable company. It can transmit at up to 30 Mbps and connect to your computer via an Ethernet connection. Like the xDSL modems we talk about in the preceding section, you generally don't buy a cable modem but rather rent it as part of the service, just like your cable set-top box. The services are typically priced in the $50 or so range for monthly service.

Why are cable modems so hot?

Cable companies are well positioned to offer cable modems, the leading-edge Internet service, for several reasons:

✔ They have plenty of money to make the investments necessary to provide more services — especially if these investments allow them to make even more money.

✔ They have a high-speed network already. Most cable television networks consist of super-high-capacity fiber-optic cable running from the central offices to local distribution points and — even more importantly — coaxial cable running from these distribution points to your home. Coaxial cable can carry a lot of data — a heck of a lot more, in most cases, than the copper wiring that connects telephone companies to your home.

✔ They have a very important booster: Microsoft, which has invested billions of dollars into the industry in an effort to move things along. In addition to Microsoft itself, Paul Allen, one of the co-founders of Microsoft, has spent a few billion dollars of his own nest egg to buy up some cable companies and turn them into providers of Net access and other advanced services.

Although many independent cable television companies are going it alone and working to offer their own versions of cable-modem services, two main brands rule for now:

✔ **@Home Networks:** @Home is actually not a cable provider at all but rather an independent network and Internet service provider that offers cable-modem services through a whole bunch of different cable companies. Many of the largest cable companies, like TCI, are or will soon be offering @Home services. You can find out whether your area is in @Home territory by checking out the @Home Web site at www.home.net.

✔ **RoadRunner:** Time Warner, one of the largest cable television providers, is offering its own service called RoadRunner. In some parts of the country — mainly in the Northeast — the local service provider is called MediaOne. Roadrunner and MediaOne are merging all of their operations, but for now, the MediaOne name remains. You can find out whether RoadRunner is available in your area at www.rrunner.com.

Regardless of your service provider, cable modems fit into one of two categories:

✔ **Telco-return modems:** These modems are used in less sophisticated cable systems and are generally much less desirable. The one-way modem receives data at high speeds over your cable system's coaxial cable, but any upstream (outgoing) data uses a standard analog telephone modem — so you send data as slowly as you would with a conventional analog modem (plus you tie up your telephone line whenever you are online). These modems are okay for e-mail and surfing Web sites, but their extremely asymmetric nature makes them less than perfect for all the neat new things you can do on the Net — like video-conferencing, Internet telephony, and online gaming.

✔ **Two-way modems:** These are the modems you hope that your service provider uses (and the big ones, like @Home and RoadRunner, do). Two-way modems both send and receive data over the coaxial cable and typically offer high speed both ways (although the reception is often still faster than the upstream data rate — the upstream is usually limited to about 1 Mbps, while the downstream is closer to 10 Mbps).

Some cable modems are internal devices (which plug into an ISA or PCI bus slot inside your PC), but most that we have seen are external, stand-alone boxes. The cable system's coaxial cable connects to the modem, and the modem connects to your computer (or your computer LAN) via a standard Ethernet 10BaseT connection (which we talk about in more detail in Chapter 15). If you don't have an Ethernet card in your PC already (and many home PCs don't come with one standard), don't worry — they're cheap, and many cable-modem service providers give you one as part of the service package. Figure 13-3 shows how a cable modem connects to the Internet.

Getting access to cable-modem access

Making cable modems the method of Internet access of choice isn't an easy home run for the cable companies. Between their current situation and the ultimate goal of a full-service network lie a couple of big obstacles:

✔ Their networks are fast, but they were designed with one-way traffic in mind — not the two-way traffic that is required for Internet access and remote connectivity to other networks.

✔ Despite their deep pocketbooks, some cable companies are wary of investing too much money in cable-modem technologies — particularly because consumers don't seem willing to add very much to their monthly bill to get the additional services.

✔ Unlike telephone-company connections, cable-modem connections make you share the bandwidth with other users in your local area. So even though the maximum speed can be pretty high, heavy usage among your neighbors can slow things down to a crawl. (Your best plan with a cable-modem is to get one and then tell everyone in the neighborhood it doesn't work.)

Oh yeah, one other "gotcha": People don't like their cable companies very much. Remember the movie *The Cable Guy*? Did it hit a nerve? Well, cable companies are working very hard to improve their image — and they may need to before people open their wallets up for additional services.

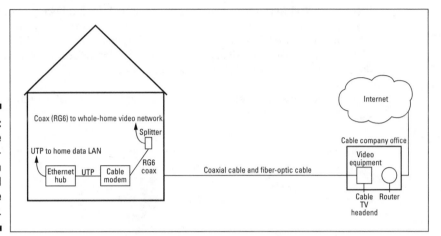

Figure 13-3:
How a cable
modem con-
nects a
home LAN
to the
Internet.

DirecPC dishes

No doubt you are familiar with the Digital Satellite System (DSS) TV system, which we describe back in Chapter 5. Hughes Electronics, the company that built the DSS system, has also developed a satellite Internet access system called DirecPC. DirecPC uses a 21-inch dish, slightly larger than but similar to the one used by DSS, to receive high-speed Internet data from the satellite and then transfers that data to your computer via an internal card in your PC (which is included in the package with the dish). With DirecPC, you can receive Internet data at up to 400 Kbps — over three times faster than ISDN and more than six times faster than the fastest analog modems. There are a couple of catches to DirecPC, however:

- The satellite connection is one-way only. The system uses an analog modem for any data going upstream (from your computer to the Internet), so you can send data at a maximum speed of only 33.6 Kbps.

- It doesn't work with your laptop computer — the special internal card used to receive the satellite data doesn't fit inside a laptop.

- You need to have a Windows 95/98 or NT computer — Macintoshes and PCs using Windows 3.11 or OS/2 need not apply.

Despite these disadvantages, DirecPC has one big advantage over most competing high-speed Internet access systems — you can use it just about anywhere in North America, something that can't be said about cable modems or xDSL. DirecPC also offers similar services in Europe and in Japan.

If you want to have both DirecPC and satellite TV from DSS, you can do so without having two dishes on your roof. Hughes has recently introduced a system called the DirecDuo. This slightly larger dish (about 21 inches, versus 18 inches for a DirecTV dish) can pick up the signals from both systems and feed them to both your PC and your televisions.

Figure 13-4 shows a satellite connection that uses a regular modem to send data out to the Internet.

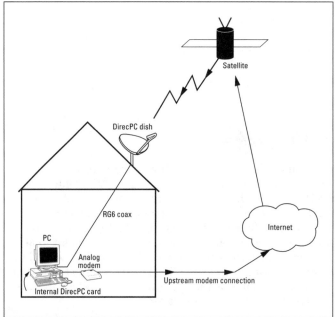

Figure 13-4:
A satellite
Internet
connection
via DirecPC.

Wireless Internet connections

While the telephone and cable television companies slowly develop and build network connections to bring data into your home at high speeds, a whole host of companies are working on ways to do the same thing without wires.

Traditionally, most of us equate *wireless* with *portable* — and indeed many wireless services companies are emphasizing this benefit of using wireless technologies.

Increasingly, however, service providers are looking toward wireless technologies as a way of quickly and cheaply providing data and telephone services to a fixed location — like your house. New advances in wireless technology are rapidly bringing down the costs of the network equipment like transmitters and receivers, and setting up a wireless service is usually pretty quick. Instead of digging trenches or putting up utility poles and running wires, wireless providers need only to put up an antenna and then provide one for each of their customers.

Many different wireless services are already available to consumers — some familiar, some not. In the next sections, we tell you about some that you may already know about and some that you may want to keep an eye out for in the near future.

Metricom

Metricom is a relatively new company that is working to develop a low-cost wireless network for Internet access. The Metricom system consists of a bunch of small, inexpensive transceivers set up on phone poles and rooftops throughout the service area. These transceivers communicate with another, even smaller transceiver that you can buy or lease when you order the service.

You can get either a fixed model, which you set up next to your desktop computer and plug into the modem port, or a portable model that attaches to your laptop via a PC card. The speed isn't blazingly fast yet — about the same as a 28.8 Kbps modem — but it may increase in the future as the network is upgraded.

Metricom service is mainly offered as an alternative to installing a second telephone line for your Internet access. The monthly price of the Metricom service is roughly the same as the combined prices of a second phone line from your telephone company and the monthly fees of an Internet service provider. Service areas are limited right now — Metricom is available in some cities on the West Coast and in Washington, D.C. — but the company plans to expand its service areas rapidly. You can keep track of availability on the company's Web site at www.metricom.com.

Warp Networks

Like Metricom, Warp Networks is a young, start-up company dedicated to offering wireless data and Internet connections. Warp's services aren't aimed at the low-cost, low-bandwidth audience served by Metricom, however. Instead, Warp plans to use unused broadcast television channels to offer data services at ISDN and higher speeds.

The initial offerings are limited to one-way service; you have to complement your inbound Warp service with a modem and phone line to send data out from your computer. But the longer-term plan is to offer high-speed, two-way services to your computer — or computer LAN — through a transceiver and antenna mounted outside your home. We're not sure how soon these services will be available, or how much they'll cost, but one of the target markets is the residential user. You can keep track of Warp Network's progress at its Web site, www.warpdrive.net.

LMDS

LMDS, or Local Multipoint Distribution Service, is a next-generation wireless data system aimed at providing tons of bandwidth to the home. You can't get it yet — it's that next-generation! In fact, LMDS will work over a group of frequencies (the 24 GHz band) that no one has had permission to use until very recently. In the past six months, the FCC conducted an auction to sell the rights to transmit these frequencies, and a whole bunch of people took the FCC up on the offer — to the tune of hundreds of millions of dollars.

Actually, we lied just a second ago — people do use the 24 GHz frequency spectrum, but they use it for different things, like communicating with satellites. And, in fact, one licensed LMDS company is actually offering service right now — in New York City, a company is using LMDS to provide a wireless cable television service.

In a nutshell, LMDS systems use an array of transceivers and antennas located throughout a service area to send and receive a high-frequency, high-bandwidth two-way signal. These systems are *line-of-sight* — meaning that the radio waves don't follow the curvature of the earth like television or radio broadcasts, so two antennas must physically see each other to communicate. This line-of-sight limitation is why LMDS is a *multipoint* system — instead of one central antenna serving a community, several antennas are spread throughout the region, each serving customers within a smaller cell (sort of like a cellular phone system).

For a homeowner, an LMDS system consists of a rooftop antenna and transceiver, a converter box (called a *downconverter*) to translate the LMDS signals into ones usable by your household equipment, and finally a Network Interface Unit (NIU), which you would use to physically connect the LMDS signal to your home's networks.

An LMDS service could conceivably connect to your home network in several different places. That's because the FCC, although controlling and auctioning the radio frequency spectrum for the service, is not forcing potential service providers to commit to sending one thing or another. LMDS could be used, for example, to provide wireless cable television services, or high-speed, multi-megabit Internet access, or local telephone service. Conceivably, it could offer you all three over the same radio connection.

Power companies

We know what you're thinking right now. "Power companies? What the heck do they have to do with the Internet, besides maybe having a Web site that tells me what to do when I have a gas leak?" (Incidentally, when you have a gas leak, run like heck.) Well, believe it or not, utility companies are trying to figure out how to jump on the Internet bandwagon themselves.

Okay, LMDS I understand, but what the heck is MMDS?

MMDS, or Multipoint Multichannel Distribution Service, is an older sibling of LMDS. This chunk of the frequency spectrum was originally allocated by the FCC for business use, but over time the primary use has migrated toward the consumer marketplace. Specifically, MMDS is being used by wireless cable television providers to provide an alternative to traditional cable and broadcast television.

While most wireless cable offerings to date have been from independent service providers, several major telephone companies (like Bell Atlantic, NYNEX, and Pacific Bell) have been making plans to use MMDS systems to provide their own cable television service. With these larger, richer players joining the fray, MMDS is changing from an analog service, providing about 33 television channels, to a digital service. Digital MMDS uses MPEG compression (like many of the DBS satellite television services we mention in Chapter 5) to provide up to 100 channels. In the longer term, Digital MMDS services may also offer two-way communications, providing services like Interactive TV and Internet access.

Just like telephone companies with xDSL technologies, cable television companies with cable modems, and wireless companies with some of the new services they're planning to offer (as we describe earlier in this chapter), utility companies want to offer you high-speed Internet access to go along with their traditional services.

Why are power companies a good candidate to jump into a business they don't have any experience in? They have a few things in their favor, actually:

- ✔ **An existing communications backbone:** You'd probably be surprised at what a complex and sophisticated communications network these companies already have — hundreds of miles of fiber-optic cable, copper wire, and wireless systems are already in place and online for these companies' internal use. The smarter ones thought ahead and laid down extra capacity while building out their own networks, so they have much of the infrastructure in place and ready to go.

- ✔ **Rights of way:** If you were to try to build your own communications network, one of the biggest problems you'd run into is getting the so-called *rights of way* to lay your fibers and cable across literally hundreds of miles of private and public property. Even wireless providers run into this problem when they try to put up antennas (seems the neighbors like having the phones, but they hate seeing all those working parts). The power companies already have these rights of way for their electrical lines — removing a big barrier of entry for them.

✔ **Ubiquity:** Think it's rare to find a home without a cable television connection or at least a telephone line? It is, but it's even rarer to find one that's not connected to electrical power. You'd have to go far out into the backwoods to find one, and even then, chances are good that those households don't have power because they don't want it — back-to-nature types, you know.

Power companies can provide high-bandwidth communications services to you in two ways:

✔ They can use their rights of way to run new wiring to your home from their network. This option isn't necessarily very cheap, depending upon how far their network access points are from their customers' homes, but it is a possibility.

✔ They can devise ways to use the existing electrical power line to also carry broadband data and communications signals into the home. If they can do this — and already some big power companies and communications equipment vendors say they can — then all they have to do is install some sort of box in your home that splits the data out from the power. The data is then sent off to your telephones, computers, and whatever else needs it in your home network. This is a pretty neat idea, and something that you may be seeing in the not-so-distant future.

Note: The first trials of this technology are being tested outside of the U.S. because of differences in how the electrical-power distribution networks are designed. Basically, the first systems being tested use a converter box at each transformer in the power network to connect the fiber-optic backbone to the power line. In the U.S., compared to Europe and Asia, fewer customers are served by each individual transformer in the network, which means that many more of these (expensive) converters would be needed. At the present pricing levels for this state-of-the-art, experimental equipment, it would just be too expensive to install here. We do think, however, that the almost inevitable increases in computer chip power, and corresponding decreases in prices, will soon make this idea an economically viable solution in the U.S. as well.

We want to point out a recurring theme here. Many different companies have sophisticated, high-speed communications networks in place right now (cable, telephone, and power utilities), but none yet have a really widespread, high-speed, two-way means of connecting your home to these networks. While it would be nice if they would all get out their backhoes and work crews to upgrade this *last mile* connection, the procedure is expensive. So most of the companies are looking at ways to reuse their existing connections in new and bandwidth-rich ways.

Chapter 14

Designing a Data LAN for Your Home

. . . .

. . . .

*I*n a simple form, a home computer network can consist of a single computer connected to the Internet or to another external network (like your office) by a modem. A network can also be two stand-alone PCs that share a printer with a simple A/B switchbox. We strongly encourage you to think beyond these examples, though.

As the number (and type) of computers in the home increases, and the price continues to decrease, consider installing (or at least preparing your home's wiring for) a full-fledged computer *local area network (LAN)* in your home to allow your computers to quickly share access to the same resources.

A home LAN provides a high-speed data connection between all the computers in your home, allowing them to do things like share files with each other, share networked peripherals (like printers), and even play networked games. Multiple computers can more easily share high-speed Internet access devices, like DSL or cable modems, over a home computer LAN.

In this chapter, we discuss some of the basics of computer LANs and discuss some of the alternative ways to set up a LAN in your home. We also talk about some of the difficulties you may encounter when you try to connect several networked computers to your Internet account at the same time.

Flipping the Wired or Wireless Coin

The first step in choosing a LAN technology for your home is to decide whether you should go with a wired or wireless solution. If you've perused other sections of this book already, you know that we usually spend most of our time talking about wired solutions, but in the case of data networks, there has been an explosion of "no new wires" networking systems. So we want to give you our opinion on the matter right up front.

Here's our take on the issue: If you're building a new home or undertaking a major remodeling of an older home, and if you have the walls open, then by all means choose the wired alternative.

Although we think that putting the right kinds of wires and cables into the right part of your home is the best solution to creating flexible and future-proofed home-networking solutions, we do live in the real world. And in the real world, you may not be able to get the necessary cabling systems installed in your home for a number of reasons, including the following:

- ✔ You rent your home.
- ✔ You live in a condominium and can't easily access shared walls/attics/basement spaces.
- ✔ You live in a historic home and have to run any changes past the planning commission.
- ✔ Your home has design problems — no crawl space, basement, or attic in which to hide wires, for instance — that keep you from easily running cables.

Whatever the reason, you may not be able to squeeze those fat CAT-5 and coaxial lines through the walls in your home. Luckily, you have some options: You can use wireless systems to do the job, or you can use the phone and electric power wires that are already in your walls. We discuss both of these alternatives in the Chapter 15.

With a few exceptions (notably telephones), most wireless systems for the home are still in the early stages of development, which means several things to you:

- ✔ **You may be unable to get what you want:** Most inexpensive wireless LAN products (see Chapter 15) have limited bandwidth and are not full 10 Mbps Ethernet today.
- ✔ **You may end up paying more:** Many of the available higher-speed wireless products are still expensive. In fact, many are really designed for business use and aren't priced at the consumer level yet.

✔ **You may not get the best product available:** The industry is still in a bit of turmoil figuring out the best wireless approach for home LANs.

✔ **You may not like the way the wireless options work:** Wireless technologies may not work as well as their wired counterparts — remember how poorly many of the early cordless telephones worked?

So if you want to go wireless in your home networks, you're going to have to pay more to get less, if you can get it at all. Still, wireless technologies already have a multitude of uses, and many smart companies are working on ways to make wireless systems cheaper, faster, and better for the home. Just remember that these technologies aren't yet mature, although they offer great prospects for the future. Both wireless and wireline data solutions can work in your home — a coexistence that can be really neat in practice.

The impact that choosing all wireless options — phone, data, audio, video, and so on — has on your home is unclear. We can tell you that many wireless technologies compete for the same spectrum in your home, though. These wireless systems are going to start interfering with one another at a certain point, so be careful about picking wireless as the catch-all for your home network.

Running Cables Here, There, and Everywhere

In Chapter 15, we spend a bit of time discussing the various methods that you can use to create LAN connections throughout your house. In this section, we want you to think about where you may want to place these network connections in your home.

Bedrooms

You may not consider bedrooms as prime locations for computer LAN outlets, but you probably should. With a bedroom outlet, you can work from your bed by plugging a laptop into the network, for example. You may also want a network outlet near the bedroom TV that allows you to connect future generations of WebTV or similar products into your LAN for some TV-based Web surfing.

Current generations of WebTV products aren't particularly networkable, but you can bet the mortgage that future versions will be.

The master bedroom isn't the only place to consider providing LAN connection points. Your kids are probably already hogging time on your PC, but with PC prices plummeting to new lows, getting the kids their own computers and connecting them to a home network is beginning to make sense.

You should also think long term here: Today's nursery is tomorrow's teenage room, and maybe — when you finally get the kids off to college — a home office someday. Or your guest room may be hosting one of your computer-geek relatives, who just can't leave home without his or her laptop. Having those rooms LAN-ready just makes sense.

Living room

Computers in the living room? Probably not in most homes, especially if you limit your concept of computers to PCs (although Pat is trying really hard to convince his wife that they need a tangerine iMac next to the living-room sofa). New devices are coming to market, however, that require LAN connections *and* fit into the living room. Leading the way is WebTV — the set-top box that lets you surf the Internet. But also think about screen phones or Internet appliances that let you read e-mail or shop on e-commerce Web sites. (We talk about some of this neat gear in Chapters 10 and 12.) Eventually, you'll probably want to access this stuff from your recliner.

You'll probably find that the first generations of information appliances are not networkable — they tend to have built-in modems rather than network ports — but as home LANs become more popular, we can guarantee you that they will be.

Home office

You obviously want to have a LAN connection in your home office. However, we suggest that you think of your home office not in terms of whether or not to include LAN connection points, but in terms of how many and where. Consider providing at least two or three network outlets in your home office — enough to support two computers and a networkable printer.

What's great about Ethernet hubs is that you can cascade them throughout your house if you run out of ports on your central hub. Say you are using all your ports to run to different rooms, but your kids want four Ethernet ports in their room instead of the two you provided. No problem: Connect your Ethernet's uplink port to the wall outlet, and the other ports are available for that room's networking — and everyone can still communicate with everyone else on the home LAN.

Home theater

You should consider including your home theater in your LAN plans for a couple of reasons. First, you may want to have some sort of TV set-top box or Internet appliance devices that we mention in the previous section, so you can take a break from movies and surf the Web on your widescreen tube. Or, you may want to install a regular PC in your home theater for Web surfing, keeping track of your movie inventory, or even for feeding streaming media (like RealAudio broadcasts) from the Web into your audio or video systems.

A future reason to make your home theater LAN-ready is the rapid melding of TVs and PCs. Compaq, Gateway, and Philips have all begun to offer PC/TV combination devices that perform both of these functions in a single unit. Forthcoming digital television will have even more computing horsepower built in, and having a way to connect to your home's data LAN nearby sure seems to make sense to us.

Kitchen

We think that having some sort of Net-connected computer device, whether a full-fledged PC or something scaled down (such as the Internet refrigerator or Internet microwave), is going to be a great way to do a whole host of kitchen tasks. Imagine accessing your network's recipe database CD-ROM from an inexpensive PC on your kitchen counter, placing your grocery order at online stores like NetGrocer (www.netgrocer.com) or Peapod (www.peapod.com) while standing next to your empty fridge, or quickly ordering your favorite pizza when you don't feel like cooking.

Some day, your kitchen appliances will use IP to send information about themselves to repair facilities and possibly to your home-automation system *(Warning! The freezer is malfunctioning!)*. Unfortunately, right now, no one yet knows how these appliances will connect to the Internet. Chances are good that they won't use the CAT-5 UTP cable that you use to connect PCs to the Internet. At this point, you shouldn't try to wire for these future needs, but having an IP connection in the kitchen (for use with a PC or Internet-browsing appliance) may allow you to connect some flavor of appliance hub to the Internet down the road. It's too soon to tell.

Other places

Where else in the home should you extend your data network? Well, personally speaking, we're big proponents of including data cabling in just about every room in the house.

Toiletly serious business

In Japan — where people evidently take certain elements of the bathroom a bit more seriously than we Americans do — high-tech toilets are all the rage. Besides stuff like heated seats and other luxury items, they actually have . . . er . . . facilities that perform medical evaluations of the . . . umm . . . contents of the toilet.

Look at the Zoë by TOTO USA, Inc. (www. totousa.com), which has an optional warm seat feature and built-in catalyzed-disk fan that freshens the air (activated by sitting down).

Also, by pressing a button on the Zoë remote control, which looks like a Nintendo control pad, you are "bathed in a gentle, aerated warm water stream." Ohhhh-kay.

We wouldn't be surprised to see this kind of thing become more common. The next step is a Net-connected toilet that can give reports to your healthcare provider (yes — really). Frankly, if these catch on in the U.S., we have no clue how you'd network them in. We'll leave that to the second edition of this book.

We're not going to give you any specific recommendations for network connections in other places in your home. Instead, we challenge you to spend a bit of time thinking about the long-term uses of each part of your home. For example, do you hope to one day finish your attic or basement? If so, you may as well get the wire there ahead of time.

Some of the wireless or existing wire (telephone or electrical) networking solutions that we discuss in Chapter 15 can also be good ways of extending a network to unexpected places. Most of these products allow you to interface with an existing wired network and get the connection to places that you just never anticipated during your planning process.

Migrating Your Computer Flock to the Net

Coming up with a general design of your home computer LAN is the first step, admittedly a big step, forward on this long march. A home LAN helps you get all of your computers onto the Internet and certainly makes your computing life easier and more fun.

Unfortunately, most consumer Internet accounts are designed and packaged, technologically speaking, to allow a single computer to attach to the Net. In other words, when you log onto your modem- or ISDN-based Internet account — which is the way that ninety-plus percent of households connect — your computer communicates with your ISP's server and is assigned a single *IP address*. (The IP address is how the Internet knows what information you've asked for and received — kinda' like your mailing address for data.)

A single IP address works fine when the modem is connected to a single computer — you don't need or want more than one IP address in this case. When you're trying to serve several computers with that Internet connection at the same time, however, you need some way to separate all those different requests so that the data doesn't get jumbled together. To solve this problem, you can choose a router, which is a hardware solution, or a proxy server, which is a software solution.

Understanding routers

If you were to go into the very dark recesses of your office's telecommunications and data center, you'd probably find several weird-looking devices mounted on racks and shelves. One of these devices is most likely a router.

A *router* is the piece of equipment that consolidates all of the Internet traffic coming in and out of your office's LAN and sends it to the appropriate computers within the public network. A router performs this bit of Net magic by looking at the *IP headers* within each packet of data and deciphering the data's ultimate destination within the network. (In case you were wondering, IP headers are specially formatted chunks of data attached to each and every packet of data sent over the Internet that identify the sender and intended recipient of the data — information which enables routers on the Internet to forward data to the right location.)

Some Internet connection methods — cable modems, for example — behave like *bridges,* which connect two separate networks together — such as your LAN and the Internet. So when you connect a cable modem to your LAN, your ISP can see the computers on your LAN and assign an IP address to them. This bridging sure makes things easier, because you don't have to worry about routing — the ISP does.

Setting up a router for a large network is a complicated procedure — another one of those reasons that IT workers in your office make such good salaries. Luckily, you can buy routers designed for small home networks — usually a modem and router in the same case — that are relatively easy to configure.

These *SOHO* (small office/home office) *routers* act as the interface between your modem (or ISDN) connection to your ISP and the rest of your home LAN, receiving all of the incoming Internet data and sending it to the correct machine on your network without any intervention from you. The first time you set up your router (or when you change the configuration of your network by adding or removing computers), you'll have to use some network management software to get things organized, but most of these routers have easy-to-understand wizard programs to lead you through this process step by step. Figure 14-1 shows how you would set up a SOHO router in a home-networking environment.

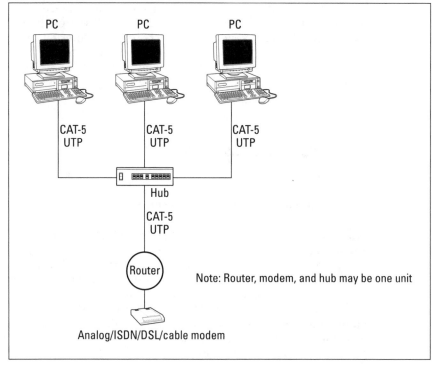

Figure 14-1:
Using a
router to
share a
modem
across the
network.

Several use your Internet browser as the software to configure the system. The configuration software is written as *HyperText Markup Language* (HTML) files — the language of Web pages. To set things up, you simply open up your Web browser software and open these files. All you need to do is fill in a few blanks, answer a few questions, and click a few buttons, and your router is ready to go.

SOHO routers range in price depending upon what kind of modem is included (if one is included at all) and how many computers they can work with. The cheapest models start at about $500. The major vendors of SOHO router and router/modem combos include the following:

- ✔ 3Com (www.3com.com)
- ✔ Cayman Systems (www.cayman.com)
- ✔ Cisco (www.cisco.com)
- ✔ Toshiba (www.toshiba.com)
- ✔ WebRamp (www.webramp.com)

Using your PC to route the packets

Routers are the hardware-based way of sharing an Internet connection. The software-based alternative is to install a *proxy server* program on one of your networked PCs. This program performs pretty much the same function as a router — that is, it distributes Internet data packets from a single connection to multiple PCs on a network.

In this scenario, you designate one of the PCs in your network (the one with the modem connected to it, generally) as the proxy server for the rest of the network. This proxy server PC collects all incoming and outgoing Internet traffic; the proxy-server software then determines which networked computer the data is intended for and sends it on its way. Figure 14-2 shows a typical proxy server setup for an Internet connection other than via an analog modem (this configuration requires two NICs in the proxy server).

Proxy-server software is usually pretty easy to set up, and the programs themselves are relatively inexpensive. The most popular software for home LAN users is made by a company called WinGate (`www.wingate.com`).

If your modem connects to your computer with an Ethernet interface, as do most DSL and cable modems, you actually need to install two separate Ethernet Network Interface Cards in your proxy server — one for the modem connection and one to connect the proxy server to the rest of your network.

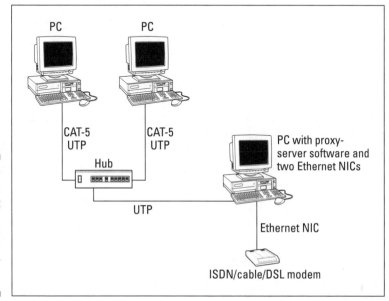

Figure 14-2:
Sharing an
Internet
connection
through
proxy-
server
software.

Luckily, most cable modems and many DSL modems give each computer on the network its own IP address without having to install a router or proxy server. The ISP does the routing at its end of the network connection, and the modem acts as a bridge.

Routing and bridging with data networks is a very complicated topic, and we've just touched on it here. As you get into your data networking plans, check out *Networking Home PCs For Dummies* — it'll help you figure out the next level of detail on this topic.

Chapter 15

Home LAN Hardware and Choices

· ·

· ·

As prices plummet and more members of your household find uses for a computer, chances are good that you will utilize several networked devices (in fact many people do already). What most people don't yet have but really need to take full advantage of the Internet, file sharing, and other computer technologies is a home computer network — a local area network, or LAN.

In this chapter, we tell you about the equipment used in a wired LAN, and how to have it installed in your house. We also tell you about products you can choose if running new wires for your data LAN isn't possible.

Home Networks of Choice (CAT-5 Data Networks)

The backbone of a computer network — regardless of what types of computers are connected to it or what kinds of network software are used to make it work — is the physical wiring and components that connect everything together. In this section, we discuss the common components of a wired computer LAN that uses a special type of copper cabling, Category 5 UTP (unshielded twisted pair).

Nearly all LAN technologies share a few basic building blocks:

✔ **Cables:** Cables usually provide the connection between networked devices. But in some cases, the physical connection doesn't take place via wires at all — many emerging LAN technologies make use of wireless communications techniques to get data around your home.

- ✔ **Network interface cards:** You must install these cards — called NICs (like the New York basketball team) — in each device that connects to the network. The NIC bridges the gap between the cables (or wireless devices) and the individual computers or other networked devices. NICs generally work with only one kind of network, such as an Ethernet card.

- ✔ **An access method — such as Ethernet:** *Ethernet* is a hardware specification that controls access to the network, allowing individual devices on the network to find and identify each other, and determines when each device can transmit and receive data.

Ethernet is the most common LAN for the home or small office (or in big business for that matter). The total bandwidth and the type of cable the network uses define different variations of Ethernet. For example, 10BaseT — the most common variation — transmits data at speeds up to 10 Mbps, and uses twisted-pair copper wires (the *T* in 10BaseT) as its physical media. (We discuss twisted pair in more detail in the section entitled "The cables" later in this chapter.)

Scores of Ethernet variations are available, but the only ones that you need to consider are the following:

- ✔ **10Base2:** 10 Mbps over coaxial cable

- ✔ **10BaseT:** 10 Mbps over twisted-pair cable

- ✔ **100BaseTX:** 100 Mbps over twisted-pair cable (two pairs of wire)

- ✔ **100BaseT4:** 100 Mbps over twisted-pair cable (four pairs of wire)

The first number in each of these names stands for the bandwidth of the cable in megabytes per second, so 10Base2 is a 10 Mbps connection. The last number or letter tells you the kind of cable that it goes over; for example, T means twisted pair.

The shortest Ethernet primer in computerdom

Ethernet — in its traditional form — is a "shared" network. That means that all of the computers and other connected, networked devices share the 10 (or 100) Mbps of bandwidth available on the network. Ethernet uses a protocol called *CSMA/CD (Carrier-Sense Multiple Access with Collision Detection)* to divide up access to the network. Basically, CSMA/CD means that all devices on the network listen for a free moment on the network before sending data. When the coast is clear, the data goes out. If two devices happen to pick the same exact moment to send their data a "collision" occurs. The devices then each wait a random amount of time to try to resend their data.

Some newer — and more expensive — versions of Ethernet are *switched.* These Ethernet networks use a sophisticated device — the switch, of course — to direct data throughout the network. Instead of sharing 10 or 100 Mbps, each device has that amount of bandwidth dedicated to it at all times.

LAN architecture options

Like the other networks we describe in this book, local area networks support different architectures. LANs are particularly flexible, however, in allowing you to mix and match architectures as you grow.

The two basic choices for how you model your LAN are the bus architecture and the star architecture. (If you've read other chapters in this book, you already know that we prefer the star architecture, hands down.)

The bus architecture for coaxial networks

Networks based upon coaxial cable (similar to the stuff that video networks use, as we discuss in Chapter 6) were the earliest Ethernet LANs; they are becoming less common as twisted-pair-based networks become the norm. These coaxial networks, however, do have the benefit of being the simplest, and lowest-cost, version of Ethernet. For example, in a 10Base2 network, the wiring topology (the way the wires are connected together) is very simple: Coaxial cable runs from station to station on the network, connecting to each individual device's NIC with a *T connector*, which sends the signals out one branch of the T to the device and out the other branch to the next computer in the network. A device called a *terminator* caps the T connectors on each end of the network.

This kind of network model — usually called a *bus* — is, in effect, all the same cable; each connected device is tapped off this common line. At each farthest end of the line, you need a terminator to tell the network to look no further for computers. Connecting the network is simple with this architecture, but its flexibility is limited. Adding new devices or moving existing ones is difficult, and these networks are more susceptible to breakdowns because problems with the cable anywhere in the network causes the entire network to malfunction. Kind of like those old-fashioned Christmas tree lights where the entire string goes dark if a single bulb burns out.

The star of the show

Twisted-pair Ethernet LANs use a network architecture called a *star*. In a star configuration, all the hardware connects to a central device called a *hub*. The hub transmits the data from each incoming cable to every other cable that attaches to the hub — and, therefore, to each device that attaches to the far end of those cables.

Using a star architecture (as shown in Figure 15-1) is a bit more complicated than the bus that coaxial Ethernet uses. A star architecture probably costs a little more, too, because of the additional lengths of cabling it requires and the cost of the hub (which is dropping by the minute — we've seen hubs for well under $50). However, this architecture greatly increases the network's reliability and flexibility.

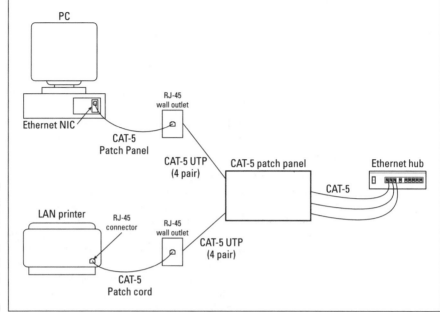

Figure 15-1:
A typical
10BaseT
network
with a
network
printer.

Need to add another device to the network? Just run another length of network cabling and connect it to the hub. Someone drive a nail through one of your network cables? Your whole network doesn't go down — just the segment that's affected.

Star architecture is a key concept in home networking because you can use it for all sorts of networks, such as a telephone system or a video-distribution system. In these systems, as in Ethernet and other LANs, the star topology greatly increases the flexibility, reliability, and expandability of a network.

Your star can grow easily by hooking a single line off of one hub to another hub, and then hooking multiple lines to that hub. Every computer in both hubs can communicate with every other hub.

The cables

If you are getting ready to create a new data network (or telephone, for that matter) within your home, you need to familiarize yourself with UTP (unshielded twisted pair) cables. UTP cables are most commonly found with four twisted pairs of wires within a single cable jacket. They are rated by their *categories,* measures of the cable's bandwidth capacity; higher-rated cables can handle higher-speed data networks. Table 15-1 shows the standard cable ratings.

What the heck is this ATM all about?

ATM. Automated teller machine? Adobe Type Manager? Well, yes, ATM is both of these things, but more importantly — at least in terms of computer LANs — ATM stands for *asynchronous transfer mode.* ATM is part of a grand vision of networking — a single, unified network protocol for LANs and WANs (wide area networks), telephone companies and Internet companies, and just about everyone else. In this vision, ATM provides a super high-speed network that can carry data, voice, and even video over a single network.

ATM's two biggest advantages are the following:

✔ **High speed:** ATM networks can transmit data at speeds reaching into the billions of bits per second, and they're getting faster.

✔ **Prioritized services:** Using a concept called *quality of service,* ATM can determine whether the data it's handling needs to reach its destination pretty soon (such as an e-mail) or right now (such as the data that makes up a phone call or video-conference).

At this point in time, ATM is used almost exclusively in WANs — phone companies use it in their networks, for example, as do some providers of the "backbone" networks that transmit data between Internet service providers (ISPs). Acceptance of ATM in the LAN environment has been much slower — mainly because of the huge installed base of Ethernet networks. Increases in speed in these networks has allowed them to pretty much keep up with the needs of their users.

That's not to say that ATM doesn't, or at least won't, have a place in a home LAN. Network service providers (like telephone companies and ISPs) are starting to move ATM closer and closer to the customer. In all likelihood, someday not too far down the road, consumers will be able to get ATM right into their homes — and when they do, they'll want to upgrade their in-home LANs to ATM to take full advantage of the technology.

Table 15-1	Category Ratings of UTP Cabling
Cable Rating	*Performance Rating*
Category 1	No performance criteria
Category 2	Rated to 1 MHz (used for telephone wiring)
Category 3	Rated to 16 MHz (used for Ethernet 10BaseT)
Category 4	Rated to 20 MHz (used for 10BaseT)
Category 5	Rated to 100 MHz (used for 100BaseT, 10BaseT, and 155 Mbps ATM)

Note: Rated cables are usually referred to as CAT-*x*, with *x* being the category rating. For example, Category 5 cable is CAT-5.

Of these categories, the ones you actually run into in the real world are CAT-3 and CAT-5:

- ✔ **CAT-3 cabling:** This cabling can carry telephone and data networks with speeds up to 10 Mbps, although high-speed data networks more commonly use CAT-5. CAT-3 works best in telephone networks and lower-speed (10BaseT Ethernet) LANs.

- ✔ **CAT-5 cabling:** The highest-rated UTP cabling, CAT-5 is capable of carrying Fast Ethernet networks (like 100BaseT) and ATM networks at speeds up to 155 Mbps. CAT-5 cable can also handle anything a lower-rated UTP cable does — like carrying telephone signals.

Because CAT-5 cabling is designed for high-speed, high-performance networks, if you use CAT-5, then the entire system — the plugs, jacks, and connectors, in addition to the cable — must be CAT-5 rated.

Although you can get away with installing CAT-3 cabling in a home LAN, we really, really recommend that you spend the few extra dollars and use CAT-5. In the long term, the extra data-carrying capacity of CAT-5 makes the higher expense well worth the trouble. Installing CAT-5 may cost a bit more now, but ripping open your walls and replacing CAT-3 with CAT-5 will cost much more when, five years down the road, you decide that you need the extra bandwidth.

If you peruse the brochures and Web sites of cable manufacturers and resellers, you may run across someone who is selling UTP cables that appear to have a higher rating than CAT-5. At the present time, CAT-5 is the highest category rating, although cable manufacturers are pressing standards organizations to create a higher category.

The shield of honor

In other countries — mainly in Europe — STP, or shielded twisted pair, cabling is often used in corporate LANs. This cabling adds metal foil shielding to the cable to provide even more protection against interference from other electromagnetic sources. Use of STP is very rare in the U.S., where most corporate and home networks use UTP (unshielded twisted pair) — any benefits that might be found by using shielded cable are outweighed by its increased cost and difficulty of installation. In fact, you'd probably have a hard time even finding STP cable and related equipment, so we're not going to be discussing this cable in any further detail.

These higher-rated cables may indeed be capable of carrying even higher-speed networks than CAT-5, but right now no standard ensures that one company's CAT-6 — or whatever they may call it — will carry the same amount of data as another company's. The good news is that CAT-5 cable is more than capable of handling home-networking needs for the foreseeable future.

Of course, cables don't do you much good when they're just a bunch of bare wires hanging out of the wall — you need something to connect them to your networked equipment. Luckily, this problem has an easy solution: Like telephone networks, computer LANs utilize a very common connector, the RJ-45. The standard jack and plug for all UTP computer LANs, RJ-45 connectors look exactly like RJ-11s, which we discuss in Chapter 10, only bigger. RJ-45 connectors are designed to terminate all four pairs of wire found in typical UTP cables — although most computer LANs don't use some of these wire pairs.

Like all cable connectors, RJ-45 comes in both male and female varieties. We'll leave the reasons for naming each variety to your own imagination, but we will tell you that you find the male version of the connector on the end of a cable, while you find the female connector on wall outlets or inside equipment like your PC.

The network components

Besides the cables and connectors, a few other pieces and parts are necessary to install a smart home LAN. This equipment is pretty universal, whether you are installing an inexpensive 10 Mbps Ethernet network or a sophisticated ATM system. The key is to use CAT-5 components throughout the network. That way, even if you start off with just a 10BaseT Ethernet system, you have wiring in place to upgrade by simply replacing a few components — no ripping down walls and starting over from scratch for you!

Punch it down!

Your home LAN's *central node* — the place from which all of your cabling runs start — begins with a device called a *patch panel* or *punchdown block.* If you read Chapter 10 on telephone networks, you are already familiar with this device. For all intents and purposes, a data network uses a punchdown block or patch panel that is identical to the one your telephone uses. The one major exception is that the punchdown block needs to be CAT-5 rated to allow high-speed data transmissions.

The main purpose of the punchdown block is to quickly and easily terminate the cables at a single point without doing much splicing and crimping. Typical patch panels come in standard designs (called the 66 or 110 panel), although some home cabling companies offer their own proprietary designs. When they reach your punchdown block, your UTP cables are unwrapped from their jacket, and individual wires are laid across the top of one side of the patch panel. You use a *punchdown tool* (clever name, isn't it?) to press the wires into connector slots on the block. Doing so strips away the insulation and creates an airtight electrical contact point. The middle portion of the patch panel uses wires called *cross connects* to create connections between your UTP cables and a series of standard RJ-45 connectors on the other side of the patch panel.

Hubs for everyone

The key component in an Ethernet network is an *Ethernet hub,* the device that ensures that data gets from point A to point B within the network. A hub is basically just a small electronic box that has a number of RJ-45 connectors (called *ports*) across the front of it. Inside the hub is a circuit board that electrically connects all of these RJ-45 connectors to each other in the proper way — *the proper way* means that the wire carrying outgoing data from one computer connects to the wires that carry incoming data to all other computers that are part of the hub. We know all this information can be confusing, but don't let it stress you out. Honestly, you don't need to spend much time thinking about how hubs work. They're simply one of those "magical" boxes that allow your computers to talk to each other.

The *uplink port,* a special RJ-45 port is another feature of a typical hub. This particular port, unlike the others, doesn't cross the incoming and outgoing data signals, but instead sends them straight through (incoming to incoming, outgoing to outgoing). This capability becomes very useful if, for example, you want to connect two hubs together or if you have an Internet connection device, such as a cable modem, that you want to connect to all of the computers in the network. In these cases, you use the uplink port instead of a standard port.

Many Ethernet hubs don't have a separate uplink port. Instead they have a switch next to one of the regular ports that lets you configure the port to act as an uplink port.

Like ice cream, hubs come in many flavors — the one you purchase is really a matter of personal taste. Be sure to look for the following, though:

✓ **Number of ports:** Be sure to buy a hub that has enough ports to connect all of the computers and networkable devices (like printers and cable modems) you plan on installing in your home LAN.

✓ **Speed:** 10 Mbps (10BaseT) is still the standard Ethernet installation, but you may want to move up to the faster 100BaseT.

Both 10BaseT and 100BaseT use the same wiring infrastructure, so you can start off with one and upgrade to the other just by changing the hub and putting new Network Interface Cards (NICs) in your PCs later.

✔ **Price:** Take a quick trip to any computer superstore, or browse through any computer equipment catalog, and you'll find an amazing range of prices for hubs that are basically equivalent (in speed and number of ports). The last time we went shopping for a small, 5-port, 10BaseT hub, we discovered that some relatively unknown companies offered them for about $19.95, while more well-known data networking companies charged well over $100. Your best bet is probably to fall into the middle range. Doing a little online detective work at a site like www. computershopper.com can really help in these cases.

NICs galore

All the cables in the world won't do your computer a bit of good if it doesn't have the right hardware installed that will let it "talk" on your LAN. That job is performed by the Network Interface Card, or NIC. NICs come in all shapes and sizes — well just a few shapes and sizes, but they are differentiated by many other factors as well.

First off, NICs come in different forms to fit the varying kinds of internal buses found in today's (and yesterday's) PCs and Macs. The most common internal buses found in new computers are the PCI (or Peripheral Component Interconnect) bus, and the ISA (Industry Standard Architecture) bus. While the PCI bus theoretically offers faster data throughput, for the NIC cards used in a home LAN there's really no difference. We recommend you utilize whichever slot you have available — just be sure to check what's free inside your computer before you buy one (or go to your local computer superstore, have one installed, and ask a lot of questions).

Second, NICs offer different interfaces to the LAN — in other words they have different connectors on the back for different kinds of LAN cabling. If you're following our advice, and we hope that you do, you should chose a NIC with an RJ-45 jack on it.

Finally, NICs are designed to connect computers to different kinds of networks. For example, some are designed for connecting to 10BaseT Ethernet networks, some for 100BaseT Ethernet, and some for ATM networks. We recommend that you install NICs that have dual capabilities — that will work on both 10BaseT and 100BaseT networks. These NICs, which cost only about $50, automatically sense what kind of network hub you have installed, and set their own speed accordingly. They also allow you to upgrade your network in the future without having to buy a bunch of new NICs.

Many PCs are now being sold with NICs preinstalled from the factory — a great thing, in our opinion. All Macintosh computers, for example, come standard with 10/100BaseT autosensing NICs standard. If you're in the market for a new computer, you should avoid the hassle of installation and get one with a NIC already inside.

Patch me in

With cables and connectors, patch panels, NICs, and hubs, you are 90 percent of the way towards putting a home LAN together. The final key to the puzzle is another set of CAT-5 cables called *patch cables.* Your patch cables fill the gap between wall outlets and computers; they also connect the patch panel to your Ethernet hub.

You usually purchase patch cables in precut lengths (usually just a few feet) with the connectors already attached, unlike the main network UTP cabling, which you buy in bulk and run inside your walls. Patch cables are also constructed differently from the main backbone cabling. Specifically, *stranded* wire — literally dozens of thinner wires wrapped together to make one, creating greater flexibility — make up each of the eight conductors (four pairs) in a patch cable. The UTP cabling that you use in the wire runs from your patch panel to individual rooms is constructed from *solid core* wires (one thicker wire for each of the eight conductors).

Software to put it all together

The one additional component to making a LAN work — probably the most difficult one for many people — is configuring all of the network protocols and software on each of your home's PCs. This used to be the domain of hard-core networking experts, but it has become less onerous with each successive release of Windows or Mac OS software.

Our focus in this book is to get you the infrastructure that you need to have a home LAN — we simply don't have the room to talk about binding protocols and configuring networking software. If you're not comfortable with doing this on your own, we recommend you check out *Networking For Dummies,* 4th Edition by Doug Lowe or *Networking Home PCs For Dummies* by Kathy Ivens (both published by IDG Books Worldwide, Inc.).

Visualizing How a Data LAN Works

In the star architecture, each *LAN station* — the outlet into which you can connect a computer to the LAN — is served by its own unique length of UTP cable radiating out from a central node, like the spokes on a wagon wheel.

Probably the best way to visualize this kind of LAN network is to follow your data from a PC all the way back to the central node of the LAN:

1. **The computer uses its networking software to send a chunk of data from a program to your NIC.**

2. **The NIC converts the data into the proper format for the network (Ethernet or ATM, for example) and sends it as an electrical signal over the patch cable.**

3. **The patch cable carries this data signal between the NIC and the nearest RJ-45 connector installed in a wall outlet.**

4. **The RJ-45 connector attaches to one end of a length of CAT-5 UTP cabling, which carries the data signal back through your walls to the central node of your LAN (in the basement, garage, or utility room — wherever you choose to house it).**

5. **The UTP cable terminates where it is punched down into the patch panel, which carries your data signal across its internal wiring to another RJ-45 connector.**

6. **Another patch cable carries the data signal from the back of the patch panel to the Ethernet hub (or ATM switch).**

The hub takes your outgoing data signal and sends it on a U-turn trip back through the patch panel and over a different UTP to its final destination on your network (another computer, a printer, or elsewhere).

Alternatives to a Wired Data LAN

A CAT-5 wiring infrastructure is the best way to build a home computer LAN — it's flexible, capable of high speeds, relatively inexpensive, and based upon proven standards. Many people, however, are unable to install this type of network in their homes because they can't rip open their walls to run new wiring. Luckily, several viable alternative methods are available:

✓ **Wireless data LANs:** These systems use radio or light waves to send data between computers. Figure 15-2 shows a wireless data LAN setup.

✓ **Phoneline networks:** These systems utilize your existing telephone wiring infrastructure for computer communications. Figure 15-3 shows a home phoneline network.

✓ **Powerline networks:** These systems use AC electrical wiring to carry data between computers.

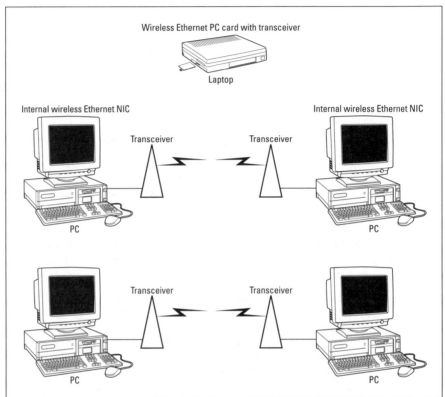

Wireless Ethernet PC card with transceiver

Laptop

Internal wireless Ethernet NIC

Internal wireless Ethernet NIC

Transceiver

Transceiver

PC

PC

Transceiver

Transceiver

Figure 15-2:
A wireless
data LAN.

PC

PC

Wireless options

Wireless data networking solutions are relative newcomers to the LAN scene compared to their CAT-5 counterparts. What does that mean to the home networker? Two things:

- ✔ Wireless systems have a worse price-to-performance ratio than wired ones. In other words, they're slower and cost more.

- ✔ Not all of the systems that we discuss in this section are currently available on your local retailer's shelves. In fact, many are still on the drawing boards, but should be available soon, assuming the manufacturers meet their production goals.

Several smart and rich companies are spending time and money to develop these wireless systems. Consequently, you should be able to take advantage of attractively priced, wireless data networks — with performance that meets all of your home LAN needs — in the very near future.

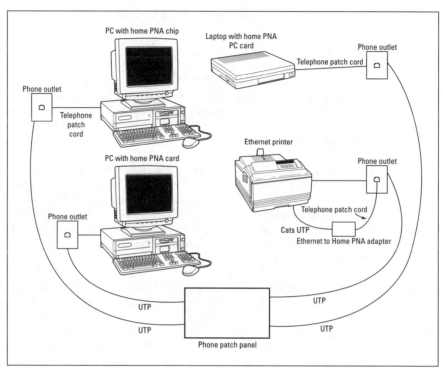

Figure 15-3:
A home
phoneline
data LAN.

Wireless Ethernet

Wireless Ethernet is an umbrella term describing a bunch of different radio frequency (RF) LAN systems that networking vendors sell. For the most part,
these systems are designed for business applications — with prices to match!
A typical Wireless Ethernet system, consisting of radio transceivers and special-purpose, internal NICs, costs somewhere in the range of $500 or more per
network station. The maximum speed of these systems is 10 Mbps (although
they often provide even less bandwidth), which is the same maximum speed as
a 10BaseT Ethernet system that may cost $75 per station. That's a whole heck
of a lot of money to a homeowner who is trying to connect two $1,000 iMacs.

Until very recently, price wasn't even the biggest obstacle to Wireless Ethernet.
The problem was that different flavors of Wireless Ethernet didn't work
together. Each vendor designed its systems by using *proprietary connection
technologies,* the networking equivalent of having one computer speak French,
and the other Russian. They just aren't going to understand each other.

Luckily, some progress has been made on this front. Manufacturers are beginning to create products that adhere to an emerging standard — IEEE 802.11
(ask for it by name). With this standard in place, a computer that uses vendor
A's product can talk to a computer that uses vendor B's.

Progress at last. The price, however, is still not right for the vast majority of home users.

HomeRF

Realizing that the full-fledged 802.11 systems that we describe in the previous section are too expensive for the average consumer, a group of powerful computer and consumer-electronics companies decided to get together and cooperate on a cheaper alternative. The result of this effort is something called the *HomeRF Working Group.*

This group (made up of Intel, Apple, Microsoft, Motorola, and literally dozens of other industry heavy hitters) is putting its collective brain to work on a "relaxed" (you can read that as "cheaper") version of 802.11 specifically designed for home use. Using a protocol known as SWAP (shared wireless access protocol — we're suckers for a catchy acronym), the HomeRF group is aiming to be *the* standard for anyone trying to create wireless LANs for the home.

In the longer term, HomeRF aims to include all sorts of home-networking stuff in the SWAP protocol — multimedia video and audio networking, telephone networking, and even home automation and control systems (for controlling lights, appliances, and other devices) — but the first step is to define the basics of SWAP in such a way that networking vendors can ship compatible computer networking products very soon. HomeRF systems should be available to consumers late in 1999.

Infrared — using light instead of radio

Infrared networking — using light waves instead of radio waves — is already a part of many computer networks. In fact, a relatively mature standard known as IRDA — which stands for Infrared Device Association — is in place. IRDA devices are commonly found in three main sets of equipment:

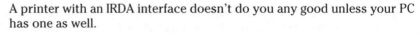

- **Printers:** Using an IRDA interface, you can *beam* print jobs from one or several computers to your printer without any cables. You find IRDA interfaces mainly on high-end laser printers — the inkjet models that most people have in their homes don't have this capability yet.

  A printer with an IRDA interface doesn't do you any good unless your PC has one as well.

- **Notebook computers:** Many laptops have a built-in IRDA interface to facilitate printing and also to make for easy synchronization of data with your properly equipped desktop PC.

✔ **Handheld computer devices:** You also find IRDA interfaces on many handheld, PDA (Personal Digital Assistant) computers, mainly for the purpose of synchronizing data with your desktop computer.

The most popular PDA to date — the 3Com PalmPilot — doesn't use IRDA, but instead uses a cradle device that connects to the PC's serial port. The cradle is physically connected to the PC by a serial cable; the PDA itself physically connects to the cradle when it's placed in it through a group of exposed electrical contacts.

Depending on its implementation, infrared networking can be quite efficient and speedy — with data throughput rates reaching several megabits per second in some cases.

Infrared does have a major downfall, however, that makes it unsuitable for a whole-home network: Infrared signals are line-of-sight only. In other words, an infrared signal won't penetrate some of those pesky things you often find in the home — like doors, walls, and giant-screen televisions. So although infrared is useful within a single room, it won't get you very far beyond that.

Other wireless systems

Wireless Ethernet and its cheaper cousin HomeRF are the main players in the wireless data-networking arena right now, but some other emerging and alternative (in other words, proprietary) systems are beginning to come to market.

These next-generation wireless products aren't on the shelves yet, but we wouldn't be surprised to see them available within a year or so. Like traditional Wireless Ethernet systems, next-generation systems will utilize radio frequency (RF) in either the 900 MHz or 2.4 GHz spectrums.

We can't give you any detailed information about these products yet, but we can share what we do know.

Home Wireless Networks

This small, start-up company based in Atlanta, has entered into a partnership with Lucent Technologies to build "digital, wireless networking" products for the home. The company hasn't announced any specific products yet, but its goal is to provide low-cost systems that will enable multiple telephone lines and data networking throughout the home.

The first generation of this product seems to be oriented toward users who need multiple POTS or IDSN telephone lines (which we discuss in Chapter 10), but don't have the wiring infrastructure in place to handle them. This product probably won't be designed to replace an internal data LAN that allows communications between computers within your home — rather it will be designed to replace the wires in your home that connect telephones and computer modems to the outside world. Future generations of Home Wireless Networks products, however, will be designed to handle data LAN duties in addition to their telephone functionality.

THiiN Line Wireless Internet Server

THiiN Line — a subsidiary of Data General Corporation, a major computer and networking company — produces easy-to-use, plug-and-play Internet appliances. In the business world, THiiN Line produces small, all-in-one Web servers designed to simplify and lessen the expense of launching a corporate Web site.

More of interest to consumers, the company has recently announced plans to produce an inexpensive ($500 seems to be the target price) *net utility box* (or NUB). This device will connect to your incoming telephone or ISDN line (with other options like cable modems or digital subscriber lines coming in the future), and distribute incoming Internet service throughout the home by using a 2.4 GHz spread spectrum RF LAN.

The NUB is designed to replace the hubs, unshielded twisted-pair cabling, and other parts of an Ethernet LAN in the home. The NUB itself will be located near the NIU (Network Interface Unit, which we cover in Chapter 11) of your telephone service, and will handle all the data distribution among computers and networked peripherals in your home. The NUB will also appropriately route incoming and outgoing Internet communications with the wider world through its interface with your ISP.

The net utility box sounds pretty cool, especially if the company meets its price targets. The only downside will likely be the maximum speed of the LAN — a bit more than 1 Mbps — which is considerably less than that of a wired Ethernet LAN.

Bluetooth

Bluetooth isn't what you get when you eat too many blueberries. Instead, Bluetooth is another major wireless networking initiative being spearheaded by a couple of wireless phone giants (Nokia and Ericsson) and computing powerhouses (IBM, Intel, and Toshiba). Bluetooth's emphasis is portability — which makes sense when you consider that Nokia and Ericsson make all their money on portable phones — but it has implications beyond the cell phone. Like the HomeRF Working Group that we mention earlier in the chapter, Bluetooth goes beyond just computer networking to include things like telephone and intercom functionality.

The main design goal of the Bluetooth group is to create inexpensive RF networking chips that can be embedded in a variety of devices — ranging from cell phones to computer mouses (or is it meeses?). Like HomeRF and the SWAP protocol, Bluetooth utilizes its own special networking protocol to enable various parts of the network to find each other and identify their purposes. So, for example, you can power up a printer and have it immediately tell all the other local Bluetooth devices that it is on the network and ready to print.

Bluetooth is still in its early developmental stages, so you won't be able to use it in your own home network any time soon. However, the companies involved do have widespread support, so we think that it will eventually become an important home LAN system. We also expect, given the interests of Nokia and Ericsson, that the first generations of Bluetooth products will emphasize the mobile rather than the home-network features of the technology.

Phoneline options

A core group of companies is behind many home LAN efforts — specifically Microsoft, Intel, and Compaq — who have much to gain if millions of consumers jump on the networking bandwagon. New software, new chips, new computers — they can already hear the cash registers ringing. So they've decided to hedge their bets by supporting several different ways to create home LANs. For example, they support not only wireless LAN systems like HomeRF and Bluetooth (see the previous sections), but also a very interesting group called the HPNA, or Home Phoneline Networking Alliance.

The HPNA is an industry association with over a hundred members, all of whom have aligned themselves behind the adoption of a home LAN that uses (as the name implies) existing telephone wires to carry data around the house.

Tut Systems, a networking and DSL (digital subscriber line) technology specialist, is developing the main technology for HPNA. Tut has designed a computer chipset that uses some fancy digital signal processing to enable computers and peripherals to use existing phone wiring — in any architecture — as a computer LAN. This system, called HomeRun, transmits data across this phone wiring at a speed of 1.3 Mbps and emulates an Ethernet network, albeit at a lower speed. (Remember that 10BaseT Ethernet, the most common kind, runs at 10 Mbps.)

As HomeRun equipment is released to the marketplace, it will come in three main forms:

- **HomeRun chipsets:** The factory can install the computer chips that make up HomeRun on computer and peripheral motherboards. To attach to the network, you can simply plug this equipment into a phone outlet with a standard RJ-11 phone patch cord.

- **HomeRun Network Interface Cards (NICs):** You can install these into an internal expansion slot inside a PC. Like equipment with a HomeRun chipset on the motherboard, computers with a HomeRun NIC connect to the telephone network with a simple RJ-11 phone patch cord.

- **HomeRun Ethernet adapters:** With these adapters, computers and peripherals that already have 10BaseT Ethernet NICs installed can connect to a HomeRun network. In this case, the adapter connects to the Ethernet port via a CAT-3 or CAT-5 RJ-45 patch cable on one end, and to the telephone wiring via an RJ-11 patch cable on the other.

The HomeRun system operates on different frequencies than analog or ISDN telephone services, so you can simultaneously use a single phone line for your computer LAN and for all of the other things you currently use it for — like making phone calls, sending and receiving faxes, or using a modem.

A particularly neat feature of HomeRun is that it doesn't need an Ethernet hub to distribute the data across the LAN. Just plug a HomeRun-equipped PC or peripheral device into any phone line in the house, and it can automatically talk to any other device on the same network. No fuss, no muss — real plug and play!

Tut isn't the only company providing technology to the HPNA. A company called Epigram, the other key technology provider, is working on providing a very similar system that can carry data at even higher speeds — up to 10 Mbps or higher. This system will also be *backwards compatible* with the Tut HomeRun system, meaning that future generations of HPNA networking equipment will run at the same speed as a purpose-built data LAN and will be able to talk to first-generation systems, albeit at the lower 1.3 Mbps speed.

We think that the HPNA is going to be an incredibly important part of the home LAN and home-networking landscape in the very near future. If the manufacturer meets all of its technical goals and delivers inexpensive products on time (which means sometime in mid-1999), these companies will offer the first widely available consumer alternative to CAT-5 LANs. If you already have a CAT-5 LAN, you can use a HomeRun-to-Ethernet adapter to expand the reach of your existing network to areas that aren't already covered — for example to an attic that was originally unfinished, but has been converted to a home office.

Powerline options

AC power lines are — electrically speaking — dirty and noisy and notoriously difficult to use for data networking. They are, however, probably the most ubiquitous set of cables in the home. Even old homes have power lines running to just about every nook and cranny. So a few brave engineers are working on ways to utilize this cabling infrastructure for home data LANs.

In fact, a product called PassPort is currently on the market. PassPort is made by a company in Utah called Intelogis. PassPort's core technologies were initially designed by Novell — the huge computer-networking company — and then spun off into an independent company, Intelogis.

Like a Tut HomeRun system for power lines, the PassPort is a plug-and-play networking system that doesn't require any particular wiring architecture or topology. All you need to do is plug the PassPort boxes into a PC's parallel port and then into a wall outlet and — *voilá!* — you have a 350 Kbps LAN for sharing files or an Internet connection. The price is pretty reasonable, too — a bit less than $200 for a two-computer kit, with additional network stations costing around $80.

Although powerline networking is generally more suitable for applications that don't need to be very high speed, such as sending control signals to lamps and VCRs, the PassPort is available now and can be useful for building or expanding a simple computer LAN.

Part V
Keeping the Bad Guys at Bay: Security

Originally we planned to have a computerized security system. But all that Y2K hysteria made us decide to just stick with the basics.

In this part . . .

Most people are familiar with some of the core concepts of home security and safety. Smoke detectors, fire extinguishers, and shrieking alarms tend to come to mind.

But a smart-home security system is much, much more. In this part, we talk about how to protect and prevent. We introduce you to a home-security infrastructure that goes well beyond just setting off any alarm when someone opens a door. We tell you about sensors galore that not only run your home security subsystem, but also lay a foundation for later use in your home-automation environment.

Chapter 16

Home Security Boot Camp

• •

• •

The earliest forms of home security systems were pretty expensive. Throughout history, leaders from kings to presidents have had their own soldiers patrolling their territory.

Most people have replaced these costly, armed guards with a dog, boa constrictor, or a fake security sticker on the door.

In recent years, home security has become cheaper, broader, and easier. A sophisticated system that covers you for fire, forced entry, and monitoring only costs a few thousand dollars — not bad for protecting your life!

You can combine security systems that go well beyond this minimal level of protection with your home network, adding a whole new perspective to the phrase, "Your home is your castle."

Guarding the House

The simplest security systems seek to protect the perimeter of your house — ensuring that someone can't open the front door, for instance, without setting off some sort of alarm.

You can install sensors that detect intrusion at every entrance (or potential entrance) to your home. These sensors can include devices like sensors that can detect glass breaking and magnetic contact sensors that can tell when doors and windows have been opened.

Cut your insurance rates

With fire and burglar alarms in your home, you are much less likely to be robbed or to lose a significant amount to fire damage. Consequently, insurance companies will give you a break on your payments if you have these in your home. If you pay a third party to centrally monitor these alarms, then your rates are even less expensive. Call your insurance company — you may find that you can finance your security subsystem on your insurance premium savings.

You can get a range of remote controls that allow you to turn your system on or off from a distance, without needing your security code. You can also program these controls to turn your lights on and off or open and close your garage door. We especially like the remotes that allow for keyless entry into your home — with the press of a button, you can unlock your front door the same way that you can unlock many car doors.

Watch for fires, floods, and other calamities

Smoke detectors, carbon monoxide detectors, flood detectors, even tornado detectors are watch dogs that eat nothing (other than a little electricity now and then) but stay alert 24 hours a day, even if your burglary system is turned off. These detectors allow you to react to an emergency as quickly as possible — hopefully even before a problem occurs.

All sorts of environmental and other sensors are available; they cover just about every contingency that most insurance companies would like to claim as "acts of God." A truly smart home has at least fire and carbon monoxide detectors inside, along with a smattering of other devices — depending on local conditions. These sensors can not only sound alarms for you, but may also do double duty in a home-automation system, triggering lights and coffee pots and all sorts of other neat stuff (we talk about this more in Chapter 23).

Detect motion

Passive infrared (PIR) and microwave detectors around the house can tell when someone is moving around in an area that should be empty. These sensors can also help keep doors and windows secured while you are at home. You can turn these motion detectors off separately from the perimeter sensors, allowing you to move freely inside while staying secure on the outside.

The areas you protect are assigned zone numbers so you can easily locate specific spots simply by reading the English or numerical display right on your keypad. If a door in Zone 4 is left open, for example, the zone's name or number appears in the keypad's display window.

See who's at the door

Both audio and video entry systems are available that help you determine who is at the door before you open it — if you open it at all. For the audio systems, a door-answering intercom replaces the standard doorbell; you can have both chime tones and intercom capabilities at the door.

For video, you can get several different types of wide-angle or close-up angle entry systems to see who's lurking at the door, trying to sell you some brooms or magazine subscriptions. A really cool smart home combines the door video with door control mechanisms to allow you to buzz your guests in.

You can even tie your video system to a VCR and record whenever someone trips an alarm in any particular area.

Tying In to Home Automation

One of the great things about these security devices is that they are multi-use. A sensor just senses something — how the system acts on a trigger event is a wholly different issue.

If you tie these sensors into a home controller, then you can set different states for these sensors.

Now that's security!

Some people know no limits when trying to secure themselves and their property. Probably the most extreme that we've seen is in South Africa, where one company will outfit your car with flame-throwers.

For a cool $655, you can buy The Blaster. This contraption squirts liquefied gas (from a bottle in the automobile's trunk) through two nozzles, located under the front doors. An electric spark then ignites the gas. You activate the system by entering a code into a dashboard keypad, and then breaking the tough plastic seal on a switch located next to the foot pedals. The manufacturer doesn't include marshmallows with this product.

For instance, if someone trips an infrared beam across your lawn while you're working at home, you may see a display video on a monitor in your office. If the same trigger occurs when you are away on vacation, the system may instead phone your alarm monitoring station.

You can also use the proximity sensors to turn on lights in your yard when someone approaches the house. This nice feature helps visitors find their way up the sidewalk, but is a disincentive to burglars who, for some reason, prefer the dark.

A totally smart home also has many preventative options for security. For instance, home controller systems (like we discuss in Part VI) can turn on your lights and other appliances while you're on vacation, giving the illusion that you're at home.

Sounding the Alarm (and Calling in Reinforcements)

Controlling and monitoring your security system is done by means of one (or in larger houses, several) keypad/display units. These wall-mounted devices let you arm and disarm your security system, display the current status, and provide a visual indication of any trouble situations (like open doors or dead batteries).

To arm or disarm your home security system, you simply enter your private 3- or 4-digit pass code when you leave or re-enter. A quick glance at the keypad's status display immediately tells you whether your system is armed, ready-to-arm, and so on (for example, if you have disabled sensors in a certain zone). If an intrusion occurs, your keypad's display visually alerts you to the alarm condition and pinpoints its location for you!

You can change your system pass codes at any time, giving additional users temporary entrance. For instance, you can give out-of-town guests temporary codes that automatically erase when you return.

Many systems allows you to use any Touch-Tone telephone in the world to operate your system. If you are on vacation, you can check the status of your system for greater peace of mind. You can also dial in and activate the system that you (oops) forgot to turn on when you left.

If something triggers one of the sensors, the system has many options, including the following:

✔ Sounding the alarm

✔ Notifying remote monitoring services

✔ Paging you

✔ Calling you on the phone and alerting you to the problem

Some monitoring companies actually monitor for sound in your house, and they have programs that listen for specific non-standard sounds when your home is in active alarm mode. Their sales agents carry around recordings of actual break-ins from clients' premises — a very effective sales pitch.

Chapter 17

Shopping for Home Security

. . . .

In This Chapter

▶ Getting the lowdown on security systems

▶ Choosing from sensors by the score

▶ Watching the world from a camera lens

▶ Controlling your safety

. . . .

An alarm system is one of those items that you definitely *don't* want to be the last person on the block to own. If a burglar is casing your neighborhood and sees an alarm on every house but yours, guess which one she's going to target? We're here with this chapter to ensure that your smart home is not the victim!

Security systems entail a great deal of specific planning to make sure that you literally cover every angle. Just one glaring hole in your security system makes you vulnerable. Still, the security component of your home network is probably one of the easiest to understand and plan because its pretty familiar and intuitive. And, because you'll likely hire out the wiring for your security system, you only have to think about where all those sensors need to be.

In this chapter, we show you how to batten down the hatches on security. Specifically, we discuss what security systems can do for you and how they work. We also talk about the components that make up a security system and how they sense conditions that might be cause for alarm.

Deciding That You Need a Security System

Even though you have to plan for all sorts of scary disasters — robbery, fire, carbon dioxide poisoning, floods, and so on, you don't need to be afraid of your alarm system. With some ingenuity and creativity, you may find that your alarm system is one of the more fun systems to plan, because you can do so much with sensors and control panels. For example, you can configure alarm systems to detect when someone is standing on your front door mat and have it turn on a light or even call you up at work and let you know you have a visitor.

An alarm system should first and foremost fit your personal style and tastes. The system design should work around your daily schedule, your kids and pets (if you have any), and the overall way you live your life. For instance, the design should take into consideration whether you have valuable possessions in your home — a stash of jewelry, mattress money, gold, silver, baseball cards, or a wine cellar. The system can also contain a medical alert capability, for example, if you are elderly or a pool alarm if young people live in the house. A smart home alarm system simply reflects you.

People install security systems for three main reasons:

- To protect their home when they are not around
- To protect their home when they are around
- A combination of the two — in other words, to protect both their home and its occupants (different sensors and sensor arrangements are necessary to protect your home and to protect occupants, and many people want both)

Protecting your house when you are not home typically serves as a baseline goal. If this goal is your only concern, you can take the minimalist approach — apply contact sensors on the doors, install a few passive infrared scanners on the interior of the house, and throw in a siren and control panel.

To protect your house when you are at home requires a more intense approach. Beyond what we just described, you have more to cover, especially the windows on the basement and first-floor levels. Security experts have determined that nearly 90 percent of break-ins involve a door. That is to say, 90 percent of the time, the burglar either enters or leaves the house using a door. When all you want to do is determine that a break-in has occurred, a simple perimeter defense like we just described is considered adequate. If, however, you want a more thorough system that can detect the presence of an intruder and immediately sound an alarm, you need additional sensors.

You may want to consider glass-breakage detectors along with contacts (the contacts only detect if a window has been opened, while the glass-breakage detectors can tell if someone smashes a window). If you don't want to see the devices for cosmetic reasons, you can install *stress detectors* — support beams mounted to the floor that can register an individual's weight and activate the alarm — which you often find in historic homes. You can also add other sensors as we discuss in the section entitled "You fill up my sensors."

Outfitting your home for this more intense protection does add dollars to your budget to the tune of about $60 a window. (The average home has 20–25 windows on the basement and first floors.)

Your choices in security will likely fall across a broad spectrum. The rest of this chapter helps you understand some of these options.

Going Through Security Basics

In this section we discuss what a security system is designed to do and how the system analyzes and responds to inputs from sensors.

A smart home's security system has at least three goals:

- ✔ **Detection:** Your system should be capable of sounding an alarm when something triggers a sensor (though you may choose *not* to sound an alarm for certain types of events).

- ✔ **Emergency response:** Your system should be able to call for appropriate help, depending on the circumstances.

- ✔ **Prevention:** Your system should be designed to help prevent problems before they occur — like scaring potential intruders away by automatically turning on outside lights at night. Well-built doors, windows, and quality locks help determine whether a criminal attempts to break into a home — alarm or not. Bringing prevention into the equation means connecting your security system with your home-automation system (see Part VI).

Your alarm system accomplishes its goals in three steps:

- ✔ **Input:** The system cannot act if it isn't aware of a problem. The sensors in your system alert your security subsystem when something deserves attention.

- ✔ **Processing:** Something has to interpret these inputs to determine whether the system needs to do something. Your security system is constantly analyzing real-time inputs from all its tethered sensors, monitoring the status of your home's health.

- ✔ **Output:** After your subsystem decides what to do, it reaches out and runs through its preprogrammed checklist of to-do items. Sirens, flashing lights, silent alarms, whatever — anything is possible with a smart system.

Examining Security Systems

Although every manufacturer has variations on the pieces and parts that make up a security system, your system should include the items we discuss in this section.

The basic elements of a standard alarm system include the following:

- ✔ A control panel
- ✔ A keypad and corresponding "key"
- ✔ Basic sensors, like an inside motion detector, door and window contact sensors, glass-breakage detectors and a smoke alarm
- ✔ A siren and/or flashing strobe light

You should also link the system to a central monitoring station (a security company in other words) for around-the-clock coverage.

Get control of your security panel

You usually find the control panel — your security system's brain — in your home's wiring closet. This room also houses your telephone and home-automation subsystems.

The control panel is basically an electronic box that serves as the core interconnection point for all the wiring (and wirelessing) in your subsystem. A sophisticated control panel has outputs that allow you to interface with X-10 home-automation systems (which we talk about in more detail in Chapters 19 and 20), for controlling lights for instance, and with RS-232 ports (a standardized communications protocol, also used to connect computer modems to PCs) for more proprietary and custom programmed automation systems. It also has ports for interfacing with telephone systems. The control panel has an internal battery for battery backup in case of a power failure.

Control pads range in size — some are the size of a telephone keypad, while others utilize several separate "boxes" mounted out of sight. You may find the keypad and control panel integrated into one unit in small systems that require only one keypad (like for apartments).

Don't panic — use your keypad!

You can use many different systems to activate and deactivate your security system. The most common interfaces for residential applications are *keypads,* which resemble telephone keypads, and *key switches,* which take a physical key. The vast majority of new installations use keypads because they offer a lot of flexibility.

To activate or deactivate the system, you enter a code into the keypad. You can also program your system directly from the keypad.

Keypads frequently have one or more function buttons that are programmed for specific tasks. The most common quickly activate an audible panic alarm, fire alarm, or medical emergency alarm.

Some alarm systems have a module that turns any Touch-Tone phone into a fully functional keypad. This feature allows you to arm, disarm, program, and check the status of the system from external locations. In addition, these modules allow all the Touch-Tone phones on the premise to become fully functional keypads, which saves you money because you don't have to distribute wired keypads all over the house.

One way to help avoid messing up at the keypad is to use remote controls, which come on keychains like you have with newer cars. One button disarms the system, turns on lights around the house, opens the garage door, and more

Aha! The key!

You use your key to arm and disarm the system, so although most people don't think of a key as a system feature, it's certainly critical to making the system work. And we're not talking only about a physical key — your key could be a code, a voice print, a fingerprint, a retinal imprint, the shape of your hand or face, or any other form of validation the system recognizes.

Most people use a four- to five-digit code to activate and deactivate their alarm system and to gain entry for maintenance. Different systems record this activity in different ways. Higher-end systems track which codes are entered at which times; lower-end ones merely record that the system was activated or deactivated on a particular date and time.

Combatting false alarms

Some sort of user error causes 90 percent of false alarms; therefore, security systems have a number of built-in features that seek to reduce false alarms. Among these are *delay tones* that beep with increasing urgency from the time that you punch your code into the system until the time the system is actually activated or deactivated, depending on whether you are coming or going.

You or your installer can also program your security system to insert delays, such as a communication delay, elsewhere in the system to give you time to react. This feature delays reporting the alarm to the central station for a set period of time, giving you a second or so to disarm the panel.

You fill up my sensors

You can use all sorts of sensors and detectors to drive your security system. And although some security-system purists try to make a strong technical differentiation between sensors and detectors, everyone that we know uses the terms interchangeably. The grammar-usage police have never stopped anyone on this charge.

Sensors are the central part of your security architecture because your security subsystem operates solely on the inputs of the sensors — it can't act on something that it can't sense.

You can surmise what most detectors do, so we won't take up your time detailing how each one works. If a given sensor is applicable to your needs, ask your security-system bidders about it. We do, however, cover the main sensors you're likely to encounter in a base system — contact sensors, passive infrared sensors, and smoke detectors. You can use the following sensors in your smart home:

- **Break sensors:** Mounted near windows to detect the specific high-frequency sounds of glass being shattered

- **Carbon monoxide detectors:** Used inside a home to detect hazardous levels of CO gas

- **Contact sensors:** Mounted in doors and windows to detect when doors and windows are opened or closed

- **Flood sensors:** Mounted in basements or other flood-prone spaces, often used to trigger sump pumps

- **Freeze sensors:** Mounted outside to detect freezing temperatures for plant protection

- **Gas detectors:** Detect the presence of gas fumes

- **Heat detectors:** Part of a smoke/fire alarm system, used to detect high temperatures

- **Ionization detectors:** The actual "smoke detector" in a smoke detector

- **Magnetic sensors:** A kind of contact sensor, using magnets to determine when a door or window is opened

- **Moisture sensors:** Mounted indoors to determine humidity, often used to trigger air conditioning or dehumidifier systems

- **Motion sensors:** Mounted in halls and stairways to detect the movement of unwanted intruders

- **Photoelectric sensors:** Shine a beam of light across a hall or doorway to detect motion (activate when a person walking by interrupts the beam

- ✔ **Plunger switches:** Another kind of contact sensor which uses a small plunger (that looks like a refrigerator or car-door light switch) to determine when a door or window is opened

- ✔ **Power status sensors:** Detect power outages to possibly start a generator

- ✔ **Pressure sensors:** Often mounted in doormats or under driveways to detect weight

- ✔ **Rain sensors:** Mounted out of doors (unless your home needs a new roof!) to trigger or cancel sprinkler systems

- ✔ **Smoke detectors:** Used for fire protection, but *smoke detector* is actually a bit of a misnomer, because most also include heat detectors

- ✔ **Snow sensors:** Mounted outside to detect snow and then do stuff like activate a heated driveway

- ✔ **Tamper switches:** Mounted in vulnerable areas of alarm systems to sound in case of tampering

- ✔ **Temperature sensors:** Unsurprisingly, used to detect temperature

- ✔ **Vibration sensors:** Mounted under floors or elsewhere in a home's structure, to detect people walking above

- ✔ **Water disturbance sensors:** Used in a swimming pool or hot tub to determine when someone or something (like a baby) has entered the water

- ✔ **Weather sensors:** Mounted outside to detect a number of weather conditions

Not only do these sensors drive your security system, but many can also drive your home-automation capabilities. For instance, you can use the magnetic detector along your driveway to note that a car has pulled in, and an infrared motion detector to note when someone walks to the door.

Contact sensors

Some 90 percent of all break-ins involve outside doors at some time — whether going in or going out. So only 10 percent of time will someone come in and leave through windows. Clearly, protection for your doors is probably the single most important element of security-system planning.

Magnetic switches are one of the most popular ways to protect doors today. You put a magnet on the edge of the door itself and then, with the door closed, place a switch across from it in the door jamb. When you open the door, the magnet loses contact with the switch, causing it to change electric states. The control panel recognizes this change and triggers an alarm or other course of action.

Passive infrared receivers (PIRs)

Passive infrared receivers are another popular security-system item. These devices literally see heat in the infrared spectrum. A series of lenses on the receiver's cover guide a PIR's vision (which is fixed in one direction). Over the years, PIR technology has been refined to the extent that false alarms are minimal. You can get different coverage areas by using different lenses on the front of the PIR. A good security team can further aim or restrict this vision by placing opaque tape over portions of the lens to reduce the opportunity for false alarms from dogs and unintended motion.

PIRs are relatively cheap and small (about the size of a light switch), can mount on a wall or ceiling inconspicuously, and go a long way toward protecting your home. The idea with PIRs is to guard your most sensitive areas, while attempting to catch a criminal early in an intrusion. A PIR covering the stairway to the second floor is always a great plan — you don't want the bad guys to get upstairs. Hallways leading to family rooms where electronics and saleable items are kept make sense, too.

Many PIRs offer different zones within the sensor's vision so that you can create "events" based on the sequence in which the sensor's zones are tripped. One of the truly neat things about sensors is that you can team them up together for unique applications. Because software drives and enables sensors, you can attach additional detectors, such as active IR beams or magnetic contacts, to trip only in special combination circumstances.

For instance, with certain manufacturers' sensors, like Optex America's VX-40A (www.optexamerica.com), you can wire two PIR detectors together and use different software modes to do different things:

✔ You can set a mode that lets the two PIRs work together to double the size of your detection area.

✔ You can use set your PIRs to activate alarms directionally — so they trip an alarm if they detect a person walking in a certain direction in your home.

✔ You can select a sequential mode to generate an alarm only if two detectors activate sequentially and separately.

The VX-40A is actually a neat sensor because you can combine it with a voice warning feature. When the system is armed, the voice warning feature (a weatherproof speaker lives inside the sensor) delivers one of two types of voice messages to anyone entering the protected area. This warning is designed to deter a would-be intruder from continuing toward the protected area.

One neat application that may save on those homeowner lawsuits is a wireless, sensor annunciator. Say you're having a party. Do people always trip on part of your walkway, or do you have areas where you don't want guests to go? When you put your security system in "guest mode," your wireless sensor can detect an approaching visitor/intruder's body temperature and then, in turn, transmit a radio frequency to the receiver(s). The receiver then gives a verbal warning to inform the guest of what you want to say — "Watch out for the cliff!"

Smoke detectors

Battery-powered smoke detectors (you know, the little jobbies that you stick to the wall or ceiling) help you get clear in an emergency, but they don't do much to protect your home when you're not around. Neither a control panel nor a central station can monitor these detectors. If no one is around when the alarm goes off, the alarm beeps, buzzes, and whirs until, well, until it melts. We think you really need to ensure that your security system monitors for fire and automatically calls for help when necessary.

These smoke detectors are hardwired back to the alarm control panel and typically offer several different levels of protection — a temperature sensor that sounds the alarm at a preset temperature, a temperature sensor that measures the rate of rise of a room's temperature and sounds the alarm when it meets its preset minimum, and an ionization detector that "smells" smoke and sounds the alarm.

In some parts of the country, these detectors may not meet your local fire regulations for hardwired smoke detectors because the security control panel itself (which powers the detector) may not be hardwired, but instead be attached to a transformer.

Smoke detectors in homes get a fair amount of press, but carbon monoxide (CO) detectors don't get enough. Such things as fuel-burning heaters or furnaces, gasoline-powered engines, charcoal grills, wood-burning stoves, fireplaces, and kerosene heaters generate CO gas. CO is particularly deadly because it's odorless, colorless, and tasteless. We highly recommend that you get this base-level security feature. Buy one with a digital read-out to help you understand what's going on when the alarm goes off. Put it where you sleep. The added cost is wort preventing the possible consequences (dying in your sleep of CO poisoning).

Sirens

You should complement your alarm system with visible and audible outputs, like the popular external sirens and flashing strobe lights. Your alarm system will probably allow different tones for different situations, such as an intermittent tone for fire but a steady tone for burglary, for instance.

Position your visible alarms in as high and as obvious a place as possible so that people coming to your aid can easily locate this beacon. Firefighters, police, and so on all look for these visible alarms first as they speed to your rescue. Remember, their siren is likely going off, too, so being an obvious target can work to your advantage.

Monitoring

You have to make the key decision of whether or not to have a central monitoring station monitor your alarm. Because this option offers the added bonus of professional security response, we highly recommend that you choose it. For a minor cost of $25 or so per month, you can give yourself peace of mind — and possibly save your life.

Most of the 12,000 plus alarm companies in the U.S. don't have their own central monitoring station. Rather, they bundle someone else's monitoring service — businesses that do nothing else but monitor systems for alarm companies — with their own installation and maintenance service.

Your control system calls out to this monitoring station when an emergency or other problem situation arises; the central station interprets the information coming from your alarm system and calls the appropriate parties.

Gathering Your 007 Security Equipment

Your security system can get quite extensive, depending on what you choose to place under the master control panel's domain. You can program your system to respond automatically or manually to almost any type of sensor or input device.

One popular application for security systems — in fact, an area of considerable growth within the industry itself — is in video surveillance.

Back in Chapters 6 and 7, we talk about distributing video throughout the home by using modulators to send video from one room to every TV in the house. You are effectively doing the same thing here. You can buy products for security and safety purposes that originate video so that you can see front, side, and back doors, garages, driveways, pool areas, play areas, valuables, babysitters, cleaners, and other people helping in sensitive areas of your home.

Video is different from many other inputs, however. Residential home systems aren't to the point where the system can automatically perform certain tasks based on the video's content, other than automatically recording the images when it sees someone coming to the door, for instance, and stopping when that person leaves the field of vision.

In fact, you can record video signals to VHS tape to review at your leisure. Have you hired a new nanny? Want to see if your cleaning person is really cleaning all day long, or just eating your food? This technology lets you see what's happening at home — whether you are inside your house or 500 miles away.

Video surveillance

Many alarm, intercom, and telephone systems have an extension capability that includes video distribution for monitoring applications, such as checking out who's at the front door or how the baby is doing in the nursery. This area is one place where the lines between security, telephones, and intercom sub-systems blur (pun intended) because any of them can provide for video distribution throughout your smart home.

You are going to want to consider two forms of video surveillance: still image and live picture. Although you may love to have live, detailed, color pictures as part of your video surveillance system, you have to determine whether the feature is worth the cost. A number of very inexpensive systems that are either black and white or still image may do the trick, and they're easier on your budget.

Most consumer-oriented imaging products for surveillance are either stand-alone, closed-circuit style cameras, or they are tethered to a local PC.

The size of today's cameras and how secretive their locations can be is amazing. Smart-Choice (www.smart-choice.com) has a line of hidden cameras that look like thermostats and PIRs; they pick up video as well as audio signals from their field of view. And they're not that expensive an add-on to your system either — a few hundred dollars per camera.

CCTV options

You used to see closed-circuit television (CCTV) only in movies and in convenience stores. This technology is ideal for surveillance — you can monitor and record CCTV to stop theft, limit liability exposure, maximize productivity, and protect yourself from safety incidents.

Smart-Choice has a line of products that fit right into the homeowner's budget. Its SecureCam Video Observation Camera connects right up to your television. You can even use the product with your TV's picture-in-picture capability (your TV must have audio/video input). The entry-level product is a low-light, black-and-white camera with a built-in microphone. It comes with 60-foot camera and TV connection cables. If you don't want to use your TV, SmartChoice offers the BabyCam wireless monitoring system. Other versions have color and quad picture displays (which show the video from four different cameras all at once on a TV screen).

You may not always have the luxury of running a coaxial cable for your video-camera signal distribution. If running a coaxial cable is out of the question, you can use a *video balun* (basically a cable converter) to convert the signals for transmission over CAT-3 or CAT-5 cabling. You use two of the eight conductors in the telephone/data cabling for each signal. Surprisingly, line noise, cross talk, and attenuation are low, approaching the performance of shielded coaxial cable. You can still use the extra conductors as a phone line if you like. You need one balun for each of the receiving and the sending devices.

PC options

Another option for viewing and storing video in a home video surveillance network is to leverage your PC investment, and put that fancy Pentium III screamer to work. You can do so in two ways:

✔ **You can use special-purpose PC video cameras that connect to the video capture card installed inside your PC:** Most of these cameras are designed for other uses, like videoconferencing, and can't really get too far away from your PC (the average cord doesn't get much beyond 12 feet in length), but a few companies are designing systems that will let you connect several cameras that are spread throughout your house.

✔ **You can install a TV card inside your PC and then connect your video surveillance cameras to your home's video network:** Using devices called modulators (see Chapter 7), you can put these cameras on unused television channels and watch them on your PC — or on any TV.

If you're a real Net expert, you can even use PC-connected video surveillance cameras and Web Cam software to watch your home remotely, over the Internet. Just set up the Web Cam software to send your home video to your personal Web site, and when you want to see what's going on at home from the office or laptop, all you have to do is punch in your URL and watch! You might want to use a password to keep that URL unavailable to prying eyes.

Other options

Moonlight Products, Inc. has a neat little $399 product called FoneCam (www.fonecam.com) — a remote digital camera with its own integrated modem, which you can easily install and access anywhere a standard phone line is available. FoneCam allows a wide range of remote image-capture applications — from checking on the yard people while they cut the grass to evaluating the weather at your vacation home before packing.

Unlike many other remotely controllable cameras, FoneCam doesn't require you to have a PC attached for operation — the camera itself contains the parts of the PC that it needs. As such, you can place FoneCam anywhere it can have access to a phone line and a power outlet, which substantially frees you to run video almost anywhere you want to in your home, without worrying about whether the PC is on or where it's located.

Although the camera doesn't require you to have a PC running, you must have one running on the remote end — to view the video sent out by the FoneCam. Using FoneCam software, you can use any remote computer with a modem to remotely control the image quality and transmission frequency of the photos. (FoneCam software is compatible with Windows 95, Windows 98, and Windows NT — and Apple/Macintosh systems running a Windows emulation such as SoftWindows.) FoneCam retrieves pictures manually, or you can schedule it to transmit automatically without user intervention. In addition, it can display images individually or in an animated sequence.

Interestingly, FoneCam incorporates a remote event trigger (RET) function that automatically downloads an image when a specified event occurs, such as when something triggers a security device. So you can combine RET with some of your other sensors to capture your thief on tape, and then have that picture sent to you or your monitoring station.

Audio surveillance

Audio surveillance is something that really hasn't taken off in most home-security installations, but it's pretty neat nonetheless. By adding a device called a *two-way audio module* into your alarm's central panel, you can send and receive audio to and from your alarm company's central monitoring station. Most two-way audio systems communicate via a microphone and speaker installed in the alarm keypad. After an alarm is triggered, the alarm system notifies the central station, and the two-way audio system automatically kicks in.

Using the same telephone line that connects you to the monitors, you can have hands-free conversations with the monitors (which could be very handy in the event of a medical emergency — you know "I've fallen and I can't get up!").

If you're not home, the monitoring station can record all of the sounds that your uninvited visitors make while they're in your home — not that you'd probably want to listen to their take on your home decorating skills.

Other cool sensors

Your security system can get even neater with the addition of more endpoint inputs to drive your "vision" around your smart home. In this section, we talk about a few of these cool sensors and how they can fit into your security network.

Temperature sensors

Mother Nature can be tough to deal with sometimes, but your smart home can help out. All sorts of sensors can warn you of impending problems.

Two popular sensors are low-temperature sensors and flood sensors. Low-temperature sensors tell you when your heat has gone out for some reason and your pipes are at risk of freezing. Flood sensors tell you when you've got water in your basement. Both are important events that you want to find out about early.

Driveway sensors

If you have a particularly long driveway or if want to have a sensor that triggers a number of automatic functions when you come home from work, you can install a driveway sensor.

There are two major types of driveway sensors:

- ✓ **Magnetic sensors** typically sit 1 inch below the asphalt or 6 inches in the ground to the side of the driveway. These are the more accurate sensors because they look for a mass that approximates a car.
- ✓ **Infrared beams** trigger the system when something breaks the beam. These sensors can pick up anything that comes up the driveway, such as a bicycle, a dog, or a UPS truck.

These sensors are great to incorporate into your smart home, however, because they can automatically trigger a number of actions designed to make your life easier. We've known homeowners who have combined intercoms at the front gate, magnetic sensors in the driveway, and home automation within the house to control the flow of people in and out of homes while they sit on a beach holding a cell phone.

Pool-disturbance sensors

Having a pool is great, but pools are a tremendous risk with small kids around. You never know when someone is going to slip through your gate and wander around the pool.

Pool-disturbance sensors solve this problem. They tell you when something has fallen in the pool. When triggered, pool sensors communicate with their wireless receivers and let out a loud alarm. They can also talk with other interfaces — such as your phone lines to call the monitoring service.

Finding the Right Security System

Security systems are easily expandable, provided that you have the right foundation. To pick a security system, look at both hardwired and wireless systems and determine how these systems will interface with your other smart-home subsystems, such as home automation.

Hardwired systems

We've heard one company compare wiring a wireline security system with wiring a train set. If you can do one, you can do the other. (If you don't have a train set, go out, buy one, install it, see if it's hard, and then come back to reading this book.)

Wireline systems are

- **Reliable:** There are no batteries to worry about; wires are hidden reliably in the walls. Control panels routinely have battery backup in case the power fails.

- **Sophisticated:** Because the alarm industry has its roots in wireline installations, wireline systems are by far the more sophisticated systems. Most of the innovations have taken place with the wireline as a foundation.

- **Supervised:** Wireline systems are constantly in touch with their endpoint devices, querying them to check their health and availability. Doing so ensures that your system is at peak efficiency at all times.

On the other hand, wireline systems are much more complicated to install and are permanent after you install them.

Wireless systems

Wireless systems are obviously easier to install than the wireline systems, particularly if you are doing the work yourself after your house has been built.

Wireless systems are

- **Portable:** If you move, simply unplug the wireless system and take it with you to your next home. You can get monitoring services from anywhere in the U.S. All you need is electricity and a phone line.

✔ **Easy to use and install:** The only tool you need is a screwdriver. Some systems come in a nice tidy do-it-yourself package, like Magnavox's Wireless Security System (www.magnavox-security.com). With that, your system is shipped to you with simple instructions, a set-up video-tape, and 24-hour customer support (for all of those 2 a.m. installations!).

✔ **Private:** No strangers come into your house, drill holes in your walls, or know your home's layout or system password.

Wireless systems require you to change batteries, so if you're the type who hates to change the batteries in your smoke detectors, you may want to opt for a wireline system.

You may hear people say that wireless systems are less reliable and more prone to false alarms. Years ago, wireless systems were inferior to wireline systems (and lower-end wireless systems are still inferior to wireline systems), but manufacturers of wireline systems are feverishly bringing high-quality, reliable wireless interfaces to market today.

An ounce of prevention

Installing a good security system only secures your house to a certain extent. For example, leaving the newspapers piling up on the front doorstep for two weeks is a sure-fire clue that you're away. You can do things to secure your home that don't involve your security system, but are nonetheless important.

Make sure that you have these critical safety items in the house:

✔ **Fire extinguishers.** They may look ugly in a white kitchen, but you need them, so plan ahead where to put them.

✔ **Night lights.** Place these in bathrooms and hallways (in-wall floor-level lights can be a neat built-in feature).

✔ **Fire escape ladders.** Multistory homes need these from upper floors.

✔ **Flashlights.** Distribute them amply around the house.

✔ **Generator.** Have one available in case of a power outage.

Also make sure that your family has a planned escape route and meeting place outside your home for emergencies. Test that plan with your family. Everyone will be calmer in an actual emergency.

Finally, on that newspaper problem, more and more newspapers, *The New York Times* (www.nytimes.com), for example, allow you to turn on and off your subscription online. With a smart home, a crafty programmer could make it very easy to turn your paper delivery on and off — as simple as telling your home controller, "Suspend the newspapers for two weeks from today," for example.

Wireless systems used to be totally unsupervised — meaning that the central control panel did not know whether the sensor batteries were running low or whether the sensors had some problem. Now, however, some of the more professional wireless systems have been outfitted with a supervision capability that makes them increasingly accepted as part of a wireline implementation. More than 25 percent of all alarm systems installed professionally are hybrid wireline/wireless now. We give you more information on supervision issues in Chapter 18.

Getting the Job Done

You have two options when installing a home security system — do it yourself or hire a professional contractor to do it for you. Most do-it-yourself projects are wireless in nature. You can buy a range of sensors and control panels from home improvement stores or electronics stores.

You can also choose a kit that offers everything in one box. Most of these kits come with a control box, an alarm siren, and various combos of wireless contact and keychain remote controls. One such vendor is Magnavox (www.magnavox-security.com), which sells a system over the Internet.

Few homeowners install wireline systems themselves (although they could do so rather easily); the wireless options are just too attractive from an ease-of-install point-of-view. Rather, most homeowners hire professionals to install wireline security systems that are designed explicitly for their homes. Professional security installers provide a proposal and make recommendations on the type and location of each sensor. They may have promotional deals that provide you with a starter system.

The choice between putting in a security system yourself and hiring a professional is a matter of budget and preference. We recommend that you seriously consider hiring a professional to install this system. Messing up the cabling of your stereo system is one thing, but messing up your security system could be life-threatening. Don't scrimp on your security system.

Some companies actually install a basic system in your home for free if you sign a long-term (usually five-year) agreement with them for monitoring services. The upside of these deals is a low initial cost. The downside is inadequate coverage and higher fees as you go along. Most of these secure-now, pay-later packages include coverage only for four doors or windows and a single motion sensor. If you want to expand your coverage, you have to pay high additional costs. Moreover, you don't own the system, you lease it. Monitoring fees are higher, and you have to agree to a long-term contract with a hefty early-termination fee. Be sure to check out comparable deals with non-free systems and figure the costs over time; you're generally better off just paying for a system up front.

The National Burglar & Fire Alarm Association (301-907-3202, www.alarm.org) offers advice on how to shop for a security system and the names of contractors who have qualified for their "Installation Quality" certificate.

Chapter 18

Wiring a Security System

● ●

In This Chapter

▶ Looping your security

▶ Controlling your sensors

▶ Playing zone defense

▶ Interconnecting with your home security brain

● ●

*H*ome security systems, in our opinion, are more suited for installation by professional specialists than by do-it-yourselfers. Too much is at stake, whether you think in terms of your family's safety or the potential troubles that an improperly installed system can cause (such as false alarms, which tend to drive people like the police and fire department crazy and can actually result in fines to the homeowner).

That said, we think it's important to have an idea what kinds of wiring and equipment make up a home security system so that you can have an intelligent conversation with potential security installers. This chapter discusses these wiring and architecture issues, and explains in some detail how security systems work and how the various pieces and parts fit together.

How to Prewire

The best place to start thinking about a home security system is to look at how you can prewire your home to meet your short-and long-term security needs. In this section, we discuss the general layout or architecture of a security system, and also the specific types of wire (or wireless systems!) that connect together the components of a security system.

Running a security loop

Your home-security system is based on the *star architecture,* in which every cable meets at a central point: the wiring control panel (see Figure 18-1). Locating your wiring control panel in the central wiring closet that we describe in Chapter 2 makes good sense; you want your control panel near the point where your telephone service comes into the house so that you can configure the system to call for help in an emergency. We cover this connection in the section "Super supervision," later in this chapter.

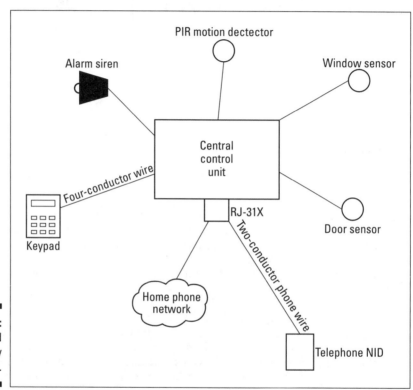

Figure 18-1:
A star-wired
security
loop.

The cables that connect to the sensors and other elements of your security subsystem all extend from the control panel. Although you can daisy-chain sensors — adding an extra sensor sometime after the initial installation to the line that runs to a nearby sensor — the control panel can't differentiate between devices that share a line to the control panel.

The cable that connects security devices generally contains multiple (generally two or four) smaller wires — known as *conductors* — within the same wire jacket. Half the wires cover the circuit that delivers information to the sensor; the other half deliver information back to the security control panel. So the signals form a loop between the control panel and each sensor. These loops enable the control panel to tell whether the sensor is functioning correctly.

Wiring choices

You use the following main types of wire in typical alarm installations:

- ✔ **Normal telephone wire:** This type is simply 22-gauge, four-conductor telephone wire. Some dealers are getting into structured cabling systems (a term used to describe all-in-one cabling systems that take care of phone, video, data, and other network needs with one bundle of wire), and some of these may utilize CAT-5 implementations for other reasons — cabling that could possibly be used as part of your alarm prewiring. Part VI provides you with more information on that situation.

- ✔ **Fire-alarm cable:** You must connect fire alarms with special fire-alarm cable that rates to 105 degrees centigrade so that it doesn't burn. You see this wiring strung as bright red cabling in your basement.

- ✔ **Intercom cable:** Some intercom systems allow you to add intercom monitoring stations to the security system. If you decide on such a system, make sure that your installer uses special 22-gauge stranded and shielded wiring and grounds on every run. Failure to do so exposes the intercom system to electrical interference, which generates an annoying hum.

Wiring for wireless

Prewiring for wireless systems may sound weird, but it does actually make sense. Few professional installations are totally wireless — you usually install some sort of hybrid system. Wireless systems don't require prewiring at each point where you install the wireless endpoints, but you need to be careful about where you install your phone-line interfaces (as we discuss later in the chapter in the section "Phone-line interfaces") and how you tie your central system into your other wireline assets.

Good news for basement dwellers

Unlike other subsystem wiring schemes, security systems are very expandable, because so much of the wiring runs through the basement ceiling and then up short distances to the first-floor terminations. (You don't need too many sensors on upper floors in most cases.) So, unless you use sheetrock or otherwise close off your ceiling in the basement, running an extra cable shouldn't be an issue if you decide to add another sensor or other end device. You don't need to "overbuild" your system, therefore, as long as you have an unfinished basement or drop ceiling. You merely install what you need today and add on to the system in the future as you want to expand.

If you trip a wireless sensor, it sends out a high-frequency coded signal to the central station, which interprets and acts on the signal as necessary. Wireless systems basically act just like wired ones, sending electrical signals to and from sensors, keypads, and central stations, but the wireless systems use radio signals instead of cabling to send and receive the signals.

Beware of all-in-one wireless security solutions. These systems are wireless designs for apartments and other smaller applications that combine a *passive infrared receiver*, or *PIR* with a siren. (We explain how these passive units monitor the infrared spectrum in Chapter 17.) All in one wireless systems are designed so that when the PIR detects a burglar, the siren sounds to alert the family or frighten the burglar away. These systems are questionable in practice, however, because many issue a beeping tone if you trip them, which enables you to disarm the unit with a user-entered code. This time delay gives a burglar a chance to locate the alarm device on entry and smash it before the siren goes off.

When placing wireless devices in your home, avoid areas that contain large quantities of metal, if metal can impede your signals. And think twice about using a wireless system if someone in your house is a ham-radio fan or because you live near a commercial broadcasting station — these radio waves can interfere with the radio signals that the sensors transmit. Avoid proximity to other electronic devices in the house as well.

All Zoned Out

The central security control panel tracks each circuit as a separate *zone,* and ideally, each circuit connects to only one sensor or device. So if you have a room with three window contacts and a passive infrared receiver, you have four zones here, not one. Typical security control panels for home applications have the capacity to monitor from 6 to 48 zones.

Zones enable the control panel to query the status of each device and to interpret the inputs from each device. By tracking triggers sequentially from three related zones, for example, you can interpret that someone is walking a specific direction down a hallway.

Still, in some cases, you may need to run multiple sensors on the same circuit, known as dividing a zone into *subzones.* The drawback to the subzone approach is that all the sensors that connect to the same circuit "appear" as a single sensor to the control panel. If you connect a door, a window sensor, and a PIR to the same circuit, you can't tell which is causing the alarm — just that *something* in that area is detecting something that shouldn't be there.

Most installers are moving away from the subzone concept and are instead installing central panels that can handle more individual sensors. This changeover means that you must install more runs of cable back to the central controller (which costs more money), but the extra wire results in a more meaningful set of alarm signals. If you have a big house, talk about the pros and cons of subzones with your installer and figure out which approach is better for your budget and needs.

Wireless systems work by zones, too. Each wireless device that's part of a professional installation has its own port on the control panel, just like on the wireline devices. The wireless devices typically communicate via the 300–900 MHz frequencies, which are highly reliable — unless you have a lot of radio activity nearby.

Super supervision

A key element of your security subsystem is the concept of *supervision*, which is the capability of an alarm system to sense the status of any attached device.

The control panel continuously monitors its attached devices — how often and which things it monitors vary from panel to panel. Among the things that most systems monitor for are power failure, telephone-line trouble, loss of internal clock, trouble in any part of the system, low-battery conditions, attempts to tamper with systems, and other internal faults.

Alarm systems send in periodic test signals to central monitoring stations — typically, once a week. You'd be amazed at the number of customers whose systems aren't functional in some fashion or another. All sorts of things can happen in a home to cause problems. People install computers on telephone lines, and the telephone installer may reroute or cause problems with the same phone line that your subsystem's on. People put additions on their houses and mess up wiring. Lots of simple things can conspire to throw part of your security system into chaos, and that's why supervision is so important.

Wireless supervision

Wireless systems need supervision to be successful, too. Control panels that support wireless systems should also enable you to supervise these devices. Unsupervised wireless systems can detect whether a sensor circuit opens. This sort of system can tell you whether someone opens the front door, for example, but can't tell you the state of the remote sensors at any particular time. It can't, for example, tell you that its batteries are low.

Phone lines — the weak link

The most vulnerable part of your security system is your phone-line interface. Your phone line isn't monitored. The alarm system relies on that phone line to call the monitoring station and implicitly assumes that it's always there. And the monitoring service, which may be located hundreds of miles away, also assumes that the line's there and working.

The result is that many phone-line-based alarm systems are vulnerable to situations in which someone cuts the phone line before entering the house and tripping the alarm. Yes — sad but true — the Hollywood movies we've seen about phone lines being cut prior to entry are accurate.

Your central panel monitors your phone line for certain levels of current and voltage to make sure that it's still operational. The panel displays a message in the LCD display on the keypad if the phone line fails. Some security systems annunciate that the line is out, using a loudspeaker. And some people install a "phone line-out" trigger siren.

As you're building your house, think about hardening the access to your telephone lines. If you're in a new home division, the builders usually bury many of these lines, which is great. Many other homes, however, have exposed NIDs (Network Interface Devices) on the outside of the house, and the telephone line is in plain view. If your telephone company requires an outside interface, work with them to protect it as much as possible with a lock box and hardened conduit.

If you feel uncomfortable that your phone line represents a line of vulnerability, you can buy a *derived channel* from your local telephone company. This item is a special alarm line. The phone company puts a little black box in the central telephone office serving you and another where the line from your house ends. This box creates a subaudible two-way communication that creates supervision. If the signal trips open, the central station gets a signal signifying that the phone line is down.

Because of its cost, which is about $45 per month, the derived-channel approach has never really taken off on any mass basis. The majority of alarms don't use this dedicated line; line seizure (the industry term for an RJ-31x system) uses the regular phone line.

Supervised wireless systems truly mimic wireline systems. Typically, the system sends each wireless zone a supervisory round every so often. If the receiver hears from the wireless device at least once during that query, it doesn't report a trouble. If it doesn't receive a response, it treats the situation just as it does any other fault and reports a problem with the system to the monitoring station.

Within the supervisory transmission, the system usually queries the device about the status of the battery. If the battery is low, the system reports a fault.

With a supervised system, if you try to jam the wireless signal, the attempt creates a trouble condition. Your keypad beeps, and the control station gets a trouble signal.

Connecting to Other Systems

The power of your security system isn't measured only in its inherent capabilities, but also in those that you can add to it by interfacing your subsystem with other subsystems in your home.

Phone-line interfaces

If you can afford it, you want a monitoring service to remotely monitor your security system. Your control panel then dials the alarm-monitoring service if any event that you programmed into your system occurs.

To dial out, your system needs access to an outside phone line. In most cases, it accesses the phone line that you use as your home telephone number, unless you opt for derived-channel service. (See the sidebar "Phone lines — the weak link," earlier in this chapter.)

The alarm system must be *inline* with your service, meaning that the telephone line physically runs through this panel on its way to your in-home telephone network. If something trips a sensor, the system seizes the telephone line to make an outbound call. The alarm system uses a piggybacked jack with a shorting bridge that disconnects the rest of the home-phone network. In doing so, the system effectively disconnects all the phones in the house while it makes that outbound call for help.

Stand-alone wireless systems — such as those you typically find at the local do-it-yourselfer outlets — enable you to merely plug them into the nearest phone outlet in the house. But if someone leaves a phone off the hook or if the phone is in use as the alarm trips, the wireless system can't seize the line and make the emergency call for help. For this reason, we recommend that you don't install a wireless system from a normal telephone extension in the house. Instead, run a phone line to the inline jack at the control box where your phone line enters the house.

Don't connect the alarm-panel communicator to telephone lines that you use with a fax machine. Fax-machine lines may incorporate a voice filter, which disconnects the line if it detects anything other than fax signals. This filter can result in partial transmissions to the monitoring center.

Your central security control panel connects with your home phone lines via an *RJ-31X connection.* This interface — called the digital communicator — transmits the signal from the control panel to the central monitoring station.

The connection is straightforward — the conductors from the local telephone line connect to the panel and then route back out of the panel to connect with the in-home telephones.

One of the big advantages of the RJ-31X interface is that it enables you to dial into your system from a phone to do stuff such as turn the system on and off or turn up the temperature inside the house.

Alternative phone-line interfaces

Having the control panel send alarm signals to a remote monitoring station is not the only way to accomplish your goal of getting help if an emergency arises. Other possibilities are the focus of this section.

One alternative to having a phone-line connection to the central security control panel is to use wireless communications — cellular-phone technologies, for example — to dial into the remote monitoring station. You can use wireless technologies as an alternative to a phone-line connection or as a supplement (in case someone cuts the phone line). At least two national networks are vying to get your wireless monitoring business: Uplink (at www.uplink.com) and Alarmnet (at www.alarmnet.com), both of which use cellular and wireless data networks to carry signals between your local control panel and the monitoring station. These networks enable two-way wireless alarm communications to any monitoring station.

Some of the service options use the digital control channels from cellular systems — that is, those channels that the cellular carriers use to authenticate the user and help set up the phone call. These control channels aren't in heavy use and have plenty of space to reliably carry this extra traffic. All these options can carry security-system signals in the event that the phone line isn't available. The radio transmitter costs around $295 with an $18 or so monthly charge.

Another way to get emergency help — one that's popular among the do-it-yourself products — is to use a *voice dialer.* This feature is an electronic tape-recording application that automatically dials out on the telephone lines to a police station, fire department, or ambulance emergency service. The upside is that you save the monthly monitoring charge by using such a system. The downside is that you have no way to ensure that the party the dialer calls actually receives the call. An automatic recording can't answer questions or give interpretation. Some localities have banned these items, too, so check your local ordinances.

If you're planning to control your security system by telephone from remote locations, you need to plan how this system is going to work with your other telephone services. You can, for example, set many security systems to answer your phone after a certain number of rings so that you can then send commands to the security system. But if you have an answering machine, central office-based voice mail, or even call forwarding on the line, you must design a way to ensure that the right device answers the phone. If controlling your system remotely is important to you, you may need to dedicate a phone line to your security system.

Home-control interfaces

Various control panels sport X-10 home-control modules that, through the addition of programming and timers, can also turn your lights on and off. By using such modules, you can program your security system so that if the fire alarm goes off, for example, you can turn on specific lights to guide you out of the house.

You can program more sophisticated systems, such as those that we discuss in Chapter 20, to utilize the inputs from your sensors to perform all sorts of tasks. You can use a driveway sensor that you connect to your security panel to issue home-automation commands that turn on the garage and porch lights, for example, or sound a chime in the home office.

Serial port connections via RS-232?

A few home security systems, such as those made by Napco (at www.napco.com), provide an electronic interface known as *RS-232*. This connection is basically the same kind that the serial port on most PCs uses (the place where you connect a Palm Pilot cradle). If you install a security panel with an RS-232 interface and you also have a home-automation controller with its own RS-232 input, you can connect them together to get even more sophisticated sensor-to-automation relationships.

Why doesn't everyone use RS232? Well, that involves a big problem, actually. Although the RS-232 interface itself is quite standardized and common, the actual programming code that works the alarms and home-automation controllers is quite proprietary. So a security panel from manufacturer X may not be capable of talking to a home-automation controller from company Y. This lack of compatibility can really be a major pain in the neck, although thankfully, some of these companies are beginning to open up their programming to each other to ensure interoperability.

Right now, however, security and automation interfacing is a pretty iffy thing. Unless you're a serial-programming expert who can get deep down into the guts of the code, you need to leave this kind of system integration to a professional installer who's trained on both alarm and automation systems.

Audio interfaces

Some alarm systems enable you to connect a number of standard interior and exterior intercom stations or sensors to your alarm system. You can use these for listening in on the babies, playing background music, seeing who's at the door, answering incoming phone calls, and paging people around the house. A neat feature of such systems is that the central station can also access these intercoms, so monitoring agents can listen and talk through these systems.

Electrical-system interfaces

Some systems use the electrical system to communicate between the control panel and remote inputs and outputs. Some wireless alarm sounders, for example, plug directly into the electrical outlet and use the electric power lines inside the home to send and receive alarm command signals. If something triggers a sensor and requires an alarm to sound, the main control unit sends an alarm command through the electric lines, triggering the plug-in alarm sounder.

Web interfaces

Although you may think that an Internet interface is a natural extension of the security subsystem, little progress has been made in that area to date.

With a constant connection to the Internet — say, through a cable modem or a DSL link — you could have constant connections to your monitoring center — and not need to rely on grabbing a dialup phone line to communicate your status. You could also set up Web-based interfaces to control various aspects of your security system, including realtime video.

Enabling Web access to the security system involves lots of, well, security issues. As the world becomes more familiar with the Internet, however, we're undoubtedly going to see some developments in this area.

Part VI
Putting It All Together: Home Automation and Control

The 5th Wave   By Rich Tennant

"It was a compromise. I gave in on the home LAN connection, but I drew the line at the two-way video feed."

In this part . . .

In a sense, we're reaching the climax of the book! This part is where it all comes together, where your home networks really hum (but your wiring doesn't). This is where you reach your true status as a "smart home."

There are two main but closely related topics in this part — whole-home-automation systems and remote-control systems for your home's entertainment networks. Both of these topics help you interconnect and take advantage of all your subsystems — audio, video, telephony, computer LAN, security, and so on— that we discuss in the first five parts of this book.

Chapter 19

Home Automation Extravaganza

*I*n preceding chapters of this book, we describe how to create a backbone that enables you to distribute various kinds of signals around your smart home. The next step — one that can make things more useful and more fun — is to install home control and automation networks that can help you take charge of your smart home's subsystems.

An amazingly wide range of home control and automation systems is available — everything from simple X-10 powerline controls that cost in the tens of dollars to custom-built proprietary networks that cost in the tens of thousands of dollars. In this chapter, we give you a taste of what's on the market and what these devices can do. We also talk a bit about some emerging standards that can make home automation and control easier, cheaper, and better than what's available today.

Where an Automated Home Begins — and Ends

An automated home can be a very simple grouping of controls, or it can be an automation extravaganza where just about anything that is plugged into electrical power is remotely controlled. You can start off small — a few lamps that turn themselves on and off — or you can go whole hog and create a system that responds to your input — or those of various sensors — and uses that input to control all sorts of stuff in your home. Where you decide to fall on this spectrum is really up to you.

Any home automation and control system includes the following basic parts:

✔ **A protocol:** The common language that all the devices in the home-automation network understand. *X-10* is the predominant protocol in home automation today.

✔ **A wiring infrastructure:** The wires that carry signals to each automation or control device in the network. Many home-automation systems (including X-10) use the existing electrical wiring to transmit signals, but a few require special wiring.

✔ **A controller device:** A device that sends signals over the infrastructure in a way that conforms to the protocol. The signals tell specific pieces of equipment what to do.

The big difference among the various implementations of home networking comes in the realm of controllers. You can start off with a small, stand-alone controller that costs only about $60, or you can go with a high-end PC-type controller that runs into the thousands of dollars (you can find cheaper PC controllers, however).

X-10 Is the Reigning Champ

X-10 actually refers to two things: a protocol and a company name. X-10 is the dominant protocol for controlling (turning on and off) electrical devices such as lights and appliances via your home's electrical lines. X-10 also refers to a company name, X-10, Ltd. (at www.x10.com on the Web), the company that bought the original patent for X-10 technology back in the 1980s and held the patent until it expired in 1997. X-10 is now an open standard, sold by both X-10 and other companies, such as Leviton.

We use the term *X-10* to refer to the protocol (or to mean a device that's compatible with the X-10 protocol), because thinking of X-10 in this way reminds you that you don't need to buy from X-10, Ltd. to get X-10. All compatible products display (on their packaging or on the product itself) an X-10-compatible logo, which ensures that they work with other products regardless of manufacturer.

X-10 basics

X-10 uses a home's existing electrical power lines to communicate between the central controller and each of the individual *modules* (the devices that receive X-10 signals over your home's power lines and directly control lamps and appliances) that turn individual lights, appliances, or other electrical devices on and off. X-10 doesn't require any specific network architecture to work in a home — by design, X-10 sends its control signals over your power lines to every outlet in the house.

The electrical wiring infrastructures of some homes isolate the circuits of some outlets from others — so a controller in the living room may not be capable of sending a signal to a module in the guest bathroom. By using a device known as a *signal bridge* (which we discuss in more detail in Chapter 20), you can overcome this problem.

Your X-10 module is a small, box-shaped device — no bigger than the "wall-wart" plug-in transformer power supplies that many home appliances such as telephones and answering machines use — with a standard electrical plug on the back and a place to plug in your lamp or other device on the front. The idea is that you place the device in the *on* mode, and after that, instead of you flipping a switch, the X-10 module turns the device on or off.

Most modules — but not all — have a *local-control* feature that enables you to manually turn devices on and off without involving your X-10 system. To activate this feature, you typically use the device's own on/off switch (not the module's) and turn it off and then back on.

Because every module in the house can "see" the control signals coming out of an X-10 controller, the system needs some way of identifying which module is which — otherwise you end up with a chaotic situation with the wrong things turning on and off. The solution to this problem is an addressing scheme that uses 16 *house codes* (using the letters A–P) and 16 *unit codes* (using numbers 1–16). Every module in an X-10 network is assigned one of each of these codes, to identify it. The house code is also used by controllers to perform multiple control actions at once — for example you can put all of your downstairs lights on a single house code (code A, for example), and then have your controller send a signal that says "turn on all lights in house code A."

The person installing each individual module programs it to a unique combination of these codes (usually just by turning a small wheel with a screwdriver) so that it answers only to signals sent to that particular code. This method of identifying modules on the network enables up to 256 (16 × 16) unique, controllable pieces of equipment within your home-automation network.

Although 256 is the maximum number of modules that an X-10 network can control, it can control a larger number of end devices. You can, for example, plug two lights into the same module with multiple outlets. These two lamps aren't *individually* controllable, but both respond to the on/off commands sent to that module. You can modify this technique for lights in different parts of the house by using two modules set to the same address.

Figure 19-1 shows a very limited X-10 network.

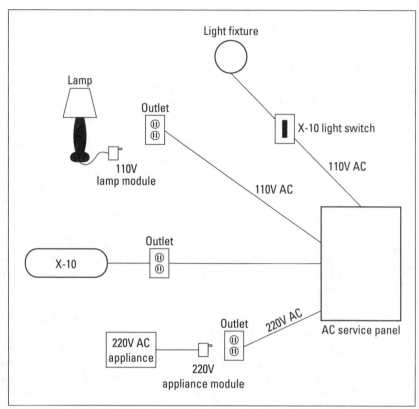

Figure 19-1:
A small X-10
network.

Modules

If you look in a home-automation catalog (we tell you about a few of our favorites in the Chapter 24), you find a wide variety of X-10 modules — ranging from generic lamp modules to specialized devices that control specific pieces of equipment. The main distinctions among modules are as follows:

- ✔ **The kind of device they control.** Modules that control devices such as lamps are cheaper (and handle less electrical current) than those that turn on and off such high-powered devices as electrical dryers.

- ✔ **The control signals they can understand.** The simplest X-10 modules simply know how to turn things on and off in response to a control signal. More sophisticated modules can perform additional functions, such as lamp dimming or brightening or ceiling-fan speed adjustments.

- ✔ **Whether they're one-way or two-way.** Most X-10 modules are one-way — that is, they receive control signals but don't respond back to the central controller to tell it that the module has performed an action. In the last year or two, however, a new breed of two-way modules has come to market that provide this status confirmation.

Sometimes electrical noise and interference on a home's power lines can prevent an X-10 module from understanding or receiving the X-10 signals. The new two-way modules tell you (or your controller) whether a command actually worked — which is a handy feature for such important commands as starting the coffee pot in the morning. Most of the modules that we discuss in this chapter are available in both one-way and two-way configurations. You can use them interchangeably in your X-10 network, but only two-way modules send confirmation signals back to a two-way compatible controller.

Some newer modules can receive something known as *extended X-10 codes* to perform additional functions, but generally speaking, a module can perform only six actions (if told to do so by a controller). Table 19-1 describes these six actions and their results.

Table 19-1	X-10 Actions
Action	*What It Does*
On combo.	Turns on the module corresponding to a house/unit code
Off combo.	Turns off the module corresponding to a house/unit code
All On	Turns on all X-10 modules within a house code range.
All Off	Turns off all X-10 modules within a house code range.
Dim combo.	Dims the module corresponding to a house/unit code
Brighten combo.	Brightens the module corresponding to a house/unit code

The following sections describe some of the modules available for your use.

Lamp modules

The simplest — and most common — X-10 modules are *lamp modules*. These modules simply plug into any standard 110-volt AC outlet, between the lamp cord and the outlet. You can use these modules only with incandescent bulbs — usually only for those bulbs that are up to 300 watts in power. (Check the labeling as you're choosing a module to make sure that it can handle the type of bulb you want it for.) Fluorescent and halogen bulbs don't work with these kinds of modules — you need to purchase an appliance module for such devices.

Lamp modules respond to On and Off commands for the particular house and unit codes that you assign to the module; they also respond to All On/All Off commands from your controller — commands that turn on or off (you guessed it) all the lights in the house that X-10 modules control. Many lamp modules also respond to dim/brighten commands that an X-10 controller issues, so you can set the mood for dinner or a movie — or whatever you have in mind.

Appliance modules

For all that stuff in your house that uses a bit more juice (electrically speaking), you want to utilize X-10 *appliance modules.* These modules can handle the higher current draws of devices such as coffeemakers, portable heaters, and other household appliances, and they also enable you to connect fluorescent lamps (something that you can't do with an ordinary lamp module).

You don't find Dim/Bright commands on most appliance modules — which makes sense, because you can't really dim a coffee pot. You also don't find an All On function on these modules, which is for safety reasons — some of the devices that connect to appliance modules are things that you *don't* want to turn on if you're just trying to light up the house. You do, however, usually find an All Off command function — if you want everything off, you generally want *everything* off.

You can find appliance modules in both 110-volt AC and 220-volt AC versions — some of a home's really heavy-duty stuff, such as hot tubs, window air conditioners, and clothes dryers, may require the 220-volt versions.

Universal modules

Universal modules are special-purpose appliance modules that control all those electrical and electronic devices in a home that a *relay* (or remote switch) turns on and off. These devices include such things as garage-door openers, electric drapery controls, sprinkler systems, and low-voltage lighting systems (such as yard lights and some track lighting).

You can set the universal module to provide a *momentary* or *continuous* relay closure. You may use the momentary mode for the garage-door opener (which creates the equivalent of pressing the open/close button) and the continuous mode for sprinklers and other devices that you want to remain on until you turn them off.

Universal modules don't receive All On signals (for the same reason that appliance modules don't) but do receive All Off commands.

X-10 receptacles

Most X-10 modules are relatively small and discreet items, but for a truly invisible appearance, you can have your electrician install in-wall X-10 receptacles.

These outlets are exactly the same size and shape as conventional power receptacles but function the same as X-10 appliance modules. The main consideration in installing X-10 receptacles is whether you want the X-10 to control one or both outlets in the receptacle. Some models have an X-10 outlet on top and an "always-live" regular outlet on the bottom — which is useful for circumstances in which you don't want X-10 control on a particular item that you plug into that outlet.

Duplex X-10 wall receptacles offer control over both outlets. We often see companies marketing these kinds of receptacles to parents who want to ensure that their kids aren't watching TV beyond certain time limits. After TV time is over, the controller can effectively turn off the outlet and disable the TV set in the children's room. Boy, is *that* going to make them mad!

Switches

Another way of making X-10 connections less visible in your home is to have your electrician install X-10 *wall switches* to control hardwired lights, fans, and other devices. These switches enable both local and X-10 control of the devices that he wires to them — so you can have your controller turn a light on or off, or you can just walk over to the switch and do it yourself.

If you use two-way X-10 switches, they can inform your intelligent controller that you manually changed the state of the switch (from on to off or vice versa). If you don't have two-way switches, you can end up getting your control system out of whack by manually controlling a switch. This system confusion arises when the switch is manually set to a different position (on or off) than the controller thinks it is set to. Without a two-way switch to let the controller know the change in status, you'll find your system turning lights on when you want it to be turning them off.

Most X-10 switches include All On/All Off command functionality as well as dimmer functionality.

You need to consider the following points when purchasing X-10 wall switches:

✔ Special switches (known as three-way *master* and *slave* switches) are necessary for applications in which more than one switch controls a particular light. Regular switches can't handle this job, because they can't keep track of the light's status when another switch turns the light on or off. Three-way switches can communicate with each other to keep track of this status.

✔ Switches with dimmer functions work only with incandescent light fixtures — not with fluorescent lighting systems.

✔ Ceiling fans and low-voltage lighting sources (such as halogen track lighting) require a specific *inductive* switch — which by design specifically controls fan speeds or dims/brightens low-voltage lights.

✔ Certain 220-volt devices, such as pool pumps, hot-tub heaters, and some air conditioners, require special heavy-duty switches because of the large amount of electrical current they draw.

Controllers

All the X-10 modules, receptacles, and switches in the world aren't very useful without some means of controlling them remotely. Luckily, you have at least as many options for controlling X-10 systems as you have module options — and probably more.

Standard X-10 controllers range from $10 mini-controllers, which provide remote control — but not automation — of a number of modules, to $500 touch-screen controllers that provide a much more sophisticated means of controlling your network. Throw into the mix wireless controllers, specialized lighting controllers, telephone-activated controllers, timers, controllers that activate by light (or darkness), controllers that your security system triggers, voice controllers, and even controllers that use your PC to run your home network, and you have quite a selection to peruse. And that's not even considering some of the high-end, proprietary systems that control X-10 systems, HVAC systems, alarms, and other controllers.

The sheer number of choices in the controller world can prove a bit bewildering, but we do have some good news: You don't need to limit yourself to just one controller. You can start small, if you want, and as you expand your X-10 network, you can supplement your controller inventory with more sophisticated models — while keeping the original controllers active in the network.

You could begin with just a simple mini-controller, for example, and then as your expand your network, use a PC-based controller system to automate your entire house. You don't need to throw the mini-controller out — you can just transfer it to the master bedroom and use it to control certain lights or appliances that you want to turn on and off from the comfort of your bed.

As we discuss controllers, we use the term *module* pretty much exclusively, but whenever we use *module*, we're also including things such as X-10 receptacles and switches. We just figure that you don't want to read "module/receptacle/switch" a whole bunch of times. Plus, we don't really want to type that lengthy term over and over again.

The following sections describe some of the various controllers available to you.

Stand-alone controllers

The simplest and most inexpensive X-10 controllers are *stand-alone* X-10 controllers. These devices don't need a PC — or anything else — to operate. Just plug them into a wall outlet, program them to match the house and unit codes, and you're ready to go.

Mini- and tabletop controllers

The stand-alone controllers that are the cheapest and easiest to install and set up are the *mini-controllers*. These small boxes simply send On/Off, All On/All Off and Dim/Brighten commands to a small number of X-10 devices — usually eight devices.

The mini-controller doesn't do any automation — that is, it requires input from a person to perform a task — but it does provide you with remote control from anywhere in the house.

Tabletop controllers do basically the same thing as mini-controllers — the only real difference is that they can control a larger number of modules.

Programmable controllers and timers

The next step up in controllers — *programmable* or *timer* controllers — begin to offer a degree of home automation to complement the home-control functions of mini-controllers. These devices, which you may either mount on a wall or sit on a desk or table, enable you to control a number of X-10 modules (usually 8 or 16) either manually or automatically.

To make the controller work automatically, you simply need to program the controller to perform an X-10 command or sequence of commands at a particular time. So you can, for example, tell your controller to turn on modules A1 (the kitchen lights) and A2 (the coffee pot) at 6:30 a.m. every Monday through Friday. This kind of automation isn't the end-all in sophistication, but it's a good way to get started down the road to an automated home.

Telephone interfaces

You don't need to be in the house to control your X-10 modules. By installing a *telephone interface,* you can dial into your network from any Touch-Tone phone and turn on the lights or get the hot tub warming up before you get home from the office.

Telephone interfaces simply plug into a phone line (using a telephone cord with a standard RJ-11 jack) and into any power receptacle in the house and utilize Touch-Tone keypad tones to perform various X-10 actions in your home. Prices for these devices range from about $70 for a simple unit that controls ten modules up to about $300 for units that can control 100 or more modules.

When choosing a phone interface for your X-10 network, you want to look for the following features:

- ✔ **Local control:** Some phone interfaces enable you not only to dial in remotely, but also to pick up any phone (on the same line) in your home and enter commands.

- ✔ **Voice annunciator:** More expensive models have built-in *voice annunciators,* which confirm your commands (a feature that can prove very handy if you're not sure whether you just turned on the porch light or the hot tub).

- ✔ **Answering-machine mode:** Some models enable you to put an *answering machine* on the same phone line as the controller. To use the controller, you just ignore the beep on your answering machine and punch in your commands. This feature doesn't work with voice-mail services, however, and may not work with every answering machine, but this feature can prove important if you have only one phone line in the house.

Sensor controllers and interfaces

Although programmable and timer X-10 controllers add some degree of automation to your home network, they're basically still dumb devices. A certain time passes, and they initiate X-10 commands that you previously programmed into them.

That's very handy, but what happens if you want an X-10 command to activate under circumstances that don't adhere to a predictable schedule? What if, for example, you want the lights in your hallway to come on whenever your children walk to the bathroom in the middle of the night. (And believe Danny when he tells you that no predictable schedule exists for that.)

For these kinds of scenarios, you may want to use *sensor-initiated* X-10 controllers, such as those described in the following list:

- ✔ **PIR controllers:** These controllers send out an X-10 signal whenever a passive infrared (PIR) motion detector picks up someone walking into a room (or past your back door in the middle of the night).

- ✔ **Photosensors:** These controllers send out X-10 signals as it gets dark outside (or, alternatively, as the sun rises).

- ✔ **Alarm interfaces:** These controllers use an input from your X-10-compatible security system and utilize the sensors from the alarm system to trigger X-10 commands.

Wireless controllers

After you start getting an automated home up and running, you're likely to find that you have less and less inclination even to get up and walk over to the controller sitting on the table across the living room from your comfy couch. (That condition's known as *couch-potato syndrome,* and it's really catching — trust us.) The X-10 standard has exactly the answer you need if you face this problem — *wireless* controllers.

Wireless controllers consist of two parts — an *RF (radio frequency) receiver,* which plugs into the wall (and does the actual sending of X-10 commands), and the handheld or tabletop *RF transmitter.* Overall, wireless controllers function basically the same as mini- and tabletop controllers but from a distance. Some of these handheld remotes also serve double duty as IR remote controls, so you can use a single remote to control the TV and audio systems as well as the lights.

You can find wireless controllers in all sizes and shapes, ranging from 16-device controllers for the living-room table to small three- or four-module controllers that can hang on your keychain. (These smaller devices are great for controlling the modules that open your garage door or turn on your porch lights.)

You can also get neat wireless X-10 wall switches that simply stick on any wall in your house and communicate with corresponding light modules via RF. These devices are great for adding light switches someplace where your electrician forgot to put them in for you.

Touch panel

The fanciest X-10 controllers are the programmable *touch-screen panels* made by companies such as SmartLinc (at `www.smartlinc.com`). For about $500, these controllers enable you to control and automate hundreds of X-10 modules by using a touch-sensitive LCD screen.

You can also use these systems to create *macros,* or sequences of X-10 actions that you want to trigger via a single touch-pad command or a timed, programmed command. Most touch-panel controllers are also compatible with two-way X-10 modules, so you can see a visual confirmation on-screen that your action has been performed.

The combination of two-way modules and macro capability also enables these controllers to precisely set devices to certain levels of brightness. If you want to set a light to a medium level of brightness, for example, this type of controller can turn on the light, send a dim signal a certain number of times (to reach your desired level of brightness), and then confirm remotely that the light is set where you want it.

PC interfaces

If you really want to get fancy with an X-10 network, you can supplement or replace your stand-alone controllers with a *PC-based control system*. These controllers use the horsepower of your PC and the familiar graphical interface of Windows (or the Macintosh) to enable you to set up and control all of your home's X-10 modules.

The vast majority of PC-based controllers are two-way capable, so they not only control, but also monitor the status of two-way modules. Many also provide inputs from external sensors such as temperature monitors and photosensors and use these inputs to trigger X-10 commands.

The two key components of a PC-based controller are:

- **The control software:** This lets you program and control your X-10 network using a graphical interface on your PC.
- **The interface unit:** This unit connects your computer to the home's powerline network.

Most interface units connect to one of your PC's serial ports (the ones labeled *Com* on most PCs), but you can find other interfaces — such as internal ISA cards. You may think that you can just use your computer's own powerline connection to the wall to do your controlling, but the internal design of a PC doesn't allow you to do so — that's why you need this interface unit to create and send X-10 signals over your home's power lines.

Most PC interface units download and save your preferred settings in their internal memory, so you don't need to keep your PC running for your automation system to work. Not all systems work this way, however — some require a PC that's always on (and always has the home-automation software running). Unless you have an extra PC that you can dedicate to your home-automation network, think long and hard about this requirement. (On the other hand, if you have an old computer sitting around, this sort of setup may be a great use for it.)

You can interface with your PC home-automation software in the following ways:

- **Keyboard:** The simplest way to set up and control PC-based automation software — and the most common method — is to use your keyboard and mouse. Using a graphical interface, you can sit in front of your computer and program timed and macro events for your controller to perform or even manually control modules (if you have the urge to turn off the kitchen lights from the home office).

✔ **Telephone:** By using your computer's modem, you can dial into your home controller/PC from remote locations and trigger X-10 commands by using Touch-Tone key commands.

✔ **Voice:** The neatest way of utilizing PC control of your X-10 network is by voice command. Systems such as the HAL2000 (check out `www.automatedliving.com` on the Web for information) and HomeVoice (at `www.appliedfuture.com`) enable you to use a telephone connection or even a microphone connected to your PC to speak commands into your computer to trigger X-10 commands. These systems not only listen to (and obey) you, but they even answer back — providing confirmation of your spoken commands.

Other Home Control Systems

Although X-10 is by far the most common protocol for controlling devices in the home, it's not the only one. A couple of other emerging standards may some day make inroads on X-10 territory, although, to date, they haven't done so. In general, these new protocols also utilize powerline communications but take advantage of more-advanced technology to make their communications faster and more robust. The following sections describe these up-and-comers.

CEBUS

CEBUS — Consumer Electronics Bus — is a standards-based effort by a group of electronics manufacturers to create a whole new paradigm for home networking. In fact, the CEBUS standard goes beyond just control and automation to encompass the entire infrastructure for home networks, including the cables for carrying audio, video, phone, and data signals. For the most part, the infrastructure part of CEBUS hasn't really been widely adopted (although it's very similar to the star-wired network infrastructure that we describe throughout the book), but a small number of manufacturers are beginning to take advantage of the CEBUS home-automation protocol.

This protocol, known as *Home Plug and Play,* is a media-independent system (meaning that you can send it over power lines, UTP cabling, or coaxial cabling) that, similar to the X-10, can provide a universal language for electrical and electronic devices in a home. The handful of CEBUS-compatible devices available on the market now pretty much mimic X-10 devices — lamp modules and light dimmer switches, for example — but because of the low volumes produced and various license fees that the CEBUS patent holders assess on manufacturers, the devices tend to cost several times as much as similar X-10 modules.

You can get more information on CEBUS equipment and availability at `www.cebus.org` on the Web. For the time being, CEBUS and Home Plug and Play are not really major players in the home-automation marketplace, but Microsoft has recently adopted the standard for future products, so it may become increasingly important in the future.

Getting fancy (and expensive) with home automation

For home automation and control that goes beyond even the functionality of most PC-based X-10 control systems, you may want to consider a high-end, proprietary home-automation system. These systems are stand-alone systems that you usually mount in a panel in your home's wiring closet. They have their own central-controller unit (usually a PC-based computer), X-10 controllers, and interfaces to a large number of other systems, such as security systems, audio and video networks, telephone and intercom systems, external sensors, and other proprietary control systems.

The most sophisticated PC-based controller systems, such as HAL2000 and HomeVoice, perform many of the same functions as these stand-alone systems but use your PC in the place of the central controller. The HAL2000 system actually includes a computer to PC interface, while the HomeVoice System offers one as an extra.

A couple of the neater high-end home control and automation systems include:

✔ **IBM's Home Director Pro System:** One of the most talked about home-automation systems is the recently introduced IBM Home Director Pro System (`www.ibm.com/homedirector`). This system is actually two interrelated parts: a structured wiring system, consisting of CAT-5 UTP and RG6 coaxial cabling and associated distribution panels, and a home

controller unit that can control lighting, security, and entertainment systems.

Home Director isn't currently available for retrofitting to existing homes — instead it's being initially marketed as a system for installation only in new construction. Home Director uses either your home's TV screens or PCs to program and control the central controller. In the case of the TV interface, the system uses an infrared remote control and an on-screen menu system similar to the type that DSS receivers use for system control.

✔ **Phast Landmark System:** Based around a device called the *Landmark MCU* (Master Control Unit), the Phast Landmark System is a modular home-automation system that provides a centrally controlled distribution system for audio and video, telephone, data, and home-automation networks in your home (check out `www.phast.com` on the Web for more information). You program the MCU remotely from any Windows computer in your home. The system is compatible with X-10 controllers and also with a wide variety of proprietary security, lighting, and entertainment control systems.

You can also control the MCU — and your home — with a wide variety of Phast products, including touch screens, handheld remotes, wall keypads, and, of course, your networked PCs.

LonWorks

LonWorks is an automation-and-control network system based on a standard that a company called *Echelon* developed (see www.echelon.com on the Web). As is CEBUS, LonWorks is a media-independent system that can operate over phone lines, power lines, or even wireless connections. The key to LonWorks systems is a chip known as the *Neuron* (which Toshiba and Motorola manufacture) that provides the intelligence in the network.

Echelon recently opened up the LonWorks standard so that other, general-purpose computer chips can utilize LonWorks, but Neuron chips are still the most common ones you find in a LonWorks system.

Although most home automators have never heard of LonWorks, it's actually a quite popular and successful protocol — in the commercial marketplace, that is, where companies use it for office and factory-building control systems. A handful of companies are making LonWorks controllers and modules for the home, but compared to X-10, it isn't widely accepted yet.

Control Networks for Entertainment Systems

Home audio and video systems present a special case for home automation and control, because you probably want to do a lot more with a VCR or CD player than just turn it on and off. In fact, you need a whole host of commands such as start and stop, pause, and fast forward that X-10 doesn't even begin to address.

In a single room, you can take care of these functions by using an infrared (IR) remote control — either the control that came with your equipment or one of the programmable universal remotes. Unfortunately, IR remote controls are line-of-sight only and can't carry signals between rooms. So unless you can somehow suspend the laws of physics in your home, pressing repeatedly on the pause button of your VCR's remote doesn't do you a bit of good if you're in the bedroom and the VCR itself is downstairs in the living room.

You have the following two common ways of getting around this problem:

- ✔ You can use a *radio frequency (RF) remote system.*
- ✔ You can use a *wired IR repeater system* to send the remote-control signals from one room to another.

You can use X-10 to control audio and video systems by buying an *X-10-to-IR converter,* such as the one that SmartLinc makes, which learns the IR commands that your system uses and maps them to certain house and unit-code combinations. Any X-10 controller in your home can then send IR signals to your audio and video equipment — the controller sends X-10 signals to the X-10-to-IR converter, which translates the X-10 into IR and sends the signals to your equipment.

We prefer to use a dedicated IR network such as the ones we describe in the following sections, but using X-10 is a perfectly legitimate solution to your remote-control needs if you're an X-10 diehard.

Using RF remotes

Radio waves have one big advantage over light waves (including those of the infrared variety) — they can get through and around obstacles such as walls, furniture, and large house pets. This particular trait makes radio waves ideal for whole-home remote-control systems. Unfortunately, because they cost more, RF remote controls are rarely part of the consumer-electronics package. If your entertainment-network needs are relatively simple (for example, you just want to watch the output of your DBS satellite dish from a different TV), you may manage to shop around and find components that are fitted with an RF remote. Sony, for example, sells a DSS receiver system with an RF remote for just this purpose.

If your network becomes a bit more complicated, or if you already have the components and are stuck with IR remotes, you do have a solution. Several manufacturers offer wireless RF repeater systems for IR remotes.

Setting one of these systems up is a piece of cake. Most consist of just two parts — a *transmitter* that converts IR signals from your remote control to radio waves and beams them out throughout your home, and a corresponding *receiver* that reverses the process and sends the reconverted IR signals to your audio and video equipment. All you need to do is plug the receiver into a wall near the equipment that you want to control and do the same with the transmitter in your remote location. Some transmitters even come in a small, battery-powered package — all you need to do is slip such a transmitter over the end of your IR remote control and carry it to wherever you want listen or watch.

We've seen another variation on this theme available as well. Consisting of the same transmitter/receiver duo, some systems plug into a wall outlet and carry your remote-control signals over your home's AC power lines instead of using RF signals.

Both these systems should work reasonably well for you, but they do have the following downsides:

✔ RF signals are better than IR at getting through and around obstacles, but as anyone with a cordless phone can tell you, they're not foolproof. Long distances, thick walls, and interference by other RF sources can cause problems.

✔ Powerline solutions can also suffer from interference and electrical noise within your electrical wiring.

✔ RF and powerline repeater systems aren't sophisticated enough for use in really elaborate, multizoned audio-and-video-distribution systems — they can't distinguish between zones or discriminate between multiple pieces of audio or video source equipment.

Using a wired IR repeater system

The best way to distribute audio and video control signals throughout your home is to install a hardwired IR signal distribution network. In this kind of system, the IR signals from a standard handheld remote or wall-mounted keypad convert to electrical signals. These signals then travel to your entertainment center over in-wall wiring that runs to your audio or video equipment room and, by using devices known as *emitters*, convert back into IR signals that can control your systems.

You can wire an IR network in either of the following two ways:

✔ You can run dedicated IR cables along with your audio and video signal distribution wiring.

✔ You can piggyback the IR signals on the RG6 coaxial cabling that you use for video distribution (as discussed in Chapter 7).

The second option, using existing coaxial video-distribution cables, requires you to have audio and video network outlets in the same locations. If you have some audio outlets (or wall speakers) in places where no video outlet is present, you can't control the system in that location.

The following components are common to any IR network:

✔ **Infrared sensors:** These devices convert the IR signal from a handheld remote into a DC electrical signal that you can distribute over your IR wiring. IR sensors come in a variety of shapes and sizes, including wall-mounted units, tabletop units, and even mini-sized sensors that you can hide in a small hole in the wall.

✔ **Infrared emitters:** At the other end of an IR network (next to your audio and video equipment), you install devices known as *emitters*. An emitter converts the DC electrical signal back into an IR signal and beams this signal to your equipment.

✔ **Emitter connecting blocks:** These devices enable you to connect IR sensors in different rooms to single or multiple emitters. If you have a multizone audio system, an emitter connecting block is an essential component of the IR control network, because it enables you to separate out IR signals by zone — so the signals from a particular zone only go to equipment that serves the same zone.

✔ **IR keypad controllers:** You can use a keypad controller in place of a handheld remote and IR sensor. Mounted on the wall, like a light switch, the keypad controller can learn the IR commands that your system uses and send them back to your emitters at the push of a button.

Chapter 20

Making Home Automation a Reality

*I*n this chapter, we talk about wiring and design strategies for home-automation systems and IR-control networks for home entertainment equipment. Neither of these networks requires much in the way of special wiring — especially X-10–based powerline networks for home automation, but certain IR networks do require installation of control wiring.

Installation is only half the battle in these kinds of systems, however. The real trick is to configure all the sensors, modules, emitters, keypads, and so on to make sure that they work together correctly. For simple networks — such as X-10 lighting controls or single-zone audio networks — this configuration job isn't too difficult a task, but more complicated systems can test your patience, diligence, and manual-reading skills. We can't simply tell you how to get your Xantech IR controller keypad, for example, to turn on and off your Toshiba VCR and Harmon Kardon amplifier — just too many variables exist for us to cover everything.

What we can do, however, is give you a good jumping-off point for getting a home automation and control infrastructure in place and, we hope, provide you with some useful tips for getting started.

X-10 Marks the Spot

The really wonderful thing about X-10 (and other home-automation standards that use powerline communications) is that the installation effects on your home's wiring infrastructure are really pretty minimal. You should, however,

consider having an electrician do a few things to optimize your home's wiring for X-10 control (and we describe such changes in the following sections), but these optimizations aren't too complicated or expensive.

After your power lines are ready for X-10, setting up the X-10 components is the epitome of plug and play. Plug a module into a power receptacle, plug the light or appliance into it, and that part of your network is complete. This simplicity, combined with the low cost of components, is the main reason that X-10 continues as the default recommendation for home-automation systems.

You can, however, take a few additional steps and precautions to ensure that everything works together in happiness and harmony: Install bridges, noise blocks, and X-10-compatible surge protectors, as well as make sure that all your receptacles have three wires rather than two.

Building bridges

Depending on the state of the electrical wiring in your house, you may need for your electrician to install a device known as an *X-10 signal coupler* in your electrical service panel. This handy-dandy little unit — which costs only about $50 — enables the X-10 signals to get around the house even if the electrical system is split into two circuits (not an uncommon situation).

The power line that comes into your home from the utility company usually consists of a two-phase, 220-volt power line. After this line connects to your service panel or breaker box, the two phases split from each other to provide 110-volt power lines to all your standard outlets, switches, and hardwired fixtures. (A few outlets in your home, such as those for clothes dryers, use both phases for 220-volt circuits.) Because of this separation, X-10 signals in some homes have a hard time getting across from one phase to the other. So a controller connecting to an electrical circuit in one room may not "see" a module in another room that runs on the other phase of the circuit. The signal coupler forms a bridge that enables the X-10 commands to jump across to the other phase.

Keep those nosy (or noisy) neighbors off your X-10

X-10 signals aren't very powerful — you don't need to worry about one traveling back up your power lines and sending your local nuclear reactor into meltdown. A possibility, however, is that X-10 signals within the small local area that your electrical company's local transformer serves can go from house to house, disrupting your carefully planned X-10 system.

Other X-10 signals aren't the only thing that can make X-10 signals act a bit funky. Electrical interference of all kinds finds its way into power lines — giving you a "noisy" power supply, which can disrupt X-10 signals.

If your X-10 network is behaving weirdly or if you're just the cautious type who already has the electrician out for a visit, you may want to have her install a *noise block* inline to your electrical power feed, just before the circuit-breaker box. This device should stop any incoming interference and keep the neighbors' controllers from triggering your modules.

Most of the noise blocks we've seen (ranging from $70 cheap ones to really fancy $500 models) all include signal-coupling functionality as well. So the electrician can make only one trip to kill these two birds (the noise block and the coupler).

Surge protectors kill X-10 dead

Surge protectors, devices that protect your sensitive electronic equipment from transient voltages (such as lightning strikes on utility poles), can be real lifesavers. Ask people who have had a power surge zap a computer or television, and they'll tell you how much they wish they'd invested $30 or $40 in a decent surge protector.

Unfortunately, many surge protectors not only filter out the bad stuff such as lightning, but also remove or disable X-10 signals. So you're left with an unpleasant choice: Protect your equipment from surges or automate it with X-10?

Luckily, you have the following two ways of getting around this problem:

✔ You can install X-10-compatible surge protector strips (which don't really cost any more than good-quality conventional ones) and plug your appliance modules into the strips.

✔ You can take a whole-home approach to surge protection and have an electrician install a whole-home surge suppressor at your breaker box. These suppressors don't cost all that much — about $200 (or the same as five or six good-quality strips) — and they protect every circuit in your home, without needing a big, ungainly power strip in every room.

When lightning strikes, no one can predict where it will hit. Your power line (safely protected behind a surge protector) may not be the thing that gets struck. There are plenty of other electrical paths to your home's other sensitive electronics — antenna and cable TV cables, phone lines, or even satellite dishes and their cables. It makes good sense to install surge protectors on all of these systems, just in case.

Wire those switches right

As your electrician is installing junction boxes and wiring for light switches in your home, tell her to do the following (and you'll *really* sound like you know what you're doing!):

> *Run the neutral wire to the light switch's junction box instead of bypassing it.*

Having all the wires run to the switch rather than some to the switch and some directly to the light gives you more freedom to install X-10 switches in the future.

Each of the 110-volt electrical circuits in a house consists of three separate wires: a *hot* wire — usually black — that supplies the current to the circuit, a *neutral* wire — usually white — that provides a return path for the current, and a *ground* wire that grounds the circuit for safety. The conventional way to install light switches is to connect the hot wire to one side of the switch and to run another wire, called the *load* (usually blue), from the switch to the light (or other device) itself. The neutral and ground wires often bypass the switch and run directly to the light. So the switch just interrupts the flow of the hot wire's current to the light: The light itself completes and grounds the circuit.

In an X-10 environment, this wiring scheme for switches limits what you can actually control with an X-10 light switch. X-10 switches can control only incandescent light fixtures if you wire the switches this way — because the lightbulb filament itself provides a path for the X-10 signals, something that fluorescent and low-voltage lights cannot do, because of their design. If you want to use a switch to control fluorescent lights, low-voltage track lighting, or appliances, you need to use a special inductive dimmer or appliance switch that connects all the wires: the hot wire, the load wire, and the neutral wire. So all these wires must be available at the junction box.

For more information on how to wire electrical switches and how not to fry yourself while working with them, please check out *Home Improvement For Dummies,* by Gene and Katie Hamilton and the editors of HouseNet (IDG Books Worldwide, Inc.).

Some of the really fancy X-10 controllable "mood lighting" switches also require this neutral wire connection, even for incandescent lights.

Controlling Your Home-Automation Systems

You can use X-10 and other home-automation protocols and equipment in one of the following two ways:

- ✔ As a simple home control system that enables you to perform actions in one part of the house while you're in another part of the house

- ✔ As part of a true automated system that performs actions on its own, based either on a schedule or on events that it detects

The modularity of X-10 and the fact that it's based on a common standard that ensures that each manufacturer's equipment works with another's make starting off with a simple home control network and gradually building your way up to fully automated system easy. You just add new components to the network as you go. So if you're not fully convinced that an automated home is for you, you can start with just a few components and — if the X-10 bug bites — go crazy with it later.

Keeping it simple

If you just want to get your feet wet in the home-automation world, we recommend that you dip your toes in the shallow end of the pool by starting off with a simple X-10 home control network. You probably don't need to worry about electrical-wiring considerations or how to connect your computer to the network. All you really need to do is to plug a few lamp or appliance modules and a mini-controller into your AC power line.

We can't promise you that you aren't going to experience some electrical-wiring difficulties, even in a simple X-10 network, but most homes don't.

For a total investment of less than about $75 ($10.95 for the controller and about $8 each for the lamp or appliance modules), you can set up a simple network that controls eight lights or small appliances from a central location.

Expanding this network is as simple as adding more modules and controllers as your needs expand. You may want a controller in the living room to set the right lighting levels for movie watching and another in the master bedroom to turn on a bunch of lights if you hear something go bump in the night.

Linking your car and home with HomeLink

Dozens of new car models are now available with a remote-control system called *HomeLink*. For most folks, the main selling point for this system is its capability to operate most garage-door openers so that you don't need to search under the seat for the door-opener remote. The HomeLink is actually integrated into your car's interior — often above the rearview mirror — and usually consists of two or three pushbuttons (each of which controls a single device).

In a smart-home environment, however, you can also use one or more of the HomeLink's RF channels (most versions have three) to trigger wireless X-10 controllers to send commands to such devices as lights and even X-10-compatible security systems from the warmth and comfort of your car. HomeLink doesn't sell as an after-market add-in — instead, it sells as a built-in, integral part of the car (although some automakers sell HomeLink as a dealer-installed accessory that you can have installed in certain car models after the fact). To find out more about HomeLink, look on the Web at `homelink.jci.com/info/homelink.htm`.

You can also expand your control network by installing X-10 wireless controllers that enable you to trigger controls without leaving the comfort of your couch — or from the front porch with a key-ring wireless controller.

You can also train some universal "learning" remotes for home entertainment systems to send X-10 commands so that you don't need both an audio/video and an X-10 remote in your home theater.

If you want to add a degree of automation to this X-10 control network, you can do so simply by plugging a programmable controller into an AC receptacle. Doing so enables you to create simple timed programs to activate or turn off various modules.

Adding a computer for more control

Adding a personal computer into the mix enables you to bring a new level of sophistication to a home control and automation network. The addition of an X-10 interface and graphical-interface software on your PC enables you to create complicated on/off schedules quickly and easily. The ease of using a computer interface for this purpose — instead of trying to fiddle with a small, somewhat unintuitive programmable controller — is worth the price of admission by itself.

But wait — there's more! (We loved those old Ginsu knife commercials.) By using the computer software, you can program your PC's X-10 interface box to perform *macros* — sets of consecutive commands, such as "turn on kitchen light," "start the coffee pot," and "open electrical kitchen window drape." After you create a macro, you can save it and use it again — create a lighting macro for TV watching, for example, and you can then schedule it for whenever your favorite shows are on. You can even download macros from the Internet and apply them to your system.

To see some neat downloadable macros, check out the X-10 ActiveHome site at www.x10.com/products/macros.htm.

Getting into computer-controlled X-10 automation is really cheap. Both X-10 and IBM (at www.ibm.com) sell starter kits for next to nothing ($84.95 for the X-10 version, and $99.95 for the IBM kit). The kits include the following components:

- ✓ A CD-ROM containing the X-10 control software
- ✓ The computer X-10 interface hardware (which connects to the PC's serial port)
- ✓ An X-10 lamp module
- ✓ An X-10 appliance module (in the IBM kit only)
- ✓ A remote-control system with a wireless controller and two remotes

Put your network on the Net

Here's a scenario for you: You have an X-10 network in your home that you control with a PC; you also have an always-on cable modem or DSL connection to the Internet. Why not put the two together and use that Internet connection to control your PC from work or even from your laptop's wireless Net connection wherever you are? Well, you can do just that with Savoy Software's CyberHouse software (check out www.savoysoft.com on the Web).

This $399 software package makes use of the Internet standard TCP/IP protocol to connect remote computers to your home's automation control computer. You don't need an always-on connection either — this software works just fine with a dial-up Internet account, although sometimes always-on connections are hard to maintain. (ISPs love to cut off people whose connections are idle for too long.)

The CyberHouse software works in both directions, too — it can actually send out e-mail messages, faxes, or pages if it senses that an event that you designate warrants this kind of attention. This software package is relatively hardware independent — so it works on just about any recent Pentium computer and works with most of the computer-to-X-10 interface systems on the market. As home automation and always-on Internet connections both become more common, we think you're going to see lots more software for this sort of setup.

Making your home interactive

Remotely controlling and scripting your home-automation systems are pretty cool ways of automating your home, but you can bring an automated home to a higher level by making it interactive and intelligent. By combining sensors with your X-10 control systems, you can program your home to react to certain events by turning on lights, alerting you with a chime, or even muting your TV.

You can integrate sensors into a home-automation system in the following three ways:

- ✔ You can keep things in the X-10 realm, utilizing sensors with built-in X-10 controllers to trigger events.
- ✔ You can integrate an alarm system with your home-automation network and use the alarm's sensors to trigger home-automation events.
- ✔ If you have a sophisticated PC-based or stand-alone home-automation controller, you can directly connect sensors to the controller.

The following sections elaborate on these three methods.

X-10 sensors

The simplest way of integrating sensors into a home-automation network is to install X-10 sensors in your home. These sensors combine the actual sensor itself (a photocell or passive infrared detector, for example) and a controller that can send X-10 commands to several different addresses. You don't need to go through a central controller for these devices — just assign some X-10 actions to them (such as turning on certain lights) and plug them into a powerline receptacle. It's that simple.

Among the X-10 sensors that we've seen are the following examples:

- ✔ **X-10 photocells:** Unless you live way up north, you can plan on the sun coming up and going down every day. By using an X-10 photocell, your home can distinguish the light from the dark and automatically turn lights on at dusk and off at dawn.
- ✔ **X-10 motion detectors:** By using a PIR, these wall-mounted sensors can send several X-10 commands if they detect motion. You may, for example, install one in the upstairs hallway and set it to automatically turn on the hall lights if someone walks by.

    Many X-10 motion detectors also have a built-in photocell so that you can set them to turn on lights only as darkness falls.

✔ **X-10 motion-detector floodlights:** These outdoor lights function just like the standard motion-detector lights that guide your path down the front walk after your dog forces you into yet another late-night walk. By using a PIR, these lights turn themselves on if someone (or something — such as that pesky dog from next door) walks into their detection field. After they turn on, the floodlights also send out a number of X-10 signals (usually up to eight) and trigger other X-10 devices such as inside lights or chime modules.

Some of the motion-detector floodlights that we've seen include photocell sensors so that you can use them to turn on other lights at dusk. Many also have X-10 functionality so that you can use any X-10 controller to turn them on manually.

✔ **The X-10 PowerFlash module:** This module accepts the output of almost any stand-alone sensor — such as a magnetic door-closure sensor, a doorbell, a driveway sensor, or even a non-X-10 burglar alarm — and sends an X-10 command if something activates the sensor.

Using an X-10 alarm

As we discuss in Chapter 11, a typical home-security system is chock-full of sensors — door-contact sensors, window-contact sensors, glass-breakage detectors, PIRs, pressure-sensitive door mats, and many more. The primary function of these sensors is, of course, to monitor your house for bad guys and trigger the alarm if necessary. By using an X-10-compatible alarm system (or by adding an X-10 controller expansion module to certain brands of existing alarm systems), you can make these sensors serve double duty.

The simplest of these X-10-compatible alarm systems simply activate an X-10 command (such as All On) in an alarm condition — in other words, they turn on your lights if the alarm siren sounds. This setup isn't really the kind of home automation we're talking about, but it does add a nice security feature. (Being able to see where you're going sure would be nice after you peel yourself off the ceiling during a middle-of-the-night alarm.)

More sophisticated systems take a more subtle approach in that they offer levels of reaction to various sensor inputs. In other words, these security systems are smart enough to know that certain sensor inputs don't necessarily spell doom. A pressure-sensitive doormat or a driveway sensor, for example, tells the system that someone is there, whether a burglar or the UPS delivery person. Obviously, the system's reaction to these sensor inputs should be something less than a full alarm. (No need to call out the cavalry if it's just the pizza guy.)

These security systems can interface with your X-10 network in the following ways:

- ✔ A sensor input can trigger a random X-10 output to create a "lived-in" look. An outdoor PIR motion detector, for example, may cause your alarm control panel to send X-10 signals to lights in several different rooms, turning them on and off at seemingly random intervals.

- ✔ In the most advanced of these systems, you can program specific sensor inputs to trigger specific X-10 outputs. So the motion detector in the backyard can turn on the rear porch lights, or the driveway sensor can turn on the carriage lights running from the driveway to the front door.

Combining sensors with a central controller

The biggest drawback to having an alarm trigger X-10 events is that these systems are somewhat limited in their capabilities. Specifically, these methods enable you to respond to a sensor input with only a limited number of X-10 commands — usually four to eight for an X-10 sensor and up to about 16 with an X-10-compatible alarm system.

If you want to create a really sophisticated interactive home-automation system — one that combines a large number of sensors with a whole bunch of potential corresponding commands — consider using a high-end PC-based or stand-alone home-control system. These systems directly accept the inputs of a number of sensors and can control literally hundreds of X-10 modules and non-X-10 hardwired systems (such as heating, ventilation, and air conditioning systems or sprinkler controls), based on the settings you enter into the system's control interface.

These intelligent home controllers can accept the following two types of sensor inputs:

- ✔ **Analog inputs:** These sensors can detect a range of measurements, such as temperature sensors or moisture/humidity detectors.

- ✔ **Digital inputs:** These sensors either detect a condition or don't detect one, such as motion/no motion sensors.

The wiring for these sensors varies — depending on the individual sensor type and manufacturer — but most utilize wiring similar to what you use for wiring alarm sensors (two- or four-conductor wiring, although some temperature sensors use three-conductor wiring). The key to integrating sensors into such a system is to anticipate as much of your sensor needs up front so that you can have your installer run the right wires ahead of time.

Voice control, the ultimate in interactivity

A few home automation control software packages on the marketplace today are beginning to include voice activation as the primary means of controlling your home's systems. Using recent developments in speech recognition, these systems (most notably the HomeVoice system by Applied Future Technologies and the HAL2000 from Home Automated Living) enable you to speak in plain English to initiate X-10 or IR commands. So you can boss your house around, *Star Trek* style, turning on lights or opening drapes without lifting a finger.

A discreet, omnidirectional microphone (or a telephone, for remote access) picks up the sound of your voice and feeds it into the microphone input of your PC's sound card. The speech-recognition software then translates your commands and correlates them with stored X-10 or IR commands and sends the appropriate control signals out over your home's powerline or IR network. These products can also use speech synthesis to talk back to you — giving you a confirmation that your command was heard and carried out. Neat stuff.

Connecting a microphone to the sound card of your PC and getting the system up and running in the same room that contains your computer and computer-to-X-10 interface is a simple task. The job becomes a bit trickier, however, if you want to use voice control throughout the house. To do so, you need to install microphones in each room and run microphone cable back to the controller location. Because most sound cards have only one microphone input, you need to combine all of the incoming microphone leads into a microphone mixer, which sends a single signal into the PC. (An alternative way on the horizon is to use distributed microphones built into light switches or other distributed devices that can process the sound at the origin and send over X-10 only the actual command inputs.)

Both systems are software-based and run on most Pentium class PCs. They're compatible with most computer-to-X-10 interfaces, so you can add voice control into an existing system pretty easily. Microphones cost about $90 each, but the mixers we've seen are a bit expensive. (The HomeVoice mixer kit, which also includes a limiter/gate device to help filter out background noise, costs nearly $700.) The software itself isn't too expensive — $239 for HomeVoice and $399 for HAL2000.

We think that voice control is a logical next step for home automation and control networks and something you're going to see more of in the future.

After you connect the sensors to your controller, you can program them (by using a computer or a television and the system's graphical-interface software) and even create *event-driven* macros that map sensor inputs to specific control outputs. The sky's the limit here — if a system is controllable, you can match it to a sensor input. We personally would like to find a way to turn on the lawn sprinklers if a salesperson comes to our door, but we haven't yet been able to find a sensor that can differentiate between the Fuller Brush man and the next-door neighbor.

Getting IR Around the House

As we mention in the Chapter 19, X-10 is a great system for controlling all sorts of devices in a home, but it's not ideal for taking care of the complicated commands that you need to control audio and video systems. You can rig up an X-10/IR converter system to perform this task, but doing so is a bit complicated and kind of a case of reinventing the wheel.

We make that last statement because you already have a great way of controlling audio and video systems — by using IR remotes. The only real problem with IR remotes is that they don't easily expand to a whole-home paradigm without a little help, because IR signals don't pass through walls and floors.

You can solve this problem by using a radio frequency IR-extender system — the cheap and easy solution. Unfortunately the RF method isn't quite up to the job of controlling multiple systems in multizone networks. To do so, you need a wired IR-repeater network.

Making your coaxial cable work overtime

If you have a coaxial cable network to distribute video signals throughout the home *and* if the endpoints of this network correspond with the endpoints of your audio network (or you don't have a whole-home audio network), you can avoid running extra wires throughout the home by running IR signals over that coaxial cable.

To do so, you need to install devices known as *IR signal injector/splitters,* which perform two tasks. In remote locations, the signal injector/splitter combines the electrical signal that an IR sensor sends with the video signals running over your coaxial network. In your media equipment room, another signal injector/splitter splits the same signal out from the coaxial cable and feeds it to an IR emitter to control your equipment. Figure 20-1 shows how these devices fit into a coaxial network.

The signal injector/splitters need electrical power to do their thing — because they're creating an electrical signal from an IR sensor output. You have the following two ways of providing this power to the devices:

✔ You can install a device known as a *remote power injector* near your coaxial distribution panel. One of these devices provides power for the entire network.

✔ You can use a video-distribution panel (discussed in detail in Chapter 7), which has a built-in power injector.

  Note: Some coaxial panel makers call this feature an *IR engine* (and no, it doesn't burn high octane fuel) because it powers all of the remote IR sensors.

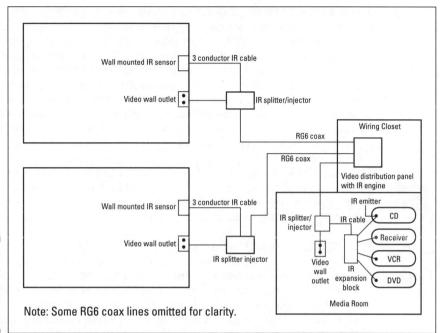

Figure 20-1:
Piggybacking
IR signals on
a coaxial
network.

Note: Some RG6 coax lines omitted for clarity.

You can configure the guts of this IR network — where the IR signal splits off the coaxial network and goes to IR emitters — in one of the following ways:

✔ If you're controlling only one or two devices (such as a single VCR or an audio receiver and CD player), you can simply connect the IR output of the signal injector (it has both an RF output and an IR output) to a single or dual IR emitter. The emitters themselves usually stick right onto the IR sensor of the equipment they control, so you need one per piece of equipment.

✔ If you're trying to control more than two pieces of A/V equipment in one location, you can connect your signal injector/splitter to an IR expansion block, which enables you to connect multiple emitters to a single injector/splitter.

Being dedicated

Using coaxial cable is a perfectly adequate method of IR distribution, but the optimal way of carrying IR signals throughout a house is to build a separate IR control network using its own wiring. This setup provides the most flexibility and reliability and makes controlling several components in a multizone audio system easier.

The majority of hardwired IR-distribution networks use simple three-conductor shielded cable (usually sold as "IR cable" in most catalogs and stores) to connect remote locations back to your audio and video network equipment. You wire this cable in a simple star architecture, with an individual run coming from each control point back to the audio/video equipment room, as shown in Figure 20-2. You can also run your IR cabling in a "daisy-chain fashion," with a single cable running from room to room, connecting all your sensors and keypads, but this type of wiring works only with a single-zone audio network, and we recommend that you don't try to save money on IR cable (which costs only about ten cents a foot) by running your cabling this way.

The MonsterCable company (at `www.monstercable.com` on the Web) sells some really neat in-wall speaker cabling that includes IR cable in the same cable jacket. If you run this cable to speaker locations, you automatically prewire these locations for IR control as well.

IR control isn't like an Ethernet or telephone network. You don't have a fixed standard that all emitters, IR receivers, or remote keypads must adhere to for their cabling. You may very well find equipment that needs some different type of cable than the three-conductor version we're discussing. Some keypads, for example, use CAT-5 cabling. Although the vast majority of equipment uses three-conductor cable, you need to make sure that you determine the requirements of your equipment *before* you prewire your house.

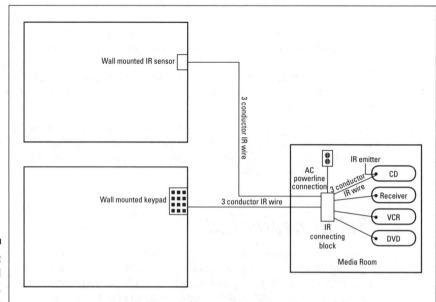

Figure 20-2:
A hardwired
IR network.

Connecting the endpoints of this network — the IR sensors and keypads and IR emitters — to the IR cabling infrastructure is a pretty easy task. Sensors and keypads connect directly to the end of the IR cable in remote locations — nothing complicated about that. On the equipment end of the network, all your IR cable "home runs" terminate on a connecting block, which then provides a number of outputs for IR emitters.

Like the IR-over-coaxial network that we discuss in the section "Making your coaxial cable work overtime," earlier in this chapter, the hardwired IR network needs a power supply to make the sensors sense, the emitters emit, and the keypads . . . er . . . key. Providing this power is a secondary job of the connecting block.

A really good idea is to use emitters, sensors, keypads, and connecting blocks from a single manufacturer to ensure that everything works together smoothly. Major manufacturers of these systems, such as Niles Audio (at www.nilesaudio.com) and Xantech (at www.xantech.com), make all these pieces and parts in matched sets.

Multizone IR considerations

If the roster of devices that an IR network controls includes a multizone audio system, you need to use a connecting block specifically designed for multiple-zone systems. This requirement stems from the fact that some of the components in this system are zone-specific, while others are common to the entire system.

The amplifier that powers the speakers in a particular zone, for example, you use only in that zone, while all zones share the CD or DVD player.

A multizone connecting block separates the common and shared IR signals by providing separate sets of emitter connections — common emitter signals and zone-specific emitter signals. This separation is especially important if, for example, you use the same type of amplifier in several different zones. By using the zone-specific emitter signal, you can direct *which* amplifier you actually want to turn up.

Getting a multizone system up and running can prove a difficult and frustrating process — and one best left to a professional. Trust us on this one.

Part VII
The Part of Tens

"Well, there goes the simple charm of sitting around the stove surfing the Web on our laptops."

In this part . . .

Top Ten lists galore! Look in this part of the book for Danny and Pat's top ten lists on all sorts of smart-home topics.

Find out where to go for more information — those extra special places where you can go to track down more ideas for your smart home. Read ways to improve your home-networking strategy with tips and tricks we picked up along the way. Find out where you can see various smart homes in action.

We also peer into our crystal balls and give you a glimpse of where smart-home technologies are heading in the near future. How your home can be turned into the Starship Enterprise — and we don't mean taking a 1,000-person crew to run it. We're talking true total integration and everything short of getting your food through an automatic replicator.

Chapter 21

Ten Neat Things You Can Network Now

● ●

In This Chapter

▶ Creating a car network that rivals your home network

▶ Roving with your MTV on top

▶ Watching the stars from your couch

▶ Watching — yes, watching — your CD collection

▶ Playing your piano the home network way

▶ Taking a shower during the movie without missing a scene

● ●

*T*hroughout this book we talk about a slew of really neat things — too many neat things to count.

But wait, there's more! (No, Ginsu knives are not available with this offer.) This chapter looks at ten or so other ways to extend the wealth of your home network to other areas of your life.

Networking the Family Sedan

You may not realize this, but your car already contains a massive computer network, similar to the type of network you find in most airplanes. Although not as sophisticated as an aircraft network, a car network touches many of the car's most critical parts — its tentacles reach out to things like brakes, airbags, monitoring systems, and so on. But you don't see most of that stuff, so it's more useful than fun.

Now you can splurge and really have fun with our idea of a car network. You start with a new automobile personal computer. These things are great. They bring together all the latest advances in computing to make your traveling experience more enjoyable, safe, and convenient.

Take Clarion's AutoPC (www.autopc.com) for instance. This computer looks like a standard piece of car-audio equipment, but looks are deceiving. With this device, you can get e-mail, driving directions from a GPS navigation system, news, customized traffic reports and weather updates, hands-free cell phone support, a programmable address book (which can work manually or with your Windows CE–based handheld or palm-sized personal PC), a CD player, an AM/FM stereo, and more. And to top things off, the system is voice-controlled. Clarion is billing this computer as "the first in-dash personal assistant."

The ability to network this system with your home network is just around the corner.

Networking on the Go

Just because you are away from home doesn't mean that you can't participate in some of the same services you get at home. Some companies are currently marketing antennas, acquisition systems (which help you aim the antenna at the right satellite), and mounting hardware for the mobile community — including boats, yachts, RVs, and buses.

If you want to keep getting your DirecTV as you tour Yellowstone Park, for example, try out the Space Scanner from FutureTrak International (www.futuretrak.com). Compatible with all Direct Broadcast Satellite (DBS) providers, the Space Scanner lets boat and RV owners receive satellite TV while parked or at dockside. You can choose from flat (like a pizza box) as well as parabolic (like a home DSS dish) antenna options.

The Space Scanner II, another system, offers satellite in-motion tracking for the mobile market. This smart system automatically rotates and maintains a connection as you travel. It provides for automatic tracking at 30 degrees per second, and by using simple arrow keys, you can program the tracking via remote control if you want to fine-tune the signal yourself.

The dockside and anchor products run $1,995, which includes everything you need to install them; the under-way tracking product runs about $3,995. If you want your MTV, you'll want your Space Scanner, too!

Getting Personal Television Service

If you travel very much, you probably have trouble keeping current on your favorite TV shows. You can always tape the shows on your VCR, assuming you remember to program the machine — for the right time and channel, no less — and stick in a tape. With all the little things that can go wrong with taping, you're lucky to successfully tape the shows 50 percent of the time.

If you're tired of battling the VCR gremlins, you may want to investigate a new service. Through a VCR-like box that sits between your video input stream (like your cable box or your DSS receiver) and your TV set, ReplayTV (www.replaytv.com) combines your telephone and video programming services — satellite, cable, or broadcast TV — to let you pause, rewind, fast-forward, instantly replay, and play back in slow-motion, live television. Replay's box is essentially a VCR with a huge hard disk inside that can store up to 28 hours of your favorite programs.

ReplayTV gives you full control of live programs as well. A friendly and highly visual interface — similar to what you experience with cable or DSS systems — guides you through the available programming options. The Replay Network Service includes complete program listings for the next seven days, of more than 12,000 DBS, cable, and terrestrial systems in the U.S.

You can also create a personalized lineup of your favorite shows ready for anytime viewing. ReplayTV's technology queries your TV preferences and puts them into a personalized channel, so you can watch your favorite shows at your convenience. Using sophisticated search software, ReplayTV intelligently searches this database of programming information to locate the shows you ask it to identify.

For example, say a viewer asks ReplayTV to create a *Star Trek* Replay Channel. ReplayTV then constantly scans the continuously updated channel guide information, searching for *Star Trek* references. When it identifies this information in the database, ReplayTV automatically configures itself to record the *Star Trek* program and make it available for on-demand viewing. With ReplayTV, your *prime time* television is essentially available whenever you want it.

In a smart home, ReplayTV dials into a secure server and downloads the latest channel-guide information every night. ReplayTV even resets the clock so you never have to worry about the perennial flashing "12:00." ReplayTV makes all its calls late at night to minimize any impact on your home phone-line usage.

We think the cost is reasonable. You can choose from three models, which differ mostly by the size of storage space onboard the ReplayTV device. The cost per box ranges from $699 (about 6 hours of storage) to $1,499 (about 28 hours of storage). You pay no monthly cost to update your schedules or to access ReplayTV's Network Service functionality.

Other, similar services are on the horizon. TiVo Inc. (www.tivo.com) has a similar service that is less expensive up-front — the hardware is about half the cost of ReplayTV's equivalent devices — but you do pay a $10 monthly fee. Competitive forces may change this practice, so check out its Web site for current pricing and availability.

Giving a Concert

Entertaining for the evening? Why not treat your guests to a stylish in-home concert of Mozart's Piano Sonatas K. 310, K. 333, and K. 533? Don't play the piano? No problem, Baldwin Piano Company (www.baldwinpiano.com) has a solution for you — ConcertMaster.

Your smart home can plug into your Baldwin, Chickering, or Wurlitzer piano and play almost any musical piece you can imagine. ConcertMaster works in several ways: as a standard piano, as a player piano that utilizes special digital data instead of the rolls used by old-fashioned ones, as a playback system (with built-in amplified speakers) for your own CDs, and even as a karaoke system. You can even plug it into your home network's VCR and watch the pianist creating the music your piano plays back for you. If you play the piano a bit yourself (which is always nice if you own one), you can also use ConcertMaster to record your own performances — a great tool for learning.

You can plan an entire evening of music from any combination of sources, to play in any order. The internal ConcertMaster Library comes preloaded with 20 hours of performances in five musical categories: Classical, Country, Jazz, Pop, and Rock. You can create up to 99 custom library categories to store your music (for example, one for your favorite Aerosmith piano solos). With up to 99 songs in each category, you can conceivably have nearly 10,000 songs onboard and ready to play, without having to insert a disk or CD.

This system is not just one-way — you can record, too. A one-touch Quick-Record button lets you instantly save piano performances. How about recording your child's piano recital? You can use songs that you record and store on floppy disk with your personal computer to enjoy the benefits of popular editing, sequencing, and score notation programs.

ConcertMaster is both easy to use and flexible. Its operation is directed by either the stationary controller that attaches to the piano or a handheld, wireless RF remote control (as discussed in Chapter 5). You can inconspicuously fit the stationary controller under the front of the piano or on the side. Small pinlights show power status, software source, and input signals at a glance. ConcertMaster can perform at extremely low volume levels, so you can have a normal conversation, even right beside the piano.

You can use your smart home's Internet connection to download the latest operating system software from Baldwin's servers, too.

Figuring Out Which CD to Play

If you're really into music, you may have hundreds — if not thousands — of CDs in your collection. You may have even splurged on a multi- or mega-CD changer than can store tens and hundreds of CDs.

But figuring out which CD is which can be tough because the CDs are in the changer all the time. You can laboriously enter CD information about each disc into your changer, but that can take a long time, and you have to do that every time you insert a new CD.

Enter Escient's TuneBase (www.escient.com), a family of electronic device products that allow you to visually catalog, select, and control your entire CD collection. TuneBase offers an intuitive user interface that enables you to play specific titles, tracks, or types of music.

TuneBase products all consist of a controller, the wireless IR remote control, and a graphical user interface. You can simply connect the controller to an existing or new system as you would any other video source component such as a VCR, DVD player, or laserdisc player.

All TuneBase products utilize Escient's IntelligentLink technology, which reads and automatically identifies the CDs in a changer and matches them to the cover art. Escient has created a master database of more than 210,000 text records and the artwork of more than 30,000 CD covers. As new records are added, you can obtain updates from the Escient's Internet database of CD and DVD covers and text information, all via your home network's phone or data connections.

TuneBase uses your TV as its user interface. You scroll through the CD covers on a normal TV display, selecting from and controlling your entire collection. You can create and save play lists, so you can preplan your entire evening's music and then have it start as soon as the first person walks in the door. Or if your friends like to select their own music, you can let them sift through your collection and choose their personal favorites.

Want to really integrate CD selection into your home network? Try connecting a TuneBase Pro MK-I into a multizone distributed audio system, like one from Audio Design Associates (ADA). You can get one-touch keypad access to an entire music collection from anywhere in your home. With this technology, you (or your guests) can access your CDs and view a text description of what you're listening to in real time, via text display, on ADA's wall keypads.

Gazing on a Starry, Starry Night!

On a beautiful, starry night, you want your child to see the space shuttle zooming across the sky, so you grab your trusty telescope and wait for it to appear across the horizon, right? Lots of luck. The space shuttle is moving at more than 17,500 miles per hour, and keeping a good focus on an object moving that fast is nearly impossible.

Impossible, that is, unless you have a smart home (wild clapping!). Imagine sitting on your couch and watching the night sky through your home-network-controlled telescope.

Start with one of the finer telescopes, say a Meade LX200 series (www.meade.com). With its super high-tech, motorized system for rotating the lens across the sky, the LX200 is a wonderful platform for satellite observing and tracking. As you use a handheld control to select specific planets or galaxies, the telescope slides over to that area of the sky.

However, if you load the proper software onto your home network's computers, software such as C-SAT from Celestial Computing, Inc. (www.skyshow.com/csat/), you can direct your LX200 to slew to any satellite that is about to come into view. The program tracks 4,000-plus satellites (including the Space Shuttle, Mir, and classified U.S. and Russian spy satellites). Of course "the perturbation algorithms built into C-SAT are very powerful, and account for gravitational influences from the sun and moon, atmospheric drag, Earth gravitational harmonics, and much more." Got that?

Once you connect digitally to your telescope, you can do a bunch of other cool stuff as well. Here's Randall Rubis from his amateur astronomer's page, www.look-inc.com/rrubis/satpage.htm: "A recent addition to my satellite observation software is the program called Iridium Flare. This is a DOS-based program that will calculate the passing of the Motorola Iridium Telecommunication Satellites. These are especially wonderful to observe because they are very frequent and very, very bright. Some of the Iridium birds will outshine Jupiter, Venus and other bright objects. The program requires the user to input local information like longitude, latitude and sun angle. I have found that the program is very accurate and you can count on seeing the 'flare' at the times stated by the program. The 'flare' is caused by the MMA 'main mission antennae' of the Iridium satellite being at the proper angle to reflect the sun's rays back to your location." Cool stuff.

Sitting Not-So-Tight in a Really Great Chair

If you live and die by online gaming, then you'll want to be buried in the Intensor video gaming chair, built by BSG Laboratories, Inc. (`www. intensor.com`). Hook this chair up to your gaming console, PC, TV, VCR, CD player, DVD player, DSS, or any product with mono or stereo audio output, and put yourself right in the middle of the action. You can feel your X-Wing bank as you evade Darth Vader's TIE fighter or feel the rumble of a NASCAR engine as you watch a race on your DSS dish.

The U.S. built Intensor is an ergonomically designed video game seat/chair with a patented, built-in audio system that creates an immersive sound field and tactile sensation for the user.

Look what it has on board:

- 5-driver audio system:
    - 5.25-inch full-range driver
    - 5.25-inch bass driver
    - 2-inch left and right mid-range drivers
    - 2-inch high-end driver (tweeter)
- Controls:
    - Volume
    - Tactile intensity
- Connectors:
    - Input: Stereo RCA connectors
    - Output: Variable mono (sub out)
    - Output: Stereo headphones
- Power:
    - 110-220 50 Hz/60 Hz switchable AC power
    - 20 watts x 4 channels
    - Total harmonic distortion (THD): .0032% at 10 watts, 70 Hz

You can purchase an optional, extra-cost sub-woofer that sports a dual 5.25-inch bass driver, tuned port enclosure, 40-watt RMS at 8 ohms, adjustable level control, and variable cross-over control.

The basic unit, which retails for about $300, includes the power unit and chair. A fully loaded system runs about $600 or so. Grab a good force feedback joystick or wheel, and you'll think you're in the middle of the action.

And you can download new software versions for your chair over your wired Internet connection. Modifications for Quake II, Deathmatch, and other games are already posted on the Intensor site. Just plain cool. Quite worth it!

You can find these at your local computer superstore. Check out BSG's dealer locator at www.intensor.com/gogetit.htm.

Singing in the Shower and Much, Much More

Okay, some people like to sing in the shower, some like to hang out in the Jacuzzi forever, and some like to watch the news in the morning. Well now, you can do all of these things, at the same time!

Introducing the J-Allure, by Jacuzzi Whirlpool Bath (www.jacuzzi.com/jallure.html). J-Allure combines a full-size whirlpool bath — which has a luxury shower system and soothing steam bath — with a television/VCR monitor. A digital control panel offers easy access to the whirlpool operation, underwater lighting, and temperature read-out. Talk about wired.

Because the tub's a Jacuzzi, it's outfitted with the total range of powerful water jet streams. J-Allure's whirlpool bath offers four PowerPro body jets and two lumbar jets. The jets are fully adjustable, ensuring personal control. They sport the WaveFlow option, which creates a variable, pulsating jet flow.

Additional luxury features include two multifunction showerheads: one is fixed in an overhead position, and the other is height-adjustable and maybe handheld. Twelve vertical jets provide an invigorating body massage.

The steam bath has a sculpted seat, which is an ideal place to enjoy soothing steam from the innovative SteamPro 120 steam generator.

But most importantly, the J-Allure comes standard with a built-in stereo/CD system, complete with four speakers. The unit is also available with an optional television/VCR monitor. Cable ready, this feature allows you to enjoy the morning news or your favorite movie. The multichannel, 9-inch unit is waterproof and includes a remote control. You can adapt the monitor for DVD or WebTV.

J-Allure was designed for corner installations. It measures 52 inches long x 52 inches wide x 94½ inches high. The unit is available in white with color-match, chrome, or brass shower attachments, in case you were wondering.

All these features for a mere $12,500 retail price. And you thought we were crazy for wiring the bathroom.

Mowing Your Lawn from the Couch!

Danny is allergic to anything green (except money). Mowing the lawn for him is like getting a root canal. He'd rather sit on the couch and watch the Duke Blue Devils play basketball.

Well, with a smart home, he can do both, at the same time, from the luxury of his living room, kitchen, or basement by using Friendly Machines Ltd.'s (www.friendlymachines.com/) robotic lawn mower, ROBOMOW. Now, you can be a couch gardener.

ROBOMOW automatically cuts your grass based on its internal programming and what it senses as its environment. And if you want, you can control the grass cutting via remote control, too.

In most instances, ROBOMOW guides itself by sensing the presence of a small wire that you place on the ground surrounding the edge of your lawn. This wire is the boundary of the areas to be cut. Don't worry, grass covers the wire pretty quickly. You won't see the wire — but ROBOMOW will. (Don't worry about the perimeter cable electrocuting you either — the current in the perimeter line is only 4.5 volts.)

You connect the wire to a small generator. By pressing the green button on the generator, you send a smart electrical pulse through the wire, which signals ROBOMOW's computer-controlled guidance system.

Just press the GO button on ROBOMOW, and sit back. When ROBOMOW encounters obstacles, it mows all around them. ROBOMOW mows in uniformly straight lines to produce a striped, manicured lawn. A special tracking mode ensures that ROBOMOW trims the edges of the lawn. ROBOMOW moves easily from the garage to the lawn and back.

If you wish, you can watch ROBOMOW through your external security cameras. Using the picture-in-picture mode on your TV, you can watch the basketball game while ROBOMOW mows away.

ROBOMOW is designed ideally to mow 5,300 square feet on a single charge. Typically, you have to recharge ROBOMOW once in order to complete the job. You may need to recharge it more often, depending on the grass height, density, and the number of obstacles that ROBOMOW has to pass.

ROBOMOW is designed to fit lawns that are relatively flat (with a slope of less than 10 degrees), do not have too many trees or other obstacles, and are mostly wider than 3 meters (10 feet). The lawn perimeter can be any shape.

By using the remote mode, you can mow any area manually, even on slopes as steep as 20 degrees.

Playing with LEGO, the 21st Century Way

Driven by PCs in your smart home, one toy — LEGO Mindstorms (www. legomindstorms.com/) — can really start to transform your kids' early life. This toy is the traditional LEGO building blocks on steroids — robotic steroids.

LEGO Mindstorms lets you design, build, and program real robots by using the standard LEGO block system along with a microcomputer core and special bricks with light and touch sensors. With the company's Robotics Invention System, you can create light-sensitive intruder alarms, line-tracking rovers, robotic beer-can retrievers, or even robots with collision and edge detection. Expansion kits allow you to create sports machines and monster creatures, too.

This new system's brain is the RCX, which looks like a big LEGO with an LCD in it. The RCX is really an autonomous microcomputer that you can program by using your smart home's PCs. The RCX uses sensors to take input from its environment, processes data, and signals output motors to turn on and off. You can also download the system's upgradeable firmware to your PC over your smart home's Internet connection, and then send it via infrared to the RCX.

The base Robotics Invention System includes over 700 LEGO pieces, the RCX, infrared transmitter, light and touch sensors, motors, gears, and a Constructopedia building guide. You can put your first robot together in an hour, and then hop on the PC and program its movements. (The robot programming software runs on Windows 95.)

You build your robot by using the RCX and LEGO pieces. Then you create a program for your invention by using RCX Code (a simple programming language), which you download to the RCX by using a special infrared transmitter. Your creation can now interact with the environment, fully autonomous from the computer. Want to get other programs? The LEGO Web site has scads of advice and downloadable software.

The LEGO Mindstorms Robotics Invention System has a suggested retail price of $219.99 each. Each expansion set runs about $50.

Chapter 22

Ten Hints for Designing a Futureproofed Home

> *Imagine a world where you can use an Internet browser to set the temperature in your home before you leave the office; or receive an e-mail message notifying you that your children arrived home from school; or deactivate your security system to allow a workman access.*
>
> —Ken Oshman, President and CEO of Echelon Corporation

Yes, you can do all the things that Ken Oshman says, but the little things can stop you dead in your tracks. Imagine if you built your ideal smart home, but forgot a few key steps. Well, we've been trying to think of lots of helpful tips throughout this book to keep you from making many mistakes. Here's a collection of some of our best tips for your home adventure.

Anticipate Your Needs

You really need to think, think, think when planning your home network. A smart home is only as good as your design.

We hope that you have found out some things in this book that have led you to consider new options with your home — running that wire into the bathroom, or planning for that access space behind the home entertainment system, for instance.

You can put lots of technologies in your home. You really need to plan ahead, because to do otherwise will cost you a bundle later on if you want to add something you forgot. We know it's hard — you never know where you're going to end up. (Ask Danny, he's got *two* sets of twins.)

So it's never going to be a perfect science, but a well-thought-out estimate of your needs is better than a wild guess.

Read Everything

In the last part of this book — as well as throughout each of the chapters — we've tried to provide a lot of sources for you to peruse when planning your smart home. Take advantage of them.

Planning a smart home is no different than getting married (someone buys all those one-inch-thick bride magazines) or buying a car (Danny still has his stacks of car magazines and auto-buying guides from his ill-fated effort to convince his wife that a GMC Suburban *really was* better than a minivan). You can find all sorts of ideas and tips by reading more. Different publications and books have different perspectives and goals, and they will each add a different aspect to your planning.

So read, a lot.

Overdo It

You start working at home and need a home office. So does your spouse. You have more kids. You need more computers. You add on a wing to the house.

For many reasons, you are going to need more. Running the bare minimum of wires only to rooms that you're sure will need them is not always enough. We admit that we overbuild our houses. There, we said it, we overbuild. Why? Because the theme of this book is to futureproof. Can you get by with other options? Yes. Can you add later? Yes, at more cost. Is it easier to do it up front? Oh yes!

So overdo it. Run that extra wire. When you figure out the cost over a 30-year mortgage, what's it really cost you day-to-day? Your home network is going to be your number-two source of primary enjoyment in your house for as long as you live there, so invest in it. (If you have to ask us what number one is, you're either not married, never going to get married, or divorced.)

Leave Room for Expansion

Look, you're going to grow your home network, period. No discussion. No matter how much you believe you are going to think of everything up front, you won't.

Plan for expansion. If you have a choice of two models, and one is slightly larger, go with the larger one. Will this add cost up front? Absolutely.

But it's going to save you money down the road.

Or, go for the smaller one, but send us an e-mail (to dummies@telechoice. com) when you are kicking yourself later on, just to let us have the "I told you so" pleasure. Hey, put "kickin' myself" in the header, and we may even automate an I-told-you-so reply.

Create an Area for Your Wiring Closet

Creating a smart home takes a lot of equipment. When you are drafting plans for your home design or redesign, make sure that you account for access panels and a central wiring closet for your gear. You will save a lot of time and money by centralizing all this equipment and wiring in one place — it makes upgrades and troubleshooting so much easier.

You don't need a lot of space — a 10- to 15-square-foot area should be sufficient. Don't put the central wiring closet in the attic because this area is subject to a lot of very high and very low temperatures. Unfinished areas like garages and basements are not recommended because of all the dust that floats around. Watch out for laundry rooms and other utility rooms because they can get warm and humid. Also make sure that wherever you choose to put the closet has good ventilation.

The best solution is a room on the main floor. Think about extra space under stairwells or at the back end of a closet. If you are going to have a major home entertainment area in one room, think about providing a walk-in equipment closet with a door accessing it in the adjoining room so you can have ready access to all the backs of the equipment. Above all, think centrally — this reduces the distance the wires have to run, improving performance as well as cutting costs.

Think about the various components you are going to have to install, and allocate about a 2-foot-wide by 5-foot-tall space for each "system" that has to go in it — video, security, phone, LAN, home automation (lighting, heating, cooling, and so on). Don't forget to leave room for lots of duplex and quad AC receptacles. Watch out for locating your gear too close to the electrical circuit breaker panel, because this can cause electrical interferences through induced static.

Also, be sure to put in wiring tubes or chases to the upper and lower floors. You don't want to be drilling holes in the floors, walls, and ceilings that might reduce the integrity of the structure itself.

Run Conduits

When the telephone company folks put in a path between two points, not knowing how much they will want to grow that in the future, they put in a big huge conduit through which they route all their cables. They leave *pull cords* in the conduit — pull cords are cords that they use to pull later cables through that conduit.

Well, the telephone companies run cables this way because they learned over time this is the easy way to do things. In setting up your home network, don't reinvent the wheel. Think about access and flexibility for future growth when you run your wires. You never know when you're going to have to run more cable for some reason or another.

One easy way to accomplish this is to run PVC conduit between floors and in the walls. Be cognizant of elbows in these PVC runs — cable, especially thicker cable, does not travel around corners well. Figure 22-1 shows how this might work.

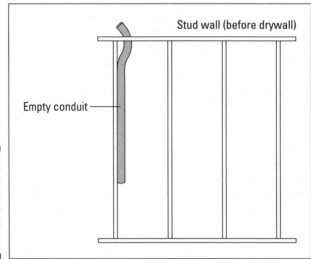

Figure 22-1:
Running
PVC pipe
between the
attic and
basement.

Stud wall (before drywall)

Empty conduit

Also be careful about what you run in the same conduit — some signals running inside the cables can interfere with each other. Never run electrical wiring inside these PVC conduits no matter how much money it saves you.

If you're planning on blowing foam insulation into your house (such as if you live in the cold North), this is even more critical to consider. Most foam insulation is blown into the wall space after the wiring is completed, so you don't get a lot of second chances if you don't run PVC.

Don't Forget the Power

Ouch. Nothing's worse than buying the latest and greatest telephone, and then bringing it home, plugging the telephone cable in, and then realizing there is no electrical outlet anywhere nearby. Argh!

When you renovate your house or build your new home, you need to talk about the location of electrical outlets with your electrician and cabling contractor. Most electrical outlets are installed every so many feet along the wall (per electrical regulations) and aren't coordinated at all with your phone lines. Although you hope that the outlets are sufficiently close to a telephone outlet, that may not be the case for your kitchen phone, for example, that's midway up a wall in a high-traffic area. The last thing you want is an electrical cable stringing across that kitchen hallway wall.

Most of the sexy new phones today require electrical power nearby. Without such power, you'll have to go wireless for your phone connection, and the quality may not be what you want it to be. So plan ahead.

Choose a Contractor Who Knows What You Want

Make sure that you get a competent contractor who has worked on a smart home before. The level of knowledge about smart homes is very low in many sectors of the contracting trade. This is all new stuff to some of them. We've given you resources in this book to track down people who have *been there, done that.* Find them and ask them questions.

Look at past examples of their work. Some are conservative and don't want to overbuild. Others are very liberal and plan for everything under the sun. Find your wired personality and match it with your contractors, and you've got a winning combination.

Don't Get Fooled by All-in-One, All the Time

A big theme in home networking, particularly home automation, is to find a single solution that does everything. True, integration is good and something to seriously look at.

But all-in-one solutions are also sometimes the lowest common denominator. Hard-core stereo buffs tend to buy a tuner from one manufacturer, a CD/DVD player from another, and an amplifier from yet another for a reason: The individual elements have enough to offer on their own to make the hassle of interconnecting them worthwhile.

So look at individual options as well as overall solutions in your buying process.

Be Creative

Now this may not seem like much of a hint, but it's sound advice. Planning a smart home is an opportunity to have fun and be truly creative. The infrastructure you put in place is going to enable the fun stuff, but it won't create it. Only by hanging neat technologies off the endpoints of that infrastructure will you see the fruits of your efforts.

You're creating an investment here. Think about it. When you go to sell your home after all the kids have left for school and they never call you anymore (sigh), the unique attributes of your home are the things that truly provide value for the buyer. Try to create something that's different (but tasteful).

Chapter 23

Ten Great Web Resources

*F*or anyone reading this book, you won't be surprised to find that you can find just about any kind of information on the Internet — especially when it comes to home networking. Such abundance makes sense, considering that Internet access is one of the main applications for home networks.

Rather than make you search high and low for related Web sites, we thought we'd offer a few of our favorites here. Please consider this chapter a jumping-off point rather than an exhaustive listing — each of these Web sites is full of links to other, related sites just waiting for your investigation.

San Jose Mercury News to the Rescue

The *San Jose Mercury News* is the daily newspaper printed (and posted on the Web, of course) right in the heart of Silicon Valley. One of its technology writers, Phillip Robinson, recently wrote a series on home networking that we think is just great. The newspaper has several good articles, dealing mainly with computer networking — which makes a lot of sense, considering the Merc's audience. You can find the whole series at `www1.sjmercury.com/compute/compute_wired.shtml`.

CNET

Everybody has a favorite Web site, one that they find themselves visiting every day (or several times a day). If we had to choose one — besides our own (`www.telechoice.com`) — we'd probably have to choose the CNET family of Web sites. CNET publishes a whole bunch of different Web sites, including a great tech news site (www.news.com), and software sites like Download.Com and Shareware.Com. The CNET News.Com site often features the latest breaking news in the home-networking arena — we check it several times a day ourselves.

The main CNET site has covered home networking several times, including a great feature piece on creating a home data network. You can find this story online at www.cnet.com/Content/Features/Howto/HomeLAN/.

Marc Henrichs' Low-Voltage Prewire Guide

One of the great characteristics about people who have been involved in wiring their own homes is that they're enthusiastic about it. Generous, too. One of these people is Marc Henrichs. He and his wife built a home that they plan to use as their retirement home, so they wired for the long run. He offers his experiences and recommendations in great detail on his Web site, and we think his advice is great. He also includes a feedback section in the form of an online bulletin board, which is full of questions, answers, and suggestions from other do-it-yourselfers. All in all, this is a great site. You can find Marc's site at www.mcdata.com/~meh0045/homewire/wire_guide.html.

John's Closet

No, this closet isn't the place where John keeps his clothes and shoes or where he hides skeletons. John's Closet is his wiring closet — which is what telcom/network pros call their wiring distribution centers. Like Marc Henrichs, John completed a do-it-yourself home network, and he also has a lot to share. Computer networkers will especially appreciate John's advice and experiences relating to his purchase and installation of an ISDN modem/router. You can open the door to John's Closet at www.digitalmx.com/wires/.

SOHO DataCom

SOHO stands for small office/home office, in case you didn't know. SOHO users — especially the home-office subgroup — are exactly the kind of people who we think are reading this book. Given that assumption, we think that you'll find a lot of good information on SOHO data and voice networking on this site. You can also find some good links and a section on home automation for all of you gadgety types. Visit SOHO DataCom at www.geocities.com/ResearchTriangle/3300/.

NetDay Installation Guide

Have you heard of NetDay? It's both an organization and an event. On NetDay, companies and individuals donate their time and money to go into public schools and install network wiring that will help get more classrooms online. Seems like a pretty good cause to us, and we support it.

That event isn't why we mention the Web site, though. It seems that the NetDay organizers realized that not everyone who volunteers is familiar with cable-installation procedures, so they published a great multimedia guide on the organization's Web site. Using Macromedia Shockwave animations, the site is a good way to get a visual representation of what all is involved in installing a CAT-5 cabling system. Check out the guide at `www.netday.org/btw/index.html`.

This Old House

Are you a fan of Steve and Norm? We sure are — we've whiled away many a Saturday morning in front of the local PBS station watching *This Old House*. Can you relate?

Well, even if you're not a fan of the show, we think you might want to check out some information on the Web site, regarding a home-office wiring the crew did on one of their "old houses." You won't find a lot of step-by-step instructions here, but you will find another perspective on the matter with some good photos. The *This Old House* Web site is `www.pbs.org/wgbh/thisoldhouse/home.html`.

Better Homes and Gardens

Better Homes and Gardens? Well, we're not really thinking along the garden lines too much in this book, but we did find that BHG has a great home-improvements Web site.

You find lots of great pictures and explanations of things like electrical wiring, telephone wiring, and the like. The networks described are often not as sophisticated as the ones we have recommended, but the basics are all covered — and covered well. You can find the *Better Homes and Gardens* home-improvement site at `www.bhglive.com/homeimp/docs/index.htm`.

The Phone-Man!

The Phone-Man knows a thing or two about telephone installation. He shares what he knows, too, on this excellent Web page. You can find lots of good illustrations and background information, as well as step-by-step instructions for adding phone jacks to existing lines, and a good tutorial on installing a star-wired system like we describe back in Chapter 17. The Phone-Man's site is www.geocities.com/SiliconValley/Pines/4116/.

Oh, by the way, there's more than one phone guy on the Net. The Phoneman (note the different spelling) has a similarly excellent site at www.users.uswest.net/~skelly2/index.html.

ChannelPlus's Guide to Watching DSS from the Bedroom

ChannelPlus is one of the leading manufacturers of video-distribution equipment — stuff like coax distribution panels, modulators, and video amplifiers. (The company also makes structured wiring systems for the home, too. It can take care of your data and telephone needs, as well.) You have to pay for this stuff, but you can get something very worthwhile from ChannelPlus for free: advice, and lots of it.

ChannelPlus recently updated its entire site and included a whole bunch of good information about designing and installing video networks. The site has the best guide we've seen yet, describing the multitude of possibilities that come into play when you're installing a DSS satellite system. Find the guide at this URL: www.channelplus.com.

Chapter 24

Ten Print Publications to Get Your Hands On

*W*e can in no way cover the entire home-networking-and-automation industry in one book. So we're leaving a few nuggets for other publications to cover. Here's a listing of those publications that we recommend you get your hands on as part of your home-networking project.

Electronic House Magazine

Electronic House — www.electronichouse.com; (800) 375-8015; (508) 358-3400 — is the bible magazine of this industry and represents a major source for cool smart-home information. It's written for the consumer who enjoys technology.

Electronic House magazine includes articles on whole-home control and subsystems such as residential lighting, security, home theaters, energy management, and telecommunications. It also regularly looks at new and emerging technologies in home control. The magazine comes out six times a year and costs $23.95 a year. Back issues are six for $30.

Electronic House also offers a series of other resources for sale through its Electronic House Store (at www.ehstore.com), including books and videos. More than a dozen books are available through *Electronic House* on various aspects of home networking, including such titles as *Build Your Own Home Theater* and *Automated Home Control*.

Electronic House offers a Planning Kit for $95 that includes a one-year sub-scription to *Electronic House,* six back issues of the magazine, the *Electronic House Planning Guide*, the *Electronic House Buyer's Guide,* and *Futureproof: Wiring and Cabling Systems Video* (VHS). The video is too basic to really get anything out of, but the other resources are great.

Popular Home Automation Magazine

Popular Home Automation — www.pophome.com; (800) 375-8015; (508) 358-3400 — also by the publishers of *Electronic House,* is a magazine for the do-it-yourselfer. It's geared more to specific product reviews and dis-cusses new technologies for the home, with a bent toward how to do them. Articles show you how to carry out home-automation projects through step-by-step instructions and cover topics ranging from "Piece by Piece: Building a Home Theater on a Budget" to "Ultimate Bachelor Pad Contest Winner: A Cool Setup For The Single Guy in All of Us. . . ."

The magazine comes out six times a year and costs $29.95 a year. Back issues are six for $30.

The www.pophome.com Web site includes Web-only articles, so check it out as well. You also find links to the www.ehstore.com shopping site for books and videos.

Home Automation Systems Catalog

The Home Automation Systems catalog — www.smarthome.com; (800) 762-7846; (714) 708-0610) — is awesome. It's a 160-page full-color cata-log that's really packed with information — good pictures and diagrams, too. This catalog is a "must have" for the smart-home enthusiast. Home Automation Systems (HAS) carries a wide variety of X-10, security, home-the-ater, video-distribution, HVAC, telephone, and wiring equipment. The catalog is free. The Web site is exceedingly friendly, with good pictures to show you exactly what you're buying. The site uses Real Audio for some introductions. You can even download the catalog from the Web site!

Home Controls Incorporated Catalog

Home Controls, Inc. — www.homecontrols.com; (800) 266-8765; (619) 693-8887 — offers a 96-page full-color catalog of (you guessed it!) home-automation gear. Home Controls concentrates on the following major areas: X-10 automation, X-10 transmitters, computer automation, security, audio, video surveillance cameras, A/V distribution, infrared devices, wireless devices, HVAC, phones and intercoms, and household automation. The catalog lists a lot of neat products, it's free, and you can order it from the company's Web site.

Stereophile Guide to Home Theater Magazine

The *Stereophile Guide to Home Theater* — www.guidetohometheater.com; (800) 666-6471; (303) 678-0354 — is another neat magazine that tracks all elements of a home-theater system and gets out on the fringe of whole-home entertainment as well. U.S. subscriptions for the *Stereophile Guide to Home Theater* are $19.94 per year. Back issues are $7 each.

Home Theater Magazine

Home Theater Magazine — www.hometheatermag.com; (800)264-9872; (800) 544-6748 — does a lot of reviews of equipment, with frequent face-off reviews between different ways to implement various technologies as well as tryout reviews of specific hardware. If you're going to spend money on a particular piece of equipment, this magazine probably can give you an in-depth review of what to look out for. Subscriptions are 12 issues for $24; back issues are $7.50 each.

Hello Direct Catalog

We look forward to getting Hello Direct Catalog — www.hellodirect.com; (800) 444-3556 — with the same fervor we used to apply to Sharper Image before we got a little more practical around the house. Hello Direct takes a problem-solving approach to home networking and offers products to match. It contains most of what you need to outfit a home office with some of the more nifty gadgets.

In Hello Direct, you can find basic phone systems, multiline phones, Caller ID boxes, music-on-hold systems, cordless phones, headsets, 900 MHz wireless intercom systems — even pay phones if you want to charge your kids to make phones calls, just like on *The Brady Bunch*. The catalog is free.

Hello Direct also owns The PhoneZone.com (www.phonezone.com), an online resource with a great interface for finding all sorts of phone and LAN networking equipment.

Radio Shack Catalog

Radio Shack is a great place to find basic X-10 and security items, as well as cable TV/DSS and telephone gadgets. In terms of Americana lore, its 300-plus-page catalog ranks up there as one of America's classics. Probably only the now-defunct Sears Catalog has more U.S.A. wrapped up in it.

The Radio Shack Catalog (www.radioshack.com) is one of those electronics publications that, if you're an electronics nerd, you tend to flip through often. Much of the stuff that Radio Shack offers, however, is basic and geared toward the do-it-yourselfer. You're not going to find the more sophisticated wiring panels, for example, in this store or through this catalog.

You can, however, get Sprint phones in the Sprint portion of the catalog and find out about computing in the Compaq portion. But the real value in this catalog is all the other "stuff" you find in its pages — the diplexers, 75-ohm connectors, RJ-11 cables, and so on. It's also got some nice Q&A sections, "How-to" hints, and informative "Buzz Words" glossaries.

Get a copy and keep it on your desk as you're planning your smart home; use it as much as a reference guide as a place to order stuff whenever you need it. The catalog is free — and well worth it!

Other nice things that you can find at Radio Shack are its various How-To publications on smart-home topics. Following is a short list of the major ones (along with their catalog numbers). These publications are typically good for the Tab-A into Slot-A stuff, but they don't really illustrate centrally homed network architectures.

- Home Theater (Radio Shack # 62-2319)
- Antennas — Selection and Installation (Radio Shack # 62-1083)
- Installing Telephones (Radio Shack # 62-1060)
- Installing TV/Video Systems (Radio Shack # 62-1393W9)

Home Office Computing Magazine

If you're going to work from home, you want to be as efficient as possible. *Home Office Computing Magazine* — www.smalloffice.com; (800) 288-7812; (212) 333-7600; back issues, (800) 544-6748 — is a great way to stay in touch with the hows and whys of working out of your home.

Home Office Computing takes sneak peeks at new technologies, offers Buyer's Guides and feature stories on key elements of your home office network, and shares tidbits of advice and information that can make your home office hum — in a good way. The magazine costs $14.97 for a one-year subscription; $25.97 for a two-year subscription; and back issues are $6.95 apiece. You can even get a free issue by asking for one at the Web site.

Black Box Catalog

Black Box — www.blackbox.com; (724) 746-5500 — is renowned in the networking industry for its data and PC-networking supplies. If you're trying to find something for your home data network, you're sure to find it here. The Black Box Catalog offers everything from cables and connectors to modems, hubs, routers, and switches — it's all here, and the catalog is free.

The Black Box Web site offers free downloads of the catalog pages in content-rich Portable Document Format (PDF). The PDF pages offer a completely interactive version of the catalog. You can click fax-back icons, for example, to request more information via fax. Definitely check this site out.

Chapter 25

Almost Ten Ways Home Networking Will Get Easier

In This Chapter

▶ Have someone else do all the work

▶ Great minds are working on solutions

▶ You don't need to run *any* wire

▶ Standards are the key

*P*eople who are building home networks now are pioneers of sorts. Just the fact that you're reading this book — even if you don't install a home-networking infrastructure in your home — puts you ahead of about 95 percent of the population. Most people haven't even begun to think about such stuff yet.

That situation's going to change — for the better — and before long, home networks are sure to be a hot topic, just as the Web was a few years ago. Already, most of the major computer, telecommunications, and consumer-electronics companies are thinking about it and developing strategies. *Convergence* — the joining together of previously separate networks — has been their buzz word for years now, and without a good home network, this network convergence is never going to happen.

Builders Are Going to Install Networks for You

Home builders and contractors haven't always shown very much concern for home wiring. Construction is a competitive business, profit margins are slim, and the added cost of home-network wiring — as small as it really is — hasn't added up in the spreadsheets of builders.

This situation is sure to change as more customers become aware of home networks and realize that the up-front costs are really pretty minor in comparison to the benefits. We don't know about your neighborhood, but where we live (near San Diego and Boston), houses cost a pretty big chunk of money, so another thousand or two on top of the price of a home is really not all that much.

Some builders are beginning to realize this truth and are offering upgraded wiring as an option or even — in a few cases — as a standard item for their new construction. Network wiring's a good selling point, in our opinion, and is only going to become more important in the future (in other words, around the time you decide to sell your home).

Electricians and Installers Are Going to Know More

Many electricians don't really concern themselves all that much with home-network wiring. Sure, they install telephone or cable television wires for you, but for the most part, their expertise — and interest — is in high-voltage, powerline wiring. Low-voltage network wiring is often not even on their professional radar screens.

We think that this educational oversight, too, is bound to change as demand for home networking increases. After all, most electricians are in the business to make money, and in the end, they try to provide what the customer wants. Helping along in this effort are groups such as the Consumer Electronics Industry Association — a trade organization that's beginning to offer seminars and training to get potential installers up to speed in the home-networking arena.

Alarm Companies Are Going to Install Networks for You

Although electricians often ignore low-voltage wiring, a sizable group of professionals out there does specialize in it — security-system installers. These guys and gals have made a career of getting low-voltage wiring to just about every nook and cranny of a home. Additionally, the alarm systems they're installing are increasingly sophisticated and capable — many security systems now include home control and automation features.

Adding wiring for phone, entertainment, and data networks is just a small step for these installers — they already know most of the tricks of the trade. Alarm-system manufacturers — ADI, for example — are beginning to include good stuff such as CAT-5 and RG6 coaxial cabling in their product lines, and they're training their installers to put it in for you. They want to become your one-stop shopping place for all low-voltage wiring.

Specially Designed Wiring Systems Are Going to Become More Available

As we discuss in Chapter 2, cabling manufacturers — many of whom have made most of their money in the commercial marketplace — want your business. To get it, they've been busy designing structured cabling systems for the home — those all-in-one bundles of cabling and distribution centers that make prewiring a home easy.

Since we've been writing this book, the number of companies offering these kinds of products has exploded. Everyone from household names, such as Lucent and Monster Cable, to commercial favorites, such as AMP, have come out with these integrated-wiring systems. Such systems save you from needing to design your own network, for the most part, and enable you to get the job done in one easy step, instead of doing it piecemeal.

Wireless Equipment Is Going to Get Better and Cheaper

Throughout the book, we tell you that wireless-networking equipment, in general, costs more and does less than it's wired equivalent. We're not backing down from that statement now, but we must qualify that statement by adding that wireless technology is still taking baby steps. You can expect spectacular increases in wireless performance and a correspondingly spectacular decrease in cost as these technologies mature.

A wired network probably is always going to be cheaper, faster, and more reliable than wireless, but if you find yourself in a situation where you simply can't wire, don't sweat it. Wireless home networking is just a few years from being a viable alternative.

The Big Players Are Getting Involved

Microsoft, Intel, Compaq, Lucent — big, successful companies by any measure, with one common goal: getting even bigger and more successful. One of the ways such companies believe that they can grow and become more successful is by putting their expertise and weight behind — yep, you guessed it

— home networks. They're not the only ones either — consumer-electronics companies, networking companies (many of which have never been involved in the consumer marketplace before), and telephone, cable, and Internet service providers all have a vested interest in making home networks take off.

Where this trend may lead we can't tell you right now — many of these companies have competing visions and interests — at least concerning the details. All we know for sure is that home networking is certain to become easier, cheaper, and more common after these big guys step into the fray.

Standards, Standards, Standards

Standards (the governmental or industry rules that ensure that equipment from different manufacturers works together) are a weird thing. On one hand, they're good for everybody — you couldn't make a phone call or plug in your television if not for consistent standards. Nor would you necessarily want to buy a telephone or a television if the manufacturer didn't assure you that it would work with the going standards. On the other hand, an innovative manufacturer has an incentive to create a proprietary solution for a new need — especially if that solution may give it a chance to dominate the market rather than share it with a bunch of other companies.

In the home-networking world, some areas — such as data communications, cabling, or telephone wiring — are pretty well governed by specific standards. Other areas, such as wireless networking, are the domain of proprietary solutions. We don't see this situation changing too much in the near future, at least for any of the official standards.

What we do expect to see are coalitions of major players getting together to support "defacto" standards that, although not blessed by any standards body in Geneva or Washington, are widely supported and ubiquitous in the marketplace. A good example of such a coalition is the HomeRF consortium that's been established to facilitate progress in the residential wireless data-networking field.

Why should you care about standards? There are two good reasons, actually. First, standards make it easier to buy and use networking equipment — since a device from one manufacturer should work flawlessly with one from another manufacturer. Second, standards help preserve your investment in equipment, because unlike proprietary equipment (which relies upon a single manufacturer's continued support), standards-based equipment usually is available from a wide variety of manufacturers.

Appendix

Glossary

● ●

10BaseT: A data networking standard for Ethernet networks that uses unshielded twisted-pair (UTP) cabling and operates at 10 Mbps.

110 Block: A termination or patch panel for data and telephone networks using unshielded twisted-pair cabling.

66 Block: Similar to a 110 Block, a termination or patch panel typically used for telephone wiring. Use this to terminate phone cabling from throughout the house in a central location and to connect this wiring to incoming telephone service feeds.

alarm system: A security system that combines various sensors, a central control panel, and signaling devices to warn of emergency situations such as a break-in, a fire, and flooding.

amplifier: A device used to increase the power or signal strength of an electrical signal. Most commonly found in audio and video systems within the home.

aspect ratio: The ratio between the horizontal measurement and vertical measurement of a TV screen. Standard NTSC televisions are built with a 4:3 aspect ration, while HDTV systems are built to a 16:9 ratio. The higher the ratio, the wider (relatively) the screen.

ATM (asynchronous transfer mode): A high-speed data networking technology.

attenuation: The loss of signal power during transmission. Usually a concern when a signal is transmitted over a long distance.

AWG (American Wire Gauge): Measurement of the diameter of a wire or cable. The lower the gauge size, the thicker the wire.

bandwidth: The transmission capacity of a cable or other media. Usually measured in bits per second or in cycles per second (hertz). A common analogy to bandwidth is a water pipe — the bigger the pipe (bandwidth) the more water that can flow through it per unit of time.

baseband: A method of transmitting signals — like video or data — in which the signal is carried on a cable without altering its modulation. Compare with *broadband*.

bps (bits per second): A measurement of bandwidth. This is the number of data bits that can be carried over a network in a second. Often measured in thousands of bits per second (kilobits per second — Kbps) or millions of bits per second (megabits per second — Mbps).

bridge: A device that connects two networks together. Often found within Internet access devices like cable modems, where it connects a home LAN to the network of the Internet service provider (and then to the Internet itself).

broadband: A method of transmitting signals where several data signals are modulated onto different frequencies and carried on the same cable or network medium. Compare with *baseband*.

cable modem: A high-speed Internet access device that uses the coaxial cable network of cable television providers to connect a home PC or LAN to the Internet over frequencies unused by television services.

Category 3 (CAT-3): A performance rating for unshielded twisted-pair (UTP) wiring suitable for telephone and 10BaseT Ethernet networks. See also *UTP*.

Category 5 (CAT-5): A performance rating for UTP wiring that is suitable for telephone and Ethernet networks up to 100 Mbps, as well as ATM data networks up to 155 Mbps. See also *UTP*.

CATV: Community Antenna TV, the original name for cable television back in the old days when a town would share a single, centrally located TV antenna. Still used on many TVs and VCRs to label connection points for cable television connections.

CCTV: Closed-circuit TV, an in-home video surveillance network.

CEBUS: Consumer Electronics Bus, an emerging standard for connecting consumer electronics devices to a home network. The most important part of the standard is the Home Plug and Play protocol, which allows compatible devices to identify and communicate with each other.

central controller: An intelligent (computer-based) home-automation controller that can monitor sensor or user inputs and control various devices throughout a house.

central monitoring station: A facility operated by a security company that remotely monitors (over telephone lines or wireless links) a home security system.

coaxial cable: Shielded cable that you can use to carry television signals or data within a network. Coaxial cable typically consists of a center conductor, a layer of insulation, another conductor wrapped around the insulation, and an outer layer of shielding and jacketing. Coaxial cables used in home video applications are designed with a 75 ohm impedance, and are rated according to their bandwidth capacity. The most commonly found coaxial cables are RG-59 and RG6.

composite video: The *baseband* video signal output of a VCR, DVD player, or other video source component.

conduit: A plastic or metal pipe that is used to contain cable runs. It is often installed empty into new homes to allow easy running of new cables in the future.

connector: A device, usually standardized, that is used to connect wires in a cable to a device or to an outlet.

current: The measure of electrical flow in a circuit, measured in amperes.

daisy chain: A method of connecting networked equipment such that each successive device in the network is connected in series from the previous device. This type of wiring is typically found in older telephone wiring installations, but it's not particularly flexible or reliable. Compare with *star*.

demarcation point: The physical point where an incoming network, such as telephone service, ends and the home's internal network begins. In most cases this point also delineates the responsibility for the network — everything inside of the demarcation point is the responsibility of the homeowner.

digital subscriber line (DSL): A new data-connection method that allows high-speed Internet connections and other network connections over a standard telephone line. Variants of DSL, such as asymmetric digital subscriber lines, are identified by a preceding initial (ADSL in this case).

distribution panel: In a video network, this is the panel that concentrates all broadband video signals from antennas, cable TV feeds, and in-home video sources and distributes them to outlets throughout the house. Often it also includes a built-in signal amplifier.

Doh!: What you'll say if you skimp on prewiring a house when you have the chance.

downstream: Data running from an external network, like the Internet into a home. Compare with *upstream*.

DTV (digital television): The next-generation digital television system that has been approved by the Federal Communications Commission as a replacement for today's NTSC system. Allows a wide variety of video resolution and quality, including HDTV. Compare with *NTSC*.

DVD (digital versatile disc *or* digital video disc): A CD-sized digital disc used for playback of movies or music.

electromagnetic interference (EMI): Interference and distortion of signals in a network caused by other electronic devices.

Ethernet: A standard data communications protocol for computers and computer peripheral devices such as printers. The most common variation of Ethernet found in home networks is the 10 Mbps 10BaseT variant, but dozens of other variations exist with speeds up to 1000 Mbps.

F connector: A standardized connector for coaxial cable, usually threaded.

FireWire: A new high-speed data communications protocol most often used for connecting digital video systems to computers. Future uses are envisioned to expand the role of FireWire to include whole-home data, video, and audio networks. Also known as IEEE 1394.

High-Definition television (HDTV): a very high-resolution, high-quality television standard that is designed to allow widescreen, film-quality video programming. See also *DTV*.

Home Phoneline Networking Association (HomePNA): An industry group promoting and developing computer data networking equipment that operates over standard telephone lines.

home run: A network architecture where each outlet is serviced by its own cable, which is run back to a central distribution point. Also known as a *star network*.

HomeRF Working Group: An industry group that is developing wireless networking standards for home applications.

house code: One of two codes used to identify devices in an X-10 network. There are sixteen possible house codes (labeled Aa–P). Combined with the other code (the unit code), there can be 256 different devices in an X-10 network.

hub: A device used in an Ethernet network that centrally connects all networked devices and distributes data among them.

HVAC: Heating, Ventilation, and Air Conditioning.

IEEE 1394: See FireWire.

IEEE 802.11: A new international standard for wireless Ethernet networks.

IEEE 802.3: The international standard for Ethernet networks.

impedance: Resistance to the flow of current in an alternating current circuit.

infrared (IR): The part of the light spectrum just below the visible portion. Often used for wireless networked devices and remote controls in a home.

Infrared Data Association (IRDA): an industry group that promotes interoperable IR networking devices.

interference: A distortion of a signal.

ISDN (Integrated Services Digital Network): A telephone system that allows two standard phone lines or medium-speed data networking over a single phone-line connection.

jack: A cable connector in the form of a receptacle, used with a plug to complete a cable connection. Compare with *plug*.

key telephone system unit (KSU): An intelligent telephone network controller that can distribute incoming calls to different extensions, act as an intercom, and provide other telephone functions such as conference calling and voicemail.

LAN (local area network): A computer data communications network used within a limited physical location, like a house. Most home LANs utilize the Ethernet protocol.

line seizure: In a security system, a technique that disconnects any other devices connected to a phone line so that the system can communicate with the central monitoring system.

MHz (megahertz): One million cycles per second. In networks, MHz is the unit used to measure the bandwidth capacity of the network. MHz is related to, but not identical to megabits per second (Mbps).

modem: A device that converts a computer's digital signals into analog tones that can be carried over a telephone network. The name comes from the function, which is to MODulate and DEModulate these signals.

modular jack: A jack used to connect twisted-pair (telephone and data cable) wiring. Generally, modular jacks come in two sizes — six position for telephones (the RJ-11), and eight position for data LANs (the RJ-45).

modulate: The process of changing the electrical properties (such as frequency) of an signal to facilitate carrying it over a network. Signals are often modulated to different frequencies to allow multiple signals to be carried over a single cable. See also *broadband*.

Network Interface Card (NIC): A device that connects to an internal bus in a PC, which provides an interface between the computer and the LAN.

Network Interface Device (NID): A small device that provides the physical connection between a telephone service feed and the home's internal telephone network. It's location defines the *demarcation point*. Also known as a Network Interface Unit (NIU).

patch cord: A short length of cable used to interconnect pieces of equipment or to interconnect cables at the patch panel.

patch panel: A device that allows the interconnection of *home runs* of data or phone cabling at a central distribution point.

plug: The part of a connector system that goes into a jack to make an electrical connection. Typically, a plug is referred to as the male connector, while a jack is referred to as the female connector. If you haven't figured out why, don't ask us. See also *jack*.

POTS: Plain Old Telephone Service, the industry term used to describe standard, analog telephone service.

power line: The electrical wiring in a home. Also used to describe networks that communicate over this wiring (powerline carrier or PLC).

protocol: A common language or specification used by devices communicating over a network.

punchdown: A method for securing cables in a patch panel or outlet. The wire is placed over a metal clip, and then punched down (with the appropriately named punchdown tool) to penetrate the wire's insulation and provide an airtight contact.

RCA jack: The standard jack used in audio-system interconnect cables.

RG-59: A 75-ohm impedance coaxial cable used in broadcast and cable TV networks.

RG6: A high-quality 75-ohm impedance coaxial cable, used for broadcast, cable, and satellite TV networks.

RF (radio frequency): The segment of the electromagnetic spectrum below visible light, used for both wireless transmission of data and for transmitting modulated signals over cable.

RJ-11: The standard six-position modular jack used for one-, two-, and three-line telephone connections. See also *modular jack*.

RJ-31x: A specialized telephone jack used in security systems to provide line seizure. See also *line seizure*.

RJ-45: The standard eight-position modular jack used in data networks.

sensor: A device that measures or detects an input (such as light, a magnetic field, or pressure) and sends an electrical signal as a result of this detection or measurement. Used in security and home-automation systems.

shielding: A protective layer in a cable that prevents electromagnetic interference from outside sources.

splitter/combiner: A device used in coaxial video networks either to split a single cable's signal onto several cables or to combine the signals from several cables onto a single one. When used to split signals, a splitter/combiner introduces a certain amount of attenuation to the signal (usually listed on the splitter).

star network: A network in which each run meets in a central hub or connection point. See also *home run*.

surge suppressor: A device that prevents damage to electrical or electronic equipment by isolating it from unexpected rises in current or voltage (like lighting strikes).

terminate: Connecting a wire or cable to something, usually a piece of equipment or a jack or plug.

tilt: (1) The tendency of higher-frequency signals in a broadband video network to attenuate faster than low-frequency ones. Often seen as an inability to clearly tune in higher channels on a television. (2) What happens when you shake a pinball machine too hard.

twisted pair: Cabling, most often used for telephone and data networks, in which individual pairs of wire are twisted around each other to reduce electrical interference. See also *UTP*.

unit code: The second code (along with the house code) used to identify a device in an X-10 network. Sixteen possible unit codes are available (1–16). See also *house code*.

universal remote control: An IR or RF remote control that can be programmed to control multiple devices. A "learning" universal remote control can be taught control signals from just about any other remote.

upstream: Data running from a home's networked equipment to outside networks like the Internet. Compare with **downstream**.

UTP (unshielded twisted pair): The cable used in most home telephone and data networks, this twisted-pair cabling contains no shielding to protect it from outside interference. See also, CAT-3, CAT-5, and twisted pair.

voltage: The measurement of electrical force in a circuit, measured in volts.

X-10: A **powerline** communications (PLC) protocol for home-automation systems.

Index

YOUR ONLINE RESOURCE

WWW.DUMMIES.COM

Discover Dummies Online!

The Dummies Web Site is your fun and friendly online resource for the latest information about *For Dummies®* books and your favorite topics. The Web site is the place to communicate with us, exchange ideas with other *For Dummies* readers, chat with authors, and have fun!

Ten Fun and Useful Things You Can Do at www.dummies.com

1. Win free *For Dummies* books and more!
2. Register your book and be entered in a prize drawing.
3. Meet your favorite authors through the Hungry Minds Author Chat Series.
4. Exchange helpful information with other *For Dummies* readers.
5. Discover other great *For Dummies* books you must have!
6. Purchase Dummieswear® exclusively from our Web site.
7. Buy *For Dummies* books online.
8. Talk to us. Make comments, ask questions, get answers!
9. Download free software.
10. Find additional useful resources from authors.

Link directly to these ten fun and useful things at
http://www.dummies.com/10useful

WWW.DUMMIES.COM

For other technology titles from Hungry Minds, go to
www.hungryminds.com

Not on the Web yet? It's easy to get started with *Dummies 101®: The Internet For Windows® 98* or *The Internet For Dummies®* at local retailers everywhere.

Hungry Minds™

Find other *For Dummies* books on these topics:
Business • Career • Databases • Food & Beverage • Games • Gardening
Graphics • Hardware • Health & Fitness • Internet and the World Wide Web
Networking • Office Suites • Operating Systems • Personal Finance • Pets
Programming • Recreation • Sports • Spreadsheets • Teacher Resources
Test Prep • Word Processing

HUNGRY MINDS
BOOK REGISTRATION

Register This Book and Win!

We want to hear from you!

Visit **dummies.com** to register this book and tell us how you liked it!

✔ Get entered in our monthly prize giveaway.

✔ Give us feedback about this book — tell us what you like best, what you like least, or maybe what you'd like to ask the author and us to change!

✔ Let us know any other *For Dummies*® topics that interest you.

Your feedback helps us determine what books to publish, tells us what coverage to add as we revise our books, and lets us know whether we're meeting your needs as a *For Dummies* reader. You're our most valuable resource, and what you have to say is important to us!

Not on the Web yet? It's easy to get started with *Dummies 101*®: *The Internet For Windows*® *98* or *The Internet For Dummies*® at local retailers everywhere.

Or let us know what you think by sending us a letter at the following address:

For Dummies Book Registration
Dummies Press
10475 Crosspoint Blvd.
Indianapolis, IN 46256

™

BESTSELLING
BOOK SERIES